Nazi-Era Provenance of Museum Collections

CRITICAL RESEARCH PUBLICATIONS FROM THE
V&A AND UCL PRESS

The V&A is a family of museums dedicated to the power of creativity. Our mission is to champion design and creativity in all its forms, advance cultural knowledge, and inspire makers, creators and innovators everywhere. We share a 5,000-year-old story of creativity through exhibitions, events, educational programmes, digital experiences, conservation, research, and an ever-evolving national collection of over 2.8m objects spanning every creative discipline.

The V&A/UCL Press titles aim to share new, high-quality research relating to the V&A's collections and practices, and to ensure that this research reaches as wide a global readership as possible through open access. While the research draws directly on V&A projects, each V&A/UCL Press title offers a critical reflection on issues of wider relevance to the cultural and heritage sector and to academic disciplines ranging from art history to museum studies to education.

Created as a new kind of museum in the 1850s and establishing a model that would be taken up around the world, the V&A is regularly the subject of museological study. Books in the V&A/UCL Press series bring new perspectives to this field by combining external contributors with rigorous, critical perspectives from practitioners within the institution.

OTHER TITLES IN THE SERIES

The India Museum Revisited
Arthur MacGregor
https://doi.org/10.14324/111.9781800085701

What Photographs Do
Edited by Elizabeth Edwards and Ella Ravilious
https://doi.org/10.14324/111.9781800082984

Botticelli Past and Present
Edited by Ana Debenedetti and Caroline Elam
https://doi.org/10.14324/111.9781787354593

Nazi-Era Provenance of Museum Collections

A research guide

Jacques Schuhmacher

UCL PRESS V&A

First published in 2024 by
UCL Press in association with the Victoria and Albert Museum, London
University College London
Gower Street
London WC1E 6BT

Available to download free: www.uclpress.co.uk

A CIP catalogue record for this book is available from The British Library.

ISBN: 978-1-80008-691-3 (Hbk.)
ISBN: 978-1-80008-690-6 (Pbk.)
ISBN: 978-1-80008-689-0 (PDF)
ISBN: 978-1-80008-692-0 (epub)
DOI: https://doi.org/10.14324/111.9781800086890

Contents

List of figures

Foreword

> ... – I note
> On a little scrap of paper the names of those
> No longer around me.
> (Bertolt Brecht)[1]

Brecht wrote four poems on the death of his friend Walter Benjamin. They are remarkable, spare texts, inventories or listings of people and places that are lost. This need to name is a kind of collection, a holding in one place of presences and absences. They recall Benjamin's own obsessional need to record: what epitaph can you write for a recorder of loss? These list-poems have the slightly ragged feeling of a grief that is very present. They feel as if they are unfinished, archival.

Jacques Schuhmacher's remarkable book is a testament to spending time with the unfinished nature of the archival. It is about finding the traces of what survives, bringing these traces into renewed focus, finding them a place in the world where their connections to lived lives have been erased or effaced, forgotten. It is about valuing the connections between people and the things that they owned, the objects or books or pictures which surrounded them in their daily life and were part of their familial identity.

Walter Benjamin was a collector. He understood that 'we are alone with particular things, which range about us in their silence ... that even the people who haunt our thoughts then partake in this steadfast, confederate silence of things. The collector "stills" his fate. And that means he disappears in the world of memory.' To care about the provenance of things is to go deeply into the world of memory, to understand that objects have a kind of agency in the world, to unlock the space between the silence of things and the silence of people. I do not mean to imply that provenance research or that restitution are a kind of closure. Tribute and restitution and memorial sound like the end, closure. 'I do not have clarity today, and I hope that I never will. Clarification would amount to disposal, settlement of the case, which can then be placed in the files of history…nothing is resolved, nothing is settled, no remembering has become mere memory,' writes Jean Amery, the survivor of Auschwitz. I feel this is true. History is happening. It is not the past, it is a continuing unfolding of the moment. It unfolds in our hands. That is why objects carry so much: they belong in all the tenses, unresolved, unsettling, *essais*.

What can we do? We follow Jacques Schuhmacher. We record traces, hand them on. We name.

It is a start. Together we find the places where the records are silent, the pages torn out, where there are only shards. Shards matter – they record a moment of disjuncture, indicate a loss. You cannot restore. To restore is to efface. To name loss, to delineate it, is a worthy act.

Edmund de Waal

Notes

1 Bertolt Brecht, 'The Losses' (1941), from *The Collected Poems of Bertolt Brecht*, trans. Thomas Kuhn and David Constantine (New York: Liveright Publishing, 2018), 836.

Acknowledgements

It was only possible to research and write this book thanks to the generous support of the Gilbert Trust for the Arts in London and of the David Berg Foundation in New York.

I would like to express my profound gratitude to the Gilbert Trustees – Nicholas Coleridge, Tristram Hunt, Antonia Boström, Edmund de Waal, Nick Hoffman, Heike Zech, Martin Levy, Erica Boyer, Martin H. Blank and Richard Ziman – for enabling me to research the Nazi-era provenance of Arthur and Rosalinde's collection and for encouraging me to share this work as widely as possible.

I am equally grateful to the David Berg Foundation, whose generous support enabled me to undertake several research trips to archives, museums and libraries in Europe. Without the opportunity to review large volumes of files and literature inaccessible elsewhere, and to discuss the challenges of various collections on site, this would be a very different book. I am particularly thankful to the Board of the David Berg Foundation for enabling this book to be published as an open access resource, making its contents freely accessible to anyone interested in embarking on this important research. I am also grateful to the V&A Americas Foundation for their support of this project.

I would also like to warmly thank The Polonsky Foundation for their generous support of the V&A's provenance research efforts.

It is difficult to imagine a more supportive and stimulating environment for provenance research than the V&A and, within it, the Gilbert Collection and the V&A Research Institute, National Art Library and Archives (VARINALA). I am incredibly grateful to Tristram Hunt (Director) for wholeheartedly embracing and championing the importance of provenance research; to Antonia Boström (former Director of Collections) for encouraging me early on to write this book and for opening so many doors to me over the years; to Alice Minter (Senior Curator of the Gilbert Collection), who has so generously shared with me her expertise, and for our rewarding and stimulating collaborations; and to Joanna Norman (Director of VARINALA) for her keen interest in this project and for enabling me to focus on finishing this book and to continue this work in a vibrant research community.

I am deeply humbled that Edmund de Waal agreed to write the foreword to this volume. Edmund's thoughtful approach to this topic has been a source of ongoing inspiration for me and I am profoundly grateful for his support.

It gives me great pleasure to express my thanks to Coralie Hepburn from V&A Publishing and to Pat Gordon-Smith, my editor at UCL Press. I could not have asked for more skilled or supportive editors; I greatly appreciate their deep engagement with the book and their patience as I completed the manuscript. I would also like to thank Robert Davies for copyediting the manuscript and Elliot Beck for assisting with the images, and to express my gratitude to every individual and archive who gave me permission to use their photographs.

I am deeply indebted to Nick Stargardt (University of Oxford) whose work and perspective has shaped how I approach the history of Nazi Germany. The training I received at the Commission for Looted Art in Europe and my many discussions over the years with Anne Webber are the bedrock upon which this book rests. I would also like to thank Gabriele Finaldi (National Gallery) and the members of the National Museum Directors' Council (NMDC) Spoliation Working Group, and Lord Inglewood and the members of the Advisory Group on Spoliation Matters, for our ongoing and always informative dialogue on Nazi-era provenance research.

I am very grateful to everyone who has, over the years at countless conferences, workshops and seminars, public talks and gallery tours, asked me the important, interesting and sometimes very challenging questions that first gave me the idea to write this book, and which directly shaped its scope, tone and approach. In particular, I would like to thank the participants of the National Museum Directors' Council (NMDC) Provenance Research Training, and of the Society for the History of Collecting's 'Provenance in Action Workshop' for the opportunity to present the entire contents of this book to the kind of audience for whom it is intended, and for providing crucial feedback.

More than other disciplines, provenance research relies on the support of colleagues from around the world. I am profoundly grateful to the provenance researchers and archivists whose generosity enabled me to include a panorama of different case studies and perspectives. In order of their appearance in the book, these are: Juliane Deinert (University of Göttingen), Marcus Kenzler (State Museum Oldenburg), Julia Eßl (Albertina), Simon Goodman, Miriam Olivia Merz (Museum Wiesbaden), Sven Haase (Prussian Heritage Foundation), Yvonne Mundt (Federal Office for Central Services and Unresolved Property Issues) and Martin Luchterhandt (State Archive Berlin).

I would like to thank the many other colleagues who each shared important insights and materials: Anna-Carolin Augustin (German Historical Institute, Washington DC), Judith Barr (J. Paul Getty Museum), Giulia Bartrum (British Museum), Uta-Christiane Bergemann (German Textile Museum), Anne Buddle (National Galleries Scotland), Mark Caldon (Department for Culture, Media and Sport), Matthias Deinert (German Lost Art Foundation), Annika Dorn (University of Bonn), Sybille Ehringhaus, Sebastian Finsterwalder (Central and State Library Berlin), Emily Gould (Institute of Art and Law), Ellen Grabowsky and Jona Mooren (NIOD Institute for War, Holocaust and Genocide Studies), Matthew Gale (Tate), Angelina Giovani-Agha (Flynn & Giovanni), Lea Grüter and Mara Lagerweij (Rijksmuseum), Nora Halfbrod (State Gallery Stuttgart), Sam Jones (Tate), Sarah Kinzel (Lindau Museum), Péter Király (Max Planck Society and University of Göttingen), Katja Lindenau (State Art Collections Dresden), Mary Levkoff (Hearst Castle), Matthias Listl (Kunsthalle Mannheim), Andrea Lehmann (Christie's), Monika Löscher and Susanne Hehenberger (Kunsthistorisches Museum Wien), Rosie Mills (Los Angeles County Museum of Art), Jane Milosch (University of Glasgow), Alexander Mirgorodsky (Taganrog Local Government), Mary-Ann Middelkoop (Pitt Rivers Museum), Victoria Reed (Museum of Fine Art Boston), Lily Sabelus (Free University Berlin), Roman Satschuk (Hesse Main State Archives), Christine Schmidt (Wiener Holocaust Library), Joachim Sieber (Kunsthaus Zürich), Antje Stahl (University of Rostock), Lucian Simmons, Julia Rickmeyer and Marie Stolberg (Sotheby's), Annette Weisner (Kunsthalle Kiel), Suzie Tucker and Kathryn Simpson (National Museum Directors' Council), Jana Jirásková (Documentation Centre for Property Transfers of the Cultural Assets of WW II Victims, Prague), Richard Winkler (Bavarian Economic Archive), Charlotte Woodhead (University of Warwick), Sandra van Ginhoven (Getty Research Institute), Brian Weightman (Glasgow Museums), Isabel von Klitzing, Till Vere-Hodge, and Matthias Weniger (Bavarian National Museum).

I cannot emphasise enough how grateful I am to two of my fellow provenance research curators – MacKenzie Mallon (Nelson-Atkins Museum of Art) and Katharina Weiler (Museum Applied Art Frankfurt) – who generously agreed to read the entire manuscript and whose thoughtful comments dramatically improved the text. I am equally grateful to the provenance researcher Pia Kainz (Commission for Looted Art in Europe), and to my V&A colleagues Alice Minter, Joanna Norman, Coralie Hepburn, Alexandra Watson-Jones and Emefa Cole for their constructive feedback on the full manuscript.

A wide range of provenance research and restitution experts and museum colleagues provided invaluable feedback on individual chapters: Anne Webber (Commission for Looted Art in Europe), Richard Aronowitz (Christie's), Alexander Herman (Institute of Art and Law), Thomas Brodie (University of Birmingham) and Arthur MacGregor (V&A). I would also like to thank Susanna Avery-Quash (National Gallery), Alexandra Gerstein (Courtauld Institute), Catherine Poust (Tate), Niklas Krawinkel (Fritz Bauer Institute), Adriana Concin, Anthony Misquitta, Sophie Morris and Jana Riedel (V&A). Needless to say, any errors of interpretation remain entirely my own.

A wide range of colleagues, both past and present, supported this project in important ways. I am deeply grateful to Jessica Eddie, for her extraordinary support as Acting Curator of the Gilbert Collection, and to Emefa Cole, for many stimulating conversations about conceptual and broader issues. I would also like to express my gratitude to: Fahema Begum, Sarah Belanger, Harriet Braine, Oliver Cox, Richard Edgcumbe, Isabella Eggert, Richard Espley, Tullia Fraser, Hannah Auerbach George, Ellen Gillespie, Claudia Heidebluth, Zoë Hollingworth, Olivia Horsfall Turner, Shanna Isaacson, Elizabeth James, Charlotte Johnson, Chloe Johnson, Chloe Kellow, Kirstin Kennedy, Jane Lawson, Clementine Loustric, Christopher Marsden, Dani Martiri, Ana Muñoz, Marta Ajmar, Tessa Murdoch, Angus Patterson, Richard Palmer, Vannis Jones Rahi, James Robinson, Spike Sweeting, Elaine Tierney, Holly Trusted, Andrew Tullis, Simona Valeriani, Matti Watton and Pamela Young. For their encouragement and help at various stages of the project, I would also like to thank: Martin Krause, Hamish Bridges, Robert Lawrence, Edward Rooney, Jeremy Baker, Benjamin Schroeder, Karis Fiorrucci, Christian Mazanek, James Dancer and Martin Kissinger.

This book would not exist without my dear friend and colleague Jonathan Waterlow (Edinburgh). I am deeply grateful to him for our many discussions; his insightful questions and critical interventions at important junctures helped me to understand what kind of book I truly wanted to write and to never lose sight of what is important throughout the project. I am also profoundly grateful to Jon for providing crucial feedback on many different draft chapters, and for his unrivalled editing skills which he so generously applied to this manuscript during our writing retreats in Brussels.

I am deeply grateful to Diamatho for her wonderful love and amazing support, which always carried me through the challenging moments.

Lastly, I would like to thank my wonderful parents, Heike and Engelbert, for their constant encouragement, which has led to the most fulfilling and rewarding job one can possibly imagine, and for their loving support and interest in this project. It gives me great joy to dedicate this book to them.

Introduction

It is disturbing to think that when we look at the artworks on display in museums around the world, there is always a real possibility that some of these objects once belonged to victims of the Nazis – and that this possibility has remained unexplored and unacknowledged for so long. If we are willing to ask the right questions about who owned these objects in the past – about their provenance – then some of these items may speak to us about the fate of individuals and families whose lives were destroyed in the name of the Nazis' racist ideology. At the very least, uncovering these stories allows us to reinsert lost voices into a historical record from which they have been erased – sometimes deliberately, sometimes by chance. In many cases, this research will raise profound moral questions, not least if it is revealed that an item would never have found its way into a museum collection had the Nazis not seized power in 1933 and then initiated a brutal campaign of persecution, conquest and extermination – a campaign that went hand in glove with the systematic dispossession of their victims (see Chapter 1). The aim of this research is not simply to add a name and date to an object's record for the sake of archival completeness; it serves to ensure that the Nazis' worldview and their actions do not live on unchallenged in the galleries and storerooms of our museums today.

If the moral imperative for this research could hardly be clearer, it often comes as a surprise to discover how difficult this work can be. Museums have historically presented themselves as the authority on the objects in their galleries, so one would naturally presume that all that would be required is to pay a visit to the museum's archives in order to learn who owned an object during the Nazi period of 1933–45. In the case of German museums, which were not only passive beneficiaries of

Nazi policy, but were often also actively involved in the dispossession process, the name of a Jewish collector in the provenance records would immediately stand out to us. Yet even if German curators in the 1930s and 1940s saw no reason to hide where these objects had come from, after the war they had every incentive to obscure this information, making the task of the provenance researcher incredibly challenging.[1] Moreover, the scale of Nazi dispossession was so vast and complex that it has left traces even in the museums of neutral countries, or of those that actively fought to defeat Hitler's regime. If we open the acquisition books of museums in North America or Britain, for example, we often find they contain no meaningful provenance information to tell us who owned, and what happened, to these objects during the Nazi period. This is a stark reminder that the goal of recording an unbroken chain of provenance for each object has only relatively recently become the norm (see Chapter 2). Even if we are lucky enough to discover a date and the name of a previous owner, this is usually only the first step on an often twisted path through the many disconnected archives across which the victims' stories have been scattered (see Chapter 3).

If museums do not hold comprehensive records that can enable us to recover and reassemble these important stories, we might naturally hope that the famously bureaucratic Nazi state would have compiled a master list of objects owned by their enemies, with the ultimate aim of seizing it all for the Reich. The Nazi bureaucracy was certainly relentless in classifying, persecuting and documenting the dispossession of their victims, and they indeed created many detailed inventories, but these were never consolidated, and many did not survive the war. Even if some of these lists have been digitised, much like the various online databases of Nazi-looted art, they can only provide small snapshots of a vast dispossession campaign that straddled the entire European continent and, on their own, will never be enough to tell us the full story of how the Nazis' actions have affected a particular museum collection (see Chapter 3). These resources can be incredibly valuable, allowing us in some cases to overcome the limitations of museum records, but it is self-evidently insufficient to cross-reference an incomplete list of objects with a museum collection, highlight any overlaps and then call it a day. Even if we recognise an object from such a list or database in a museum collection (and are sure it is not a duplicate), it is crucial to dig much deeper if we are to recover and do justice to the full human story of what happened to an object and its owners. There is no way around it: if we want to understand the true history of a museum collection during and after the Nazi period, then we must begin with the objects themselves and, with the museum records as our starting point, begin to trace their journey through time and space by drawing on as many resources as possible.

There is so much to gain by treading this difficult path: we can tell a more complete and accurate story of one of the darkest chapters in human history; we can better understand how its reverberations continue to affect our culture today; and, in light of this information, we are challenged to consider what the role of museums has been and should be in our own countries. Fundamentally, this research is the essential foundation for us to ensure that museums act as ethical stewards of our shared history (see Chapter 2).

As we begin this work, it can certainly feel that we are doing it 'too late', and we cannot help but wonder why it has not already been completed. In 1945, the Allies did initiate a major research effort into the origins of the millions of artworks and other cultural property that the Nazi state had hidden in salt mines, remote castles and caves as the Reich began to crumble. This important research was carried out by curators and art historians – later known as the Monuments Men and Women – whose work culminated in the largest provenance research and restitution effort in history (see Chapter 2). Donning the uniforms of the victorious Allied armies, they drew on their training and expertise with the aim of reversing the Nazis' campaign of plunder. Instinctively, they approached this task as if they were cataloguing a museum collection, yet remarkably these efforts were not thereafter replicated in the museum world – not in Germany, not in the formerly occupied territories, nor in the Allied or neutral countries. By this point, many objects that carried a Nazi provenance had long since entered museum collections across the world, often after a complex journey through the international art market. Not only were existing museum collections not scrutinised with respect to the Nazi past, but over the ensuing decades museums also continued not to ask in-depth questions about the new items that they added to their collections. As a result, the scale of this unexamined legacy only grew larger.

It is surprising that it would take more than 50 years after the end of the Second World War before museums began to confront this legacy in earnest. In 1998, a major international conference held in Washington, DC, at the US State Department and the US Holocaust Memorial Museum, shone a dramatic spotlight onto the fact that museum collections had never been systematically studied with respect to the Nazi period (see Chapter 2). The revelations of the conference would be a powerful call to action. It created the expectation that museums should carry out research into the Nazi past of their collections, that they should publicly acknowledge what they found, and that they must ensure that they are not the beneficiaries of Nazi policies. But the conference had effects that reached far beyond the walls of museums: it galvanised research into persecution and dispossession under the Nazis, drawing large numbers of researchers to museum collections, where the consequences of the Nazi period become very concrete as they looked upon material objects, knowing that they were once held by both victims and perpetrators. As journalists, filmmakers and scholars have continued to highlight the Nazi past and its legacies, museum visitors now expect to be told not only about the aesthetic qualities of objects on display, but also about their unvarnished histories. They also rightfully expect museums to take appropriate decisions on the basis of this information, including a fully transparent engagement with questions of restitution. It is reassuring to see that the Nazi past is no longer a topic confined to history museums, but is increasingly taken up by art museums through exhibitions, talks and gallery tours.

Now, decades after the Washington Conference energised the sector, its vision remains only partially fulfilled, which is a stark testament to just how difficult this work can be. At its core, this research must be truthful, accurate and complete. This book seeks to equip anyone interested in researching museum collections with the knowledge necessary to embark on this journey. It is not only aimed at curators who wish to confront the provenance of their collections, but also seeks to empower anyone interested in using the objects on display in our museums to confront and engage the Nazi past.

The first two chapters of the book focus on providing the essential background and historical context for undertaking this work. Although this research shares many similarities with traditional provenance approaches, in that it aims to reconstruct who owned objects in the past, it rapidly and inescapably pulls us into a far more complex realm. Traditional provenance research was largely an exploration of past cultural climates, describing the tastemakers and trends, the interconnected world of art dealers and prominent collectors, and in doing so often kept a cautious distance from matters that might cast a troubling light on the objects studied.[2] Although Nazi-era provenance research often involves the records of dealers, auction houses and collectors, it is fundamentally about reconstructing the lives of helpless individuals tormented by a brutal dictatorship. Here, the objects are the gateway into the human realities of what it meant to live under the Nazi regime.

As Chapter 1 shows, in order to make the objects reveal this history to us, it is essential that we have a clear understanding of Nazi ideology and how it was put into practice; without this, the sources can remain deceptive or deeply confusing.

As Chapter 2 explores, researchers have now been analysing Nazi-era provenance issues and the modes of persecution and dispossession for far longer than the Nazi regime itself existed. For this reason, as part of our orientation, it is essential that we grasp the nature and extent of the post-war restitution effort, which produced a wealth of knowledge in the most difficult circumstances, and which remains the bedrock upon which all future efforts are constructed. It is equally important that we are aware of the restitution and compensation mechanisms that were available to the survivors after the war. Through these records, we can sometimes recover their desperate pleas for redress and uncover the human stories that were ignored in the cold documents generated by the Nazi bureaucracy. As we will be focusing on museum collections, it is crucial to understand how the Washington Conference transformed the field of provenance research and the very idea of how museums should fulfil their role as civic spaces.

The third chapter of the book deals with how we can best approach research into particular collections – the strategies, methods and resources we can use to explore the moving stories behind the objects. Museum collections can certainly appear overwhelming. Depending on the institution, they may have thousands of items of various kinds in the collections, and it is simply impossible to know by looking at any object, ancient or modern, whether it carries a Nazi-era provenance. And while we must look at the objects that entered the collections between 1933 and 1945, we must not ignore the records of the following decades. The Nazi empire was vast, and its mechanisms of dispossession were at times overt and brutal, while at others they were creeping and sinister. Despite the magnitude of the task and the complexities of Nazi policy, it will be reassuring to realise that the fundamental research strategy always remains the same: we need to closely examine the object and then carefully think about where it may have left archival traces that will enable us to fill in the gaps. In some cases, this will mean tracing an object back from the present and into the Nazi past; in others, it will mean picking up the trail before Hitler came to power and following the object into the 1930s–40s. As we do so, we are able to call upon many rich resources that help us to bypass apparent brick walls and make connections that would otherwise be impossible if we had only followed the limited or opaque information in museum acquisition files.

This book aims not only to provide the tools and references essential to this work, but also through vivid case studies to bring to life the research process as it plays out in practice. The goal of this research is always to discover the name of an individual, whom we can then investigate further. In doing so, we recover a crucial sense of their agency and bear witness to them as far more than victims of a brutal and repressive regime.

Notes

1 On the erasure and obfuscation of provenance records, see, for example: Weiler and Weber 2019, 49.

2 On the remarkable development in recent decades of provenance research from an often optional or auxiliary field into an prominent, dynamic and thoughtful discipline, see, in particular: Feigenbaum and Reist 2012; Milosch and Pearce 2019.

1 Persecution and dispossession, 1933–45

As our goal is to research the Nazi-era provenance of objects and the fate of their previous owners, it is essential that we have a firm and nuanced grasp of the Nazi ideology that defined the regime's brutal campaign of persecution and conquest. At the core of the Nazi movement's worldview was its hatred for the Jews. After the Nazis seized power in 1933 and crushed their left-wing opponents, they mobilised the might of the German state to torment the Jewish community. The regime issued a series of escalating decrees, accompanied by waves of violence, designed to exclude Jews from public life and the economy, forcing them into a state of isolation and despair. As the social, economic and legal pressure continued to build, many Jews were left with no choice but to part with their possessions, either needing to raise funds in order to survive this hostile environment, or to finance their escape from Hitler's regime. As the Reich expanded, the Nazis exported their ideology and its mechanisms of persecution and dispossession, all of which were further radicalised in the violent environment of war, and would lead ultimately to the systematic mass murder of millions of innocent Jewish men, women and children.

The Nazi worldview

In 1933, Nazi activists clustered around a Berlin tram stop, eagerly distributing an election pamphlet which aimed to provide a straightforward summary of the key elements of their ideology.[1] It was penned by Johann von Leers, one of the most prolific antisemitic writers of the Nazi movement, with a talent for capturing the essence of Nazi ideology in a far more concise fashion than Hitler and other prominent leaders could manage.[2] The Jews played a central role in this worldview, as the title of the pamphlet made plain – 'Juden raus!' (Jews out!).[3]

The central premise was that the salvation of the German people depended on the removal of Jews from their midst. Leers' pamphlet was infused with the 'scientific' racism of the day. He claimed that the Jews had convinced the world of a great lie: that all humans are equal, when in fact they belonged to distinctly different races, the members of which were forever bound together by blood. Leers painted a disturbing and lurid picture of world history as a Darwinian struggle between races for supremacy. If any race allowed its blood to be diluted, it would eventually, inevitably perish.[4]

Leers urgently wanted Germans to wake up to the terrifying fact that members of an alien and hostile race were living among them. He claimed that, unlike other races, the Jews never built anything of their own but instead operated as parasites that extracted the vitality and wealth from other races, until their victims had been sucked dry. Their ultimate goal, Leers claimed, was world domination – a goal they ceaselessly pursued through any and all means. This is why he could simultaneously claim that the Jews were the puppet masters behind both capitalism and communism. Both systems were a mere façade for the larger Jewish mission which would, all too soon, cease to operate in the shadows and become an overt grab for total power – unless, of course, the German people voted for a party that recognised this existential threat and promised to address it in a ruthless fashion.

Leers described a scenario that he found truly horrifying, in which the members of this 'foreign race' had occupied key positions within German society and culture, using their malign influence to erode and subvert the strength of the German nation. One of the many ways the Jews were supposed to be undermining the German people was by promoting democracy and, thus, discord, which the Nazis saw as antithetical to racial unity. Leers believed that in the face of increasing protests by workers against their 'Jewish capitalist' masters, the Jews had swiftly invented Communism in order to hold onto their power. By replacing the unifying force of 'race consciousness' with 'class consciousness', the workers' anger was neatly diverted away from the rich Jews behind the scenes and now turned German 'racial comrades' against each other. And if culture was a race's truest expression of itself, Leers believed that the Jews were infecting German culture by fostering degenerative, self-destructive values, not least by promoting forms of art, literature, films and pornography that were all designed not to inspire German greatness, but to confuse and gaslight Germans into believing that ugliness was beauty. At the same time, these enemies of racial purity were allegedly conspiring with Jews in other countries to humiliate and exploit the German nation on the world stage.

Following this diagnosis, Leers insisted that the only effective treatment would be the systematic and uncompromising removal of the Jews by stripping them of their undeserved influence and citizenship, before unceremoniously expelling them beyond the borders of the Reich. Leers was well aware that his audience would know many individual Jews who seemed nothing like the nightmarish figure he described. With this in mind, he insisted that even the most assimilated Jews in German society were always inescapably defined by their Jewish blood: 'In the case of a nation that wants to dominate us, what matters is not the character of the individual, but the threat of the whole.'[5] This single pamphlet crystallised the essence of Nazi ideology – radical, dehumanising and ruthless – and, when put into practice, it would lead to rapidly escalating persecution, dispossession and – ultimately – mass murder.

Persecution and dispossession of Communists and Social Democrats

On 30 January 1933, Adolf Hitler was appointed Reich Chancellor. In the ensuing months, the Nazis unleashed a wave of violence against their left-wing opponents.[6] When the Reichstag burned on 27 February, the Nazis swiftly blamed the conflagration on the Communists and accused them of plotting to overthrow the government. The accusation was followed by an immediate and brutal crackdown, the legal basis of which was an Emergency Decree ostensibly 'for the protection of state and people'. It expressly authorised arrests and confiscations 'outside the usual legal norms'.[7] At a Nazi party rally in Frankfurt, Hermann Göring pulled no punches as he publicly revealed how he intended to use these powers. In order 'to root out Communism from our people', he declared that he would use both the powers of the state and of the Nazis' stormtroopers (the SA) 'to deliver the death blow' to the Communists.[8] Göring was Reich Commissar for the Interior in Prussia and had already elevated the stormtroopers to the status of 'auxiliary police officers'. A wave of mass arrests duly spread across the Reich. At the same time, stormtroopers abducted political opponents, snatching them off the streets and invading their apartments. These early victims

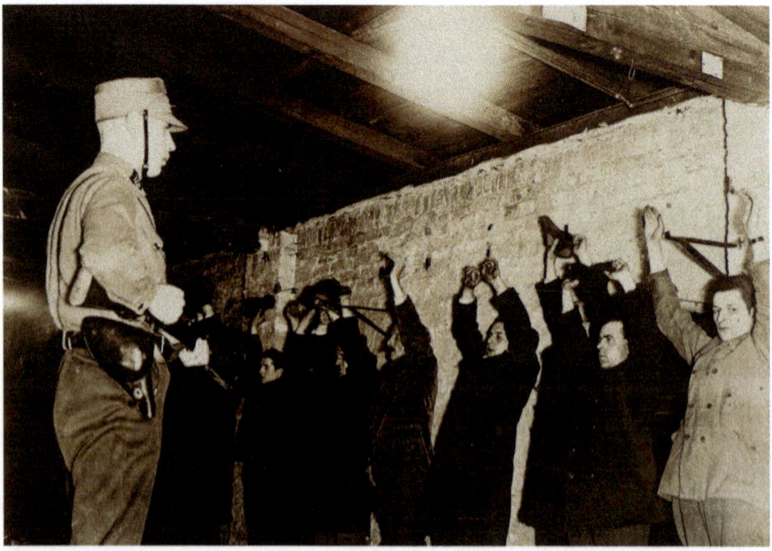

Fig. 1.1. Political prisoners abducted by stormtroopers and held under guard in a makeshift concentration camp in a basement beneath Friedrichstrasse in Berlin. © Bundesarchiv, Bild 102-02920A/Georg Pahl/ CC-BY-SA 3.0 (Source: Wikimedia Commons, https://bit.ly/3QFJki2).

were taken to makeshift concentration camps in barracks and empty buildings, and to torture chambers hidden beneath stormtrooper-controlled pubs (Figure 1.1).[9] There, they were beaten and brutalised; we will never know exactly how many were murdered.

During raids on the offices of left-wing organisations and the private homes of their functionaries and activists, the police seized documents and Marxist literature as evidence of alleged treason (Figure 1.2).[10] In this early violent campaign, we can already see the pattern which would define the Nazis' approach to their enemies: direct force and arrests went hand in glove with dispossession.[11] While the Emergency Decree had provided the legal justification for arbitrary arrests, the 'Law on the Confiscation of Communist Assets' enabled the seizure of Communist Party property, as well as any other assets that 'could be used for the purposes of Communist agitation'.[12] This law was soon followed by the 'Law on the Confiscation of Assets Hostile to the People and the State', which was aimed at the Social Democrats.[13] These laws allowed the state not simply to confiscate material to be used as evidence in a trial, but to take full and permanent possession of any assets it deemed 'hostile', from Marxist literature to socialist realist artworks hanging on the walls of Party offices.[14]

Fig. 1.2. Books and documents confiscated as 'evidence' of treason being loaded onto a truck outside the Berlin headquarters of the German Communist Party. Public domain (Source: United States Holocaust Memorial Museum).

Although Nazi student activists burned publications they considered Marxist and Jewish (and thus a corrupting influence on impressionable minds), the Nazi state believed that it had 'to study' its enemies in order to combat them effectively.[15] While Communists and Social Democrats were incarcerated in prisons and concentration camps, their libraries entered the collections of the newly minted institutions of the Nazi state and many universities; there, they were secured in 'poison cabinets' and served as a vital resource for 'enemy research'.[16]

We can see this grim process play out in the dramatic story of Walter Heise, a tailor and Communist from Hannoversch Münden. On 25 April 1933, the local police carried out a large-scale raid on Communist Party members in the city. During the raid, officers confiscated more than 50 books from Walter's personal library. On the official form, they justified these confiscations by Walter's membership in the Communist Party and the subversive political nature of the books. Several months later, Walter received a letter from the local government president, informing him that the books now belonged to the state because they were evidently designed to 'promote hostile tendencies'.[17]

This personal invasion and seizure were repeated countless times across the Reich. After the initial confiscation, lists were created and sent to the state libraries, which were given first refusal of the titles before they were distributed across the new network of poison cabinets housed in university libraries.[18] Walter stayed true to his Communist beliefs, despite being persecuted and arrested multiple times for 'treason'. He was a broken man when he was released for the last time in 1939; he took his own life, leaving behind his wife and children. A book carrying his name remained on the shelves of the University of Göttingen's library for decades. It was only when the university decided to investigate the origins of its collections that a provenance researcher discovered Walter's name on the first page and, after careful research, was able to restore the book to his heirs, and Walter's story to the historical record.[19]

Antisemitic violence and laws

In the spring of 1933, in the climate of escalating political persecution, Nazi stormtroopers not only brutalised their political opponents, but also felt empowered to strike against Jews, whom they believed were the hidden hand behind Communism.[20] A trade unionist who survived torture in a makeshift concentration camp recorded his shock when he had to look on as a Jewish doctor was beaten to death.[21] In this moment, he suddenly realised what would soon become emblematic of the regime: that the Nazis persecuted people not only for their beliefs, but even for who they were. Indeed, in the Nazi worldview, a Communist or Social Democrat could repent and eventually return to the fold, but this was a door firmly closed to Jews, who were persecuted irrespective of their political or religious beliefs.[22]

With the destruction of the Left, Nazi activists increasingly turned the terror upon the Jews, abducting prominent members of the Jewish community, invading homes, disrupting synagogues, smashing shop windows and interrupting lectures given by Jewish professors.[23] In Breslau (now Wrocław in Poland), Nazi activists stormed the court building and demanded the removal of Jewish judges, state prosecutors and lawyers, incensed that these 'alien elements' could hold legal power over German citizens.[24] If the Reichstag fire had served as a pretext for the violence against Communists, the international outcry

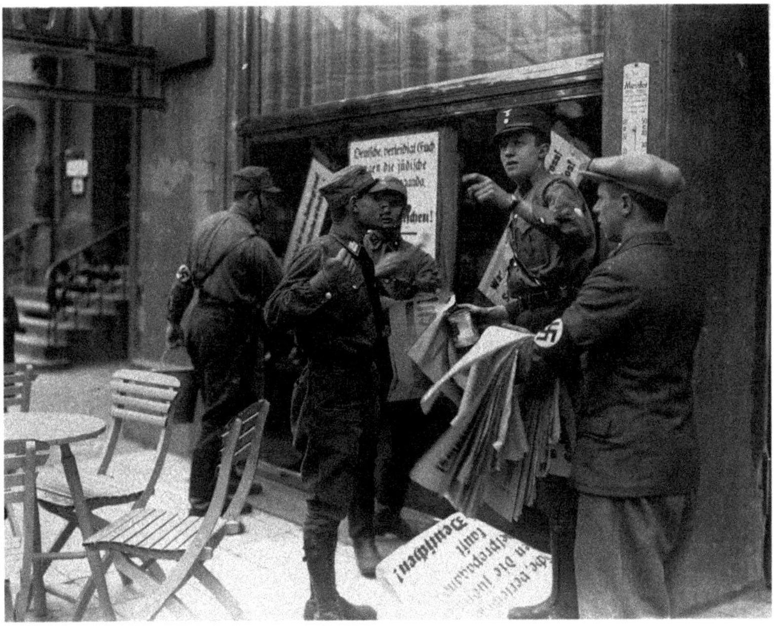

Fig. 1.3. Stormtroopers glueing boycott posters to a shop window and discussing which Jewish businesses to target next. Public domain (Source: United States Holocaust Memorial Museum).

against the mistreatment of Jews now became the justification for a Reich-spanning boycott. On 1 April 1933, stormtroopers carrying placards appeared outside Jewish businesses, legal offices and medical practices, menacing and often assaulting anyone coming in or out of the premises (Figure 1.3).[25] Despite the terror of these experiences, many Jews still hoped that this upswell of violence and prejudice would be temporary, that it was merely the result of the Nazis still feeling drunk on their political victory.[26]

If the Reichstag Decree had formally enabled the Nazis to arrest opponents 'outside the usual legal norms', then the 'Enabling Act' went much further: it allowed them to pass laws that openly violated the Weimar Constitution, which had previously guaranteed the equality of all citizens, irrespective of their ethnic background.[27] In April, the first directly antisemitic law came into force as the Nazis moved to cleanse the civil service – the heart of any state – of all elements that they considered a political danger, which carried the deceptively bland title 'Law for the Restoration of the Professional Civil Service'.[28] On the one hand, this law enabled the exclusion of any civil servants whose political history meant they could not be trusted to act 'ruthlessly' in service of the new racial state. On the other, even if their past record may have seemed beyond reproach, this law was inherently racist: it stipulated that civil servants who were not 'Aryans' could be forcibly retired from their posts.[29] For the enforcers, a directive spelled out what 'non-Aryan' meant, namely anyone who had a Jewish parent or even a single Jewish grandparent.[30]

When thinking of the civil service, we should not imagine only a select number of ministerial or legal officials, for in Germany the service encapsulated a huge range of different professions – from postal workers, municipal workers, judges, teachers and professors to museum curators and even train conductors.[31] They were all forced to confront the chilling possibility that their careers, their financial security and their hopes for the future could now all be abruptly terminated. There were some exceptions to the racial rules spelled out in the law. To appease the Reich President (still technically the head of state), veterans were excluded from the purge, but even they faced increasing hostility from the Nazi activists like Leers, who filled the now-vacant posts.[32]

One of the many promising and established careers cut short by the law was that of Curt Glaser, a former museum curator and now Director of the Berlin Art Library. Even before the 'Law for the Restoration of the Civil Service' was passed, he was placed on administrative leave; for this experienced cultural professional, it soon became all too evident that every door in the field was now closed to him. It was in this climate that he made the decision to leave his homeland. After the war, Glaser's sister-in-law recalled that Curt was just one of many 'non-Aryans' who 'rushed to escape from Germany', and that before he fled, he sold his private art collection at the Max Perl auction house.[33] Curt's wife remembered that he described this last-minute auction 'as a total fire-sale'.[34] At the auction, his possessions were acquired by German museums and, via private collectors and art dealers, many items would ultimately end up in museum collections around the world.[35]

To the delight of the Nazi activists who had boycotted and protested outside the practices of Jewish lawyers and doctors, a series of additional laws was introduced which targeted the so-called 'free professions'. These were the professions for which the state could issue and rescind licences, directly controlling who had the right to practise.[36] Among those affected was Ismar Littmann, a lawyer and notary who lived and worked in Breslau, the site of some of the earliest protests against Jewish professionals. Within months, this accomplished lawyer and philanthropist of the arts had his professional existence destroyed; as his son recalled after the war, 'from the April boycott onwards, his income was dramatically reduced', putting the family in financial jeopardy and curtailing his ability to support artists.[37] 'This double blow drove my father to [attempt] suicide in 1933. He was rescued, but he never recovered.'[38]

Ismar died the following year, leaving behind his wife and four adult children to live on in an environment that was now so hostile that it had already cost them the life of their beloved Ismar. Facing immense financial difficulties, his widow, Käthe, was compelled to sell his art collection at auction and, like Curt Glaser, she turned to the Max Perl auction house which, at this point, was still under Jewish ownership.[39] To initiate the auction, she had to specify the reason for the sale. She was clear and direct: 'lack of funds' – a simple phrase that did no justice to the personal tragedy that had driven her to the auction house.[40] Like Glaser's collection, many of the objects were dispersed and ultimately entered museum collections.[41]

Emigration

The violence and discrimination against the Jews prompted many to escape from Nazi Germany. Leaving a country to start a new life elsewhere was a daunting task that required great courage, optimism and connections, and the financial means to do so.[42] If persecution and increasingly antisemitic legislation was what drove many to seek emigration, the laws that would have the most devastating impact actually predated the Nazi period. These laws were born of the economic crisis of the 1930s and were designed to dissuade or prevent taxpayers and capital from leaving the country. The increasingly terrorised Jews found themselves caught between antisemitic legislation that wanted to drive them from the Reich, and pre-Nazi laws that had been designed to make this financially crippling (Figure 1.4).[43] In 1931, a law had been passed which became known as the Reich Flight Tax, the name heavily implying that relocating to a different tax jurisdiction was tantamount to treason. It applied to anyone who owned taxable assets exceeding 200,000 Reichsmarks, or whose annual income exceeded 20,000 Reichsmarks. People falling into these categories had to hand over 25 per cent of their net worth to the state.[44]

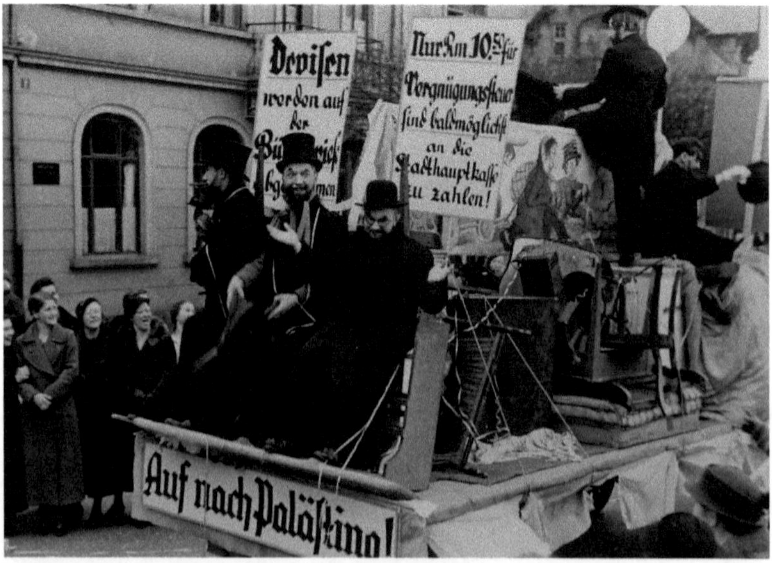

Fig. 1.4. An antisemitic 1936 carnival float mocking the discriminatory taxes that Jewish refugees were forced to pay. Note the household goods stacked at the rear. © Stadtarchiv Marburg, with permission from Gerhard Unkel.

While the Reich Flight Tax was designed to prevent taxpayers from leaving, the Foreign Exchange Control Law of the same year was intended to prevent capital from leaving the country. This decree meant that Reichsmarks could only be exchanged for foreign currency through the Central Bank and only for the official value set by the Berlin stock exchange – in short, giving the state direct control over citizens' ability to prepare for a life elsewhere.[45]

Two years later, the Nazis had seized power and were fixated on the idea that Jews should leave the Reich and never return. In their hands, tools originally designed to discourage emigration became weapons used to extract as much wealth as possible from these persecuted people as they tried to flee.[46] In 1934, the Nazis tightened the screws by issuing an amendment to the Reich Flight Tax which lowered the asset threshold from 200,000 to 50,000 Reichsmarks, and the income threshold from 20,000 to 10,000 Reichsmarks.[47] Only a few months later, the income threshold was slashed to an absurd 10 Reichsmarks, allowing the Reich to siphon off assets from even the poorest emigrant.[48]

Crucially, this amendment gave sweeping powers to the Finance Offices.[49] At the same time that the police were putting individuals in 'protective custody' on the mere suspicion that they might commit a crime, finance officials could now block and seize individuals' assets based on the mere suspicion that they might emigrate in the future.[50] In essence, a freeze was placed on assets to ensure that, if they did leave, the Reich Flight Tax would be paid. In practice, this meant that innocent acts like moving to a smaller apartment, applying for a passport or selling pieces from an art collection could seriously exacerbate the financial distress so many were already experiencing.[51]

Once they saw how effective these harsh measures could be, the Nazi lawmakers would rapidly take it to the extreme. They exploited and tightened the currency laws in order to seize as much as possible of what remained. Reichsmarks could not be taken out of Germany, which forced emigrants to exchange what little they had left for foreign currency. They had no choice but to make this exchange via the state's German Gold Discount Bank (Deutsche Golddiskontbank), which would buy Reichsmarks for 50 per cent of their true value.[52] In other words, in addition to the 25 per cent Reich Flight Tax they had already paid, the refugees lost a further 50 per cent of their wealth as they attempted to leave Germany. This rate was gradually worsened until it reached a shocking 96 per cent in 1939, which amounted to an act of almost total dispossession.[53] It was only after all tax bills had been settled that the German state deigned to issue an exit permit, without which it was impossible to leave the country.[54]

'Aryanisation'

Many Nazi activists, who had gleefully boycotted Jewish businesses, now hoped that the Nazi state would not only 'Aryanise' the civil service and certain professions, but would apply the same racial logic to the economy at large.[55] Although there was for now no equivalent legislation enacted against private businesses, this should not blind us to the reality that both Jewish employees and Jewish business owners faced significant grassroots hostility, the impact of which could be easily as devastating as the antisemitic laws printed in the pages of the state newspaper.[56] Shortly after the Nazi seizure of power, many Jewish employees were served notice, sometimes after their Nazi colleagues had staged protests to demand their removal.[57]

In the new antisemitic climate, many business owners forced out their Jewish partners or employees to ensure their companies would remain on good terms with the new rulers. Whether these individuals were ideologues or opportunists, the choices they made had the same painful impact on the people who were pushed out. At the local level, Jewish business owners were assailed from all sides. Arrayed against them were Nazified administrative and professional bodies; local Nazi leaders and activists eager to see businesses in 'Aryan'-only hands; competitors who sought to capitalise on the new orthodoxy as a means of eliminating and taking over their rivals; and even customers who did not want to be seen frequenting a Jewish business.[58]

The hostility was tangible and could come in many forms. Public contracts could be cancelled, financial agreements terminated, and many businesses died by degrees as local authorities strangled them in red tape. Behind this loomed the ever-present threat of violence and arbitrary arrest.[59] In this climate, many Jewish business owners understandably could see no future for themselves. They felt compelled to sell their businesses to competitors, to their former employees and often to the very people who had harassed and denounced them to the authorities.

At the national level, the pressure came in different forms. In 1933, the Nazis seized direct control over the cultural sector by creating the Reich Chamber of Culture (Reichskulturkammer).[60] Membership of this body was a prerequisite for anyone wishing to do business in the cultural sector, which meant that all art dealerships and auction houses had to become members. One of the many disorienting signals received by the Jewish community (and which gave many a temporary but false sense of security) was that they were likewise compelled to become members.[61] However, the Chamber always reserved the right to strip people of membership if they were considered to be 'unreliable'. This was a Sword of Damocles that hung over the head of every Jew in the sector. What shielded some was simply the fact that their continued existence was considered beneficial to the Reich, for example if an art dealership generated revenue in the form of much-needed foreign currency.[62] Even this would prove only a temporary reprieve.

One of the many businesses to be 'Aryanised' was the Max Perl auction house, where both Curt Glaser and Ismar Littmann's widow had sold their collections. In 1935, its Jewish owner received a notice excluding him from the Reich Chamber of Culture. Like so many others, he sold his business to a non-Jewish employee, the proceeds of which would then be slashed to a fraction of their value as he emigrated from Germany.[63]

Legitimising the new order in museum galleries

By this point, the ideological vision that Johann von Leers had outlined in his pamphlet had firmly become reality. In 1937, a major exhibition opened in Munich which invited visitors to look back on the four years since Hitler had come to power, aiming to recap and reaffirm what the regime had done to eliminate the 'Jewish menace'.[64]

'Der Ewige Jude' (The Eternal Jew) first opened at the Deutsche Museum before touring widely across the Reich. Outside the exhibition hall, visitors were greeted by an enormous poster depicting a crude caricature of 'the Jew' (Figure 1.5). As they entered the first gallery, the tone shifted from simplistic imagery to the seemingly more respectable ideas of 'scientific' racism that underpinned Nazi ideology. Visitors were confidently informed that the Jews had always been a distinctly different race, a claim illustrated by photographs of 'typical Jews' and plaster casts of their allegedly typical racial characteristics, such as long noses and enlarged ears (Figure 1.6). Large quotations on the wall hammered home the idea that Jews would always be Jews – no passport, language, political credo or baptism could ever change this fundamental biological fact. In the gallery that followed, visitors were supposed to learn that the Jewish presence among other peoples had been a problem throughout history because they systematically exploited the other races around them.[65]

In the museum, visitors could have used Johann von Leers' antisemitic publications as an exhibition catalogue. His diatribes had been brought to life in the exhibition halls, where visitors could be left in no doubt that the Jews, whether they wore the mask of capitalist or Communist, or had converted to Christianity, should always be viewed as a lethal cancer within German society. Like a malignant tumour, the only possible treatment was surgical removal, and so the exhibition celebrated how the Nazi state had excised the Jews in all areas crucial to the health of the nation, using statistics to show how the numbers of Jews in key professions had been drastically reduced.[66]

The climax of the exhibition would be a room dedicated to the Nuremberg Racial Laws. Like the first antisemitic decrees, the Nuremberg Laws were preceded by a wave of grassroots violence against Jews across the Reich.[67] The persecution and brutalisation familiar from 1933 was now accompanied by the open humiliation of 'mixed' couples, who were paraded through the streets with placards strung from their necks which denounced them as 'race traitors'.[68]

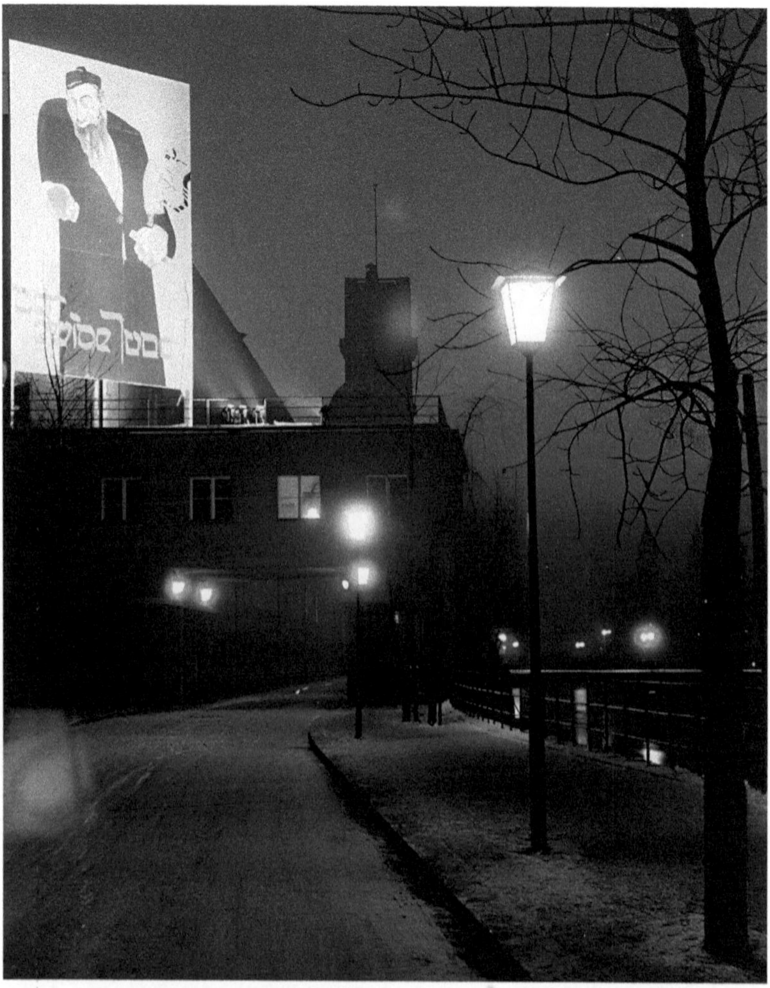

Fig. 1.5. An enormous, illuminated poster advertising the 'Eternal Jew' exhibition looms above the German Museum in Munich. Public domain (Source: Wikimedia Commons, https://bit.ly/3s7aHIm).

The Nazi Party had declared in 1920 that only pure Germans should be granted citizenship, and the 'Reich Citizenship Law' unveiled at Nuremberg in 1935, delivered on this racist vision.[69] The law drew a sharp distinction between 'citizens of the Reich' and those who merely lived within its borders.[70] The 'First Decree' provided an explanatory note, formalising the criteria: a person was classified as fully Jewish if they had at least three Jewish grandparents.[71] In order to ensure their segregation, the 'Law for the Protection of German

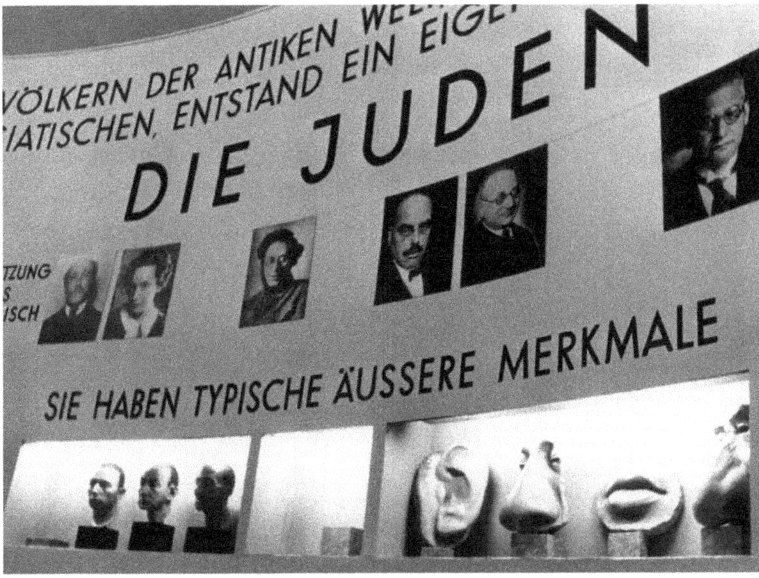

Fig. 1.6. A scene from the 'Eternal Jew' exhibition in Munich. Note the plaster casts of supposedly 'typical physical characteristics'. © Stadtarchiv München.

Blood and German Honour' made it illegal for German citizens to 'weaken' their race by marrying Jews.[72]

Acquisitions and complicity

Our goal is to understand the effects and legacies this relentless persecution had on museums, so we must turn to these institutions directly. Like the civil service, museums were directly controlled by the state and were therefore 'cleansed' in 1933. Jewish museum professionals were abruptly forced from their posts, while those allowed to remain embraced the new political reality and, in many cases, capitalised upon it.[73] As in the business world, this was a golden moment for denouncers, careerists and ideological purists – many of whom went beyond what was required by the regime. They organised their own purges of Jews from cultural organisations, deleted their names from mailing lists, and some even enquired whether it was possible to bar Jews from entering museums entirely.[74] Museum professionals may in private have looked with bourgeois disdain upon the former Nazi street fighters who now suddenly held influential posts in the cultural sector, but their private sentiments could not change the facts on the ground.

Even if these professionals tried to take a 'business as usual' approach to their work, it was nearly impossible for a German museum that expanded its collection in the 1930s not to become the beneficiary of Nazi persecution. Many individuals were compelled to sell their collections on the art market in the desperate attempt to raise funds to survive the destruction of their livelihoods, or to prepare to flee.[75] For museums looking to expand their collections, this human tragedy created an unparalleled opportunity to buy pieces that would otherwise never have entered the offices of art dealerships and auction houses. Naturally, the directors and curators in charge of acquiring new pieces would often have known the collectors whose treasures suddenly came up for sale – they had moved in the same circles and sometimes even acted as their advisers, so they could be under no illusions concerning the grim reality behind deceptively normal-seeming art market sales. If they did not know them personally, the names of famous collectors were often published to drum up interest in particular sales, which made plain the disproportionate number of Jews who suddenly parted with their collections. From 1938 onwards, any object that came up for auction from a Jewish collection had to be identified as such in the catalogues.[76]

But museum professionals did not merely turn a blind eye to the realities behind these sales. Many of them directly offered their art-historical and curatorial expertise in the service of the Nazi state. This did not just mean providing professional advice or acting as agents for Hitler, who tasked the Dresden museum director Hans Posse with building up the collections of a vast new Führer Museum.[77] It increasingly meant that the museum sector was directly and consistently complicit in the dispossession of the Jews: when the finance and customs authorities confiscated Jewish property, they needed experts to tell them what exactly they had seized, how much it was worth and whether it should be placed in a state museum, or simply sold at auction to satisfy the frequently enormous tax demands levied upon those who sought to escape the Reich.[78] These curators were often not merely analysts in this situation; they were also given first refusal on artworks that they might want to add to their own museum collections.[79] As the process of dispossession escalated, art dealers and curators would find themselves sifting through the contents of apartments that had belonged to Jews who, sometimes just moments before, had been forced onto trains bound for the extermination camps in the East.[80] None of this was secret: throughout the 1930s and 1940s, curators diligently recorded the names of the objects' previous owners. In acquisition books and card indexes, they scribbled the names of countless Jewish collectors whom they knew would never return, or they recorded the names of the Nazi organisations that sometimes dumped crates of artworks on museum doorsteps that were simply and openly labelled as 'Jewish Property'.[81]

In light of this practice, research into German museum collections has been particularly urgent and necessary.[82] But we must always remember that if objects torn from their former owners did not end up in German museums, they were acquired by art dealers and private collectors. In time, by often twisted paths, many have come to rest in museum collections all over the world, their full histories forgotten or erased along the way.

'Degenerate' art

Nazi ideology also affected the art world in other ways. At the same time as German museums were adding new pieces to their galleries from former collections of persecuted Jews, they were made to surrender other objects the Nazis deemed 'degenerate' and which would then enter galleries and private collections outside the Reich. If Leers had provided a concise summary of the Nazis' general worldview, it was the architect and Nazi activist Paul Schultze-Naumburg who crystallised how this ideology should be enacted in the art world. In his 1928 book *Kunst und Rasse* (*Art and Race*), he applied the racial 'science' of the day to establish a disturbing connection between artistic expression and mental or physical disabilities, both of which were supposed to be eradicated from a healthy 'racial community'.[83] According to this perspective, all artworks inherently mirrored the 'racial quality' of the artists themselves. This meant that artists who were considered to be racially healthy would produce art that celebrated and furthered the advancement of the German race as a whole. By extension, individuals with mental or physical 'defects' were thought to be capable of only producing art that mirrored their 'racial deficiencies'.[84]

To drive home this point, Schultze-Naumburg juxtaposed photographs of disabled individuals with modernist art to demonstrate that they were both ultimately the outcome of negative hereditary traits and were symptomatic of a 'racial degeneration' that must be immediately curtailed.[85] If such art implicitly celebrated the degeneration of the

German race, then, in the Nazis' view, its promotion could only serve the interests of those seeking to undermine the 'racial community'. The chief culprits were predictably thought to be Jewish art dealers and critics, who used their supposedly disproportionate influence to harm the community, aided by wayward Germans seduced by their money and influence.

In June 1937, Joseph Goebbels, the Reich Minister for Propaganda and Enlightenment, authorised the Director of the Reich Chamber of Culture, Adolf Ziegler, to select and confiscate paintings and sculptures from public collections in order to create a major exhibition on 'degenerate art'.[86] Ziegler promptly assembled a commission which, over the course of a mere ten days, confiscated artworks deemed guilty of promoting degeneracy. A selection of these artworks was displayed in the 'Degenerate Art' exhibition, which opened in July at the Archaeological Institute of Munich (Figure 1.7).[87] It was only fitting that Ziegler himself made the opening address, leaving no room for doubt as to how the artworks should be interpreted: 'Look around you at these monstrosities of insanity, insolence, incompetence and degeneration.'[88]

As visitors made their way through the exhibition, they were soon confronted by a selection of paintings said to exemplify the 'revelation of the Jewish racial soul'. This was intended to provoke disgust at the Jews' artistic creations and, by extension, their racial 'otherness' (Figure 1.8).[89] The exhibition drew large crowds and would soon go on tour across the Reich. Later incarnations contrasted modernist art with paintings and drawings made by patients in a psychiatric hospital in order to hammer home the connection between biological and artistic degeneracy.

Energised by a Hitler speech, in which he had announced a 'ruthless war of cleansing against the last elements of our cultural decomposition', Goebbels decided to complete the mission by clearing out the remaining unacceptable artworks.[90] This time, the screening process did not have to be rushed for the sake of an upcoming exhibition and aimed to remove the last vestiges of Germany's shameful 'period of decay'. Ziegler's commission visited more than 100 museums in 74 cities, confiscating more than 16,000 works of art.[91] These were stored in a grain silo in Berlin. The next step would be their 'liquidation': if they could not be shown in Germany outside the context of 'shaming exhibitions', they could yet be sold abroad to generate revenue for the Nazi regime. They were sold through the regime's most trusted art dealers, auctioned off in neutral Switzerland

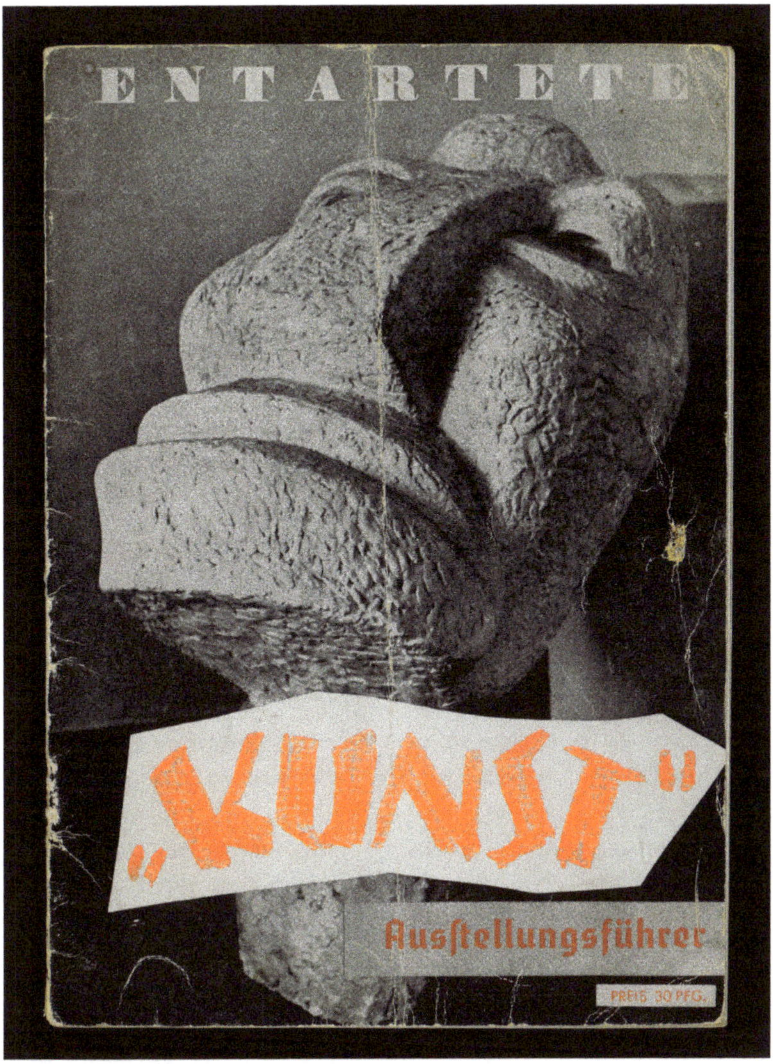

Fig. 1.7. Otto Freundlich, who created the sculpture on this title page of the 'degenerate art' exhibition guide, was murdered in 1943 in the Majdanek extermination camp. © Victoria & Albert Museum, London.

or exchanged for artworks deemed racially appropriate.[92] The items that could not be 'liquidated' in this manner were destroyed in a bonfire that turned perhaps 5,000 artworks to ash.[93] The pieces that survived this fate eventually entered art collections around the world, where they now stand as an often forgotten testament to the Nazis' uncompromising ideological campaign – a campaign that not

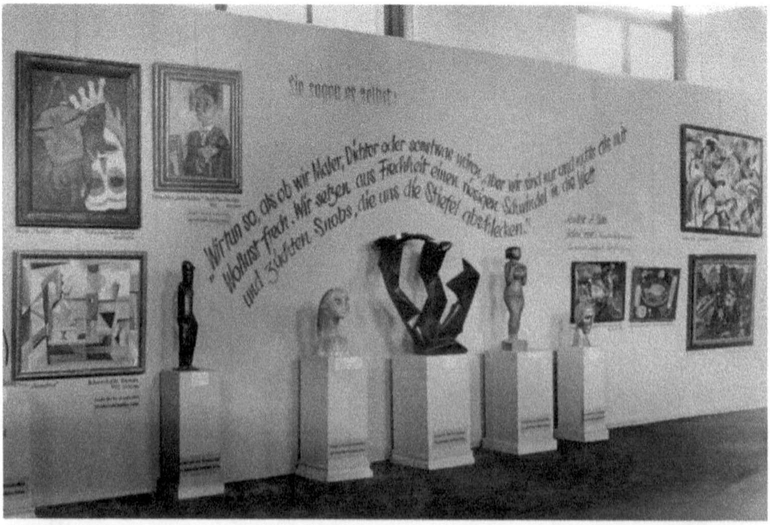

Fig. 1.8. A scene from the 'degenerate art' exhibition, showing a gallery designed to appear chaotic and disturbing to the German audience. On the walls, quotations were chosen to present modernist art as a Jewish conspiracy. © Stadtarchiv München.

only changed German museums forever, but also carried the stories of Nazi cultural policy into the museum galleries that became their safe haven.[94]

Researching the provenance of these pieces enables us to tell the story of the artworks excommunicated from Hitler's Germany, and invites us to learn about the fate of the artists who made them. The case of Elfriede Lohse-Wächtler draws into focus the consequences of the worldview that lay at the heart of Schultze-Naumburg's eugenic equation of modernist art with mental illness. In 1929, Elfriede suffered a nervous breakdown and was admitted to a psychiatric hospital where she continued to make drawings and to paint watercolours, many of which depicted her fellow patients.[95] In 1932, she was diagnosed with schizophrenia; two years later, under the Nazi regime, she was forcibly sterilised in order to prevent her from passing on her 'degenerate traits'.[96] Not long after Ziegler's commission had confiscated her earlier works from museum collections, the Nazi regime began to systematically murder the mentally and physically disabled.[97] In 1940, Elfriede was gassed in the Pirna nursing home.

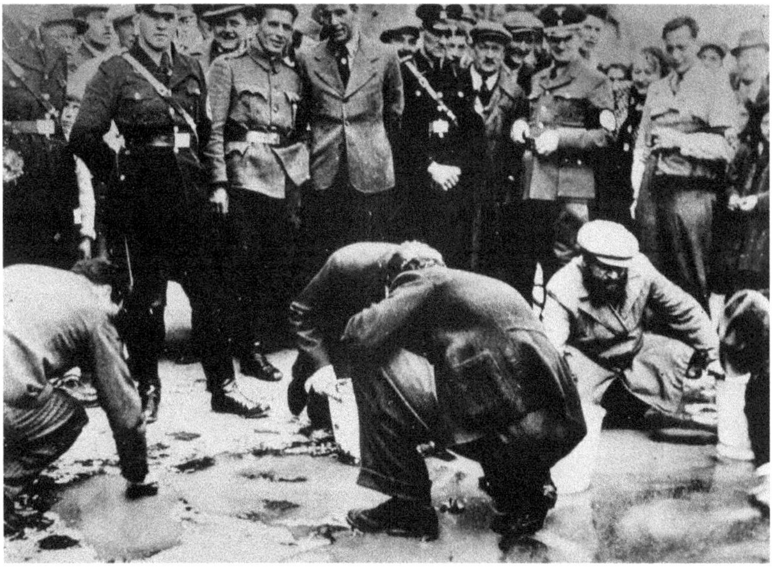

Fig. 1.9. Austrian Nazis forcing Jews to get on their knees and scrub the pavement in front of a large crowd of bystanders. Public domain (Source: United States Holocaust Memorial Museum).

Radicalisation

Both the 'Eternal Jew' and the 'Degenerate Art' exhibitions would soon be shown in Vienna, after Nazi troops had swept into Austria and 'restored' it to what was now called the Great German Empire.[98] The arrival of the new order meant that Nazi activists unleashed an inferno of violence against the Jewish population in Vienna, making the events of early 1933 pale in comparison. In March 1938, Jews were dragged from their homes, assaulted in the streets and subjected to brutal rituals of humiliation: they were stripped, their beards were forcibly shaved, and many were forced to clean the streets in front of laughing bystanders, or even made to dance like carnival animals for the amusement of the Nazi faithful (Figure 1.9).[99]

While Jews were brutalised on the streets and Nazi activists filled their own pockets during ad hoc 'confiscations', a curator from the Kunsthistorisches Museum in Vienna became deeply concerned about the fate of significant private art collections owned by Jews. Having been appointed Interim Director, Fritz Dworschak pushed the Nazi party to 'secure' these collections from the rampaging mobs (and, of course, from their Jewish owners, who he feared might take them out of the country).[100] The seizures in Vienna soon drew Hitler's personal attention. Having spent his formative political years in the city, Hitler had a keen interest in the artworks now 'liberated' through the confiscations of 'property hostile to the state, and particularly Jewish property'. He made it known that he would be the ultimate decision-maker concerning the fate of these artworks.[101] Dworschak wasted no time: he proposed to create 'in coordination with the Gestapo a Central Office for the Review and Registration of Confiscated Cultural Property in Austria'. Driven by self-interest and practical considerations, he volunteered his own institution as the central location at which these confiscated items would be 'stored, catalogued and where necessary conserved'.[102]

In the Neue Burg, curators from the Kunsthistorisches Museum and other major Viennese museums now brought their art-historical expertise to bear, cataloguing and processing the artworks the Gestapo had removed from Jewish homes.[103] In the process, they created an inventory (emblazoned with the handwritten word 'confiscations' in bright red ink), which began with the personal details of the Jewish collectors, effectively making it an address book of the dispossessed. For each of the thousands of confiscated works, the curators also created an individual index card that described the objects and their location within the overflowing crates stacked in the museum's offices and hallways. These 'acquisition records' contained information not only about the objects, but also about their next intended destination. Often these cards contained reference to the 'Kunstmuseum Linz', which meant that the object had been earmarked for a museum that did not yet exist. This was to be the public home of Hitler's personal art collection; to befit the stature required by such an institution, his existing collection had to be vastly expanded to fill the enormous halls and galleries that his architects envisioned.[104] Hitler had already announced that he would have first refusal over the objects 'seized' by the Gestapo in Austria, but to make the initial selections he turned to the museum director Hans Posse. This whole enterprise would become known as the 'Sonderauftrag Linz' (Linz Special Commission), under whose auspices Posse was not only authorised to select items from the loot assembled at the Kunsthistorisches Museum, but also equipped with an acquisition budget to expand the collection via his network of art dealers.[105]

After the first wave of violence in Vienna in March 1938, the racist policies that had developed gradually in Germany over months or even years were now imported wholesale and implemented with staggering speed. Not only did the Nazis have a blueprint to work from, they could also now perfect and streamline the mechanisms of implementation.[106] Nowhere was this more apparent than with regard to dispossession and emigration. Jewish observers would later recall how so many lives were transformed during a single visit to the Nazi administrative building in Vienna (seized from a prominent Jewish family):

> At one end you put in a Jew who still has some property, a factory, or a shop, or a bank account, and he goes through the building from counter to counter, from to office to office, and comes out at the other end without any money, without any rights, with only a passport on which it says 'You must leave the country within a fortnight. Otherwise you will go to a concentration camp.'[107]

While Vienna was rocked by the orgy of violence, Hermann Göring laid the foundations for a comprehensive and coordinated seizure of Jewish assets across the Reich.[108] A series of decrees was issued in rapid succession that, together, would form a ruthlessly efficient instrument for seizing what wealth remained from this tormented community. The first step was to meticulously catalogue what they owned.[109] The 'Decree on the Registration of Jewish Assets' forced all Jews who still possessed assets worth more than 5,000 Reichsmarks to complete a detailed declaration, in which they listed their bank accounts, savings, insurance policies, interests in property and companies, and any artworks and precious metals they owned.[110]

Göring had long been frustrated that the 'Aryanisation' of Jewish companies had often produced no direct financial benefit to the Reich; although a company's ownership might pass into 'racially pure' hands, this did nothing to fill the pockets of the Reich directly. For this to happen in a systematic fashion, it was necessary to clearly define and identify Jewish businesses. Following the spirit of the Nuremberg Laws (which had defined who was classified as Jewish), the 'Third Ordinance to the Reich Citizenship Law of 1938' applied the same logic to companies. If a Jew owned a business, or was part of the senior management, or if just one-quarter of the capital was owned by Jews, this company was now earmarked for hostile takeover.[111]

Armed with this encyclopaedic information concerning Jewish assets and companies, all that remained was to act upon it. If the Reichstag fire had been used as the pretext to terrorise Communists and Social Democrats and to seize their organisations' assets,

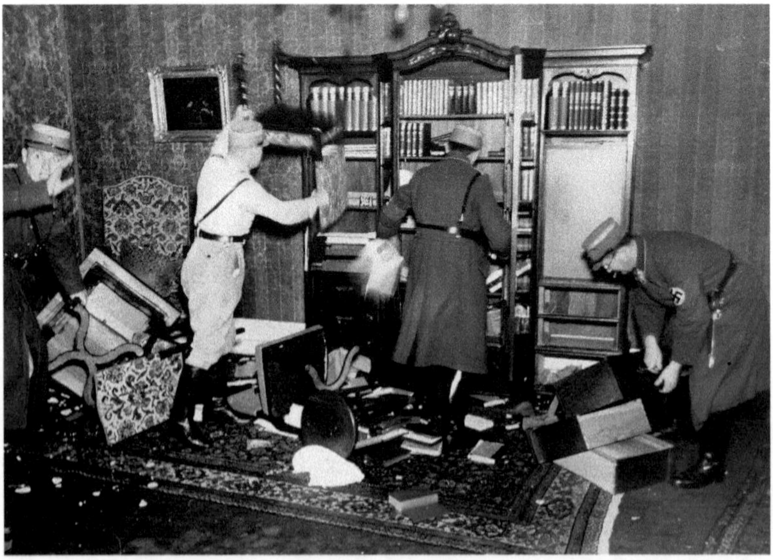

Fig. 1.10. Stormtroopers invading and ransacking a Jewish apartment during the November pogrom in Fürth (Bavaria). © Yad Vashem.

the assassination of a German diplomat in Paris by a Polish Jew in November 1938 was the spark that set in motion the complete destruction or seizure of what little the Jewish community had left.[112] After the news broke, Goebbels gave an inflammatory speech to party leaders, declaring that the Jewish community in the Reich needed to be punished for this act. The party leaders rushed to the telephones and insisted to their underlings that the time had come to strike. Shortly thereafter, police stations across the country were ordered not to stand in the way of the expression of 'righteous anger' that the Nazis sought to orchestrate.[113] The single proviso was to ensure that only Jewish interests were damaged. This was the signal to begin what became known as 'Kristallnacht'.

Following the familiar playbook of previous violence campaigns, not least the hitherto unprecedented violence in Vienna, Nazi activists in every corner of the Reich gathered together as a mob. They marched into the homes of terrified Jews, destroying everything they found and brutalising everyone they encountered. Businesses were ransacked and synagogues were set ablaze as firefighters looked on, anxious only to prevent the fire spreading to non-Jewish properties (Figure 1.10). That night, 100 Jews were murdered, tens of thousands were abducted to concentration camps and more than 7,000 businesses were destroyed.[114]

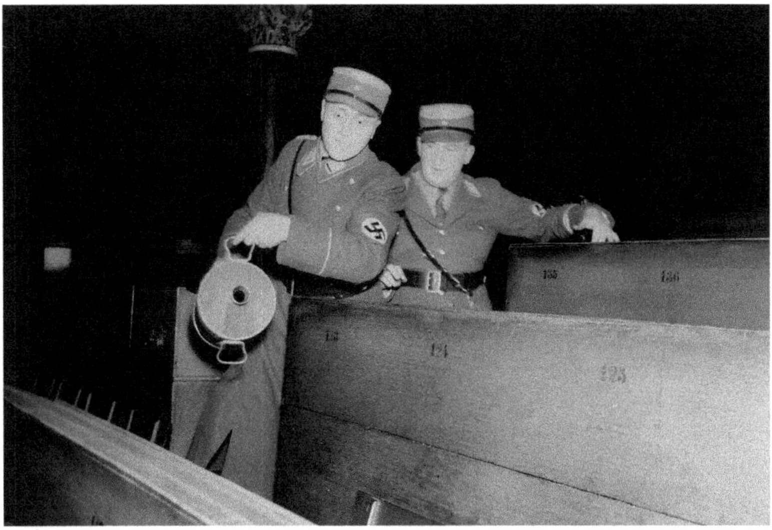

Fig. 1.11. Stormtrooper pouring gasoline on the benches of the synagogue in Fürth (Bavaria) before setting it ablaze. © Yad Vashem.

As in Vienna, this unrestrained violence opened the door to 'wild' confiscations (Figure 1.11). It is no surprise that men who were capable of brutalising innocent people in their own homes frequently stole items to personally enrich themselves, and that this included valuables and works of art that could be easily slipped into a pocket. For museum directors, who often viewed these rough Nazi street fighters with cultured condescension, this moment likewise presented a huge opportunity to enrich themselves. In Frankfurt, the Nazi mayor threatened an almost 100-year-old Jewish collector with stormtroopers, forcing him in fear for his life to sell off his entire collection to the city's museums.[115] As in Vienna, curators invaded his home to catalogue the collection. In a nearby town, the director of the local museums and archives waded through the ruins of the synagogue in order to 'collect' nine Torah scrolls and other religious items. He proposed to create a museum on the site of the ruined synagogue which would house local Jewish history and would, naturally, be 'antisemitically interpreted'.[116]

In a move that was as perverse as it was cruel, the regime punished the Jews for the damage caused by the frenzied brownshirts. Göring demanded compensation payments from the Jews, calculated on the basis of the asset declarations they had been forced to submit earlier that year.[117] In other words, the same people who had just survived the largest pogrom in German history were now forced to pay a substantial portion of their remaining resources to the perpetrators. As the smoke cleared and the ash settled, some Jews naturally turned to their insurance policies to help them rebuild their homes and businesses, but Göring swiftly ordered the confiscation of all pay-outs.[118]

Kristallnacht was followed by more antisemitic laws which would sound the death knell for Jewish economic activity in Hitler's Reich. The First Decree on the 'Elimination of the Jews from the German Economy' stipulated that Jewish businesses had either to be sold off, or would be forcibly dissolved.[119] As Jews were barred from virtually all professions, the machinery of dispossession was ratcheted up still further. They were ordered to surrender all precious metals in their possession, which meant taking not only bags of cutlery, but also ritual objects important to their religious practice, to Nazi pawn shops – which paid them a pittance in return. Once again, this haul was inspected by museum directors and curators, who were given first refusal before the rest was melted down and used to finance German rearmament.[120]

In the wake of Kristallnacht, Jews were not merely comprehensively dispossessed, they were also subjected to another series of sadistic laws designed to segregate them still further. If their first name was not on a list of 32 names that the Nazis believed to be distinctly Jewish, they had to add Sara or Israel to their names; they were no longer allowed to visit museums.[121] And if they did not manage to flee, they plummeted into abject poverty, forced to live in overcrowded 'Jewish houses', which were in essence mini-ghettoes scattered across the cities.[122]

The war

Within a handful of years, the Nazi regime had dramatically reshaped German society, crushed internal opposition, converted all institutions to its racist ideology and embarked on a remorseless campaign of ethnic cleansing and dispossession. The outbreak of the Second World War in 1939 would now enable the regime to export this ideology, along with its mechanisms of confiscation and extortion, to the territories seized through conquest. In the violent environment of war, the Nazis took these practices to new extremes.

In September 1939, Germany invaded Poland; it soon rapidly brought vast swathes of Europe under its control, before launching a war of extermination against the Soviet Union.[123] As the troops and death squads took control over ever more territory, they were shadowed by Nazi institutions whose agents had become masters of seizing the possessions and assets of their political and racial enemies.[124] In the ruins of the Polish state, they enthusiastically implemented radical policies designed to expand the Reich into the East, using their favoured tools of violence and ethnic cleansing to achieve this goal.[125] As before, this was accompanied by policies designed to extract as much wealth as possible from their defeated enemies. As always, the Nazi state made laws to legitimise this campaign of terror and dispossession: they issued a law that declared the death of the Polish state, and announced that all it contained now belonged to the Reich.[126]

As the 'Degenerate Art' and 'Eternal Jew' exhibitions made plain, the Nazis consistently valued the role museums could play in rewriting history and justifying their actions. Narratives of Polish nationhood told through the collections of Polish museums were eradicated. The museums were closed and their galleries reshaped to tell the Nazis' story that these territories had always belonged to Germany.[127] Just as the possessions of the Communists and the Social Democrats had found their way into the 'poison cabinets' of German university departments and Nazi organisations dedicated to 'enemy research', cultural property considered emblematic of Polish identity would now suffer the same fate. The storerooms of these Polish museums (and the collections of the Polish aristocracy) also contained many treasures that drew the eye of Nazi agents, who, armed with the experience of Vienna in 1938, now swooped in.[128]

While the occupation of Poland was from the outset characterised by unprecedented brutality, the Nazis had a different vision for their new territories in Western Europe. The citizens of the Western states were, unlike Poles, considered to be 'racial comrades', provided they were not Jewish. Western hostility to Nazi Germany was not ascribed to race, but to indoctrination at the hands of a Jewish global conspiracy that had long sought to sow racial discord among non-Jewish peoples. For this reason, the Nazis would create a version of the 'Eternal Jew' exhibition for audiences in Paris.[129] The regime would also pursue the same strategy that it had implemented domestically in 1933, namely the purging of its political and racial enemies. In the shadow of the German armies, Nazi organisations arrived in France dedicated to 'studying' these foes. Among them were men who worked for the Nazi party's chief ideologue, Alfred Rosenberg, who, in the previous year, had established the Institute for Research into the Jewish Question in Frankfurt; its library's founding stock consisted of thousands of Jewish texts confiscated from across the city and deposited in Rosenberg's hands.[130] In Paris, Rosenberg's men saw a golden opportunity to become more than the passive recipients of Nazi dispossession and sought actively to expand their collections in order to furnish the library of the massive Nazi university that they planned to establish.[131]

They arrived late on the scene, as the German Embassy had already 'secured' some Jewish collections, but Rosenberg's men soon became a major force. After the confiscation of Jewish organisations' libraries and files, they became determined to seize Jewish art collections as well. In light of the magnitude of the task they had set themselves, it is no surprise that a new unit was created which became known as the Einsatzstab Reichsleiter Rosenberg (ERR). This organisation would become notorious for its massive role in the confiscation of archives, libraries and private collections (Figure 1.12). To achieve its goal, the ERR could rely on experienced Gestapo officers (who now donned the uniforms of the Wehrmacht's Secret Field Police), their colleagues in the French police (who helped to identify abandoned Jewish apartments), Göring's Currency-Protection Commandos (tasked with the seizure of enemy assets) and the SS apparatus (which had its own department dedicated to 'enemy research').[132]

After storming an apartment, the ERR officers took any artworks discovered to temporary storage facilities at the Louvre. From there, the seizures were taken to the Jeu de Paume, a Parisian museum whose own collections had been conveniently evacuated prior to the invasion.[133] In keeping with the spirit of this location, the staff of the ERR approached their task as if they were cataloguing new acquisitions for a museum collection. Following the practice established in Vienna, they compiled detailed inventories and index cards, on the back of which they recorded the information they deemed important, showing off their knowledge of the literature, of similar works found in other collections, as well as details of the objects' previous owners.[134] Crucially, the index cards contained a field for the 'Verbleib' (whereabouts), which allowed them to record the next destination or the ultimate fate of the item in question. Some of these items would be earmarked for the Linz Museum, or were 'selected' by Hermann Göring for his private collection (which, he claimed, would one day become public).[135] Others that were deemed 'lesser works' were sold or exchanged; those deemed 'degenerate' were singled out for destruction. The majority, however, were freighted up for delivery to the Reich, where they awaited the end of the war in Bavarian castles and monasteries.[136]

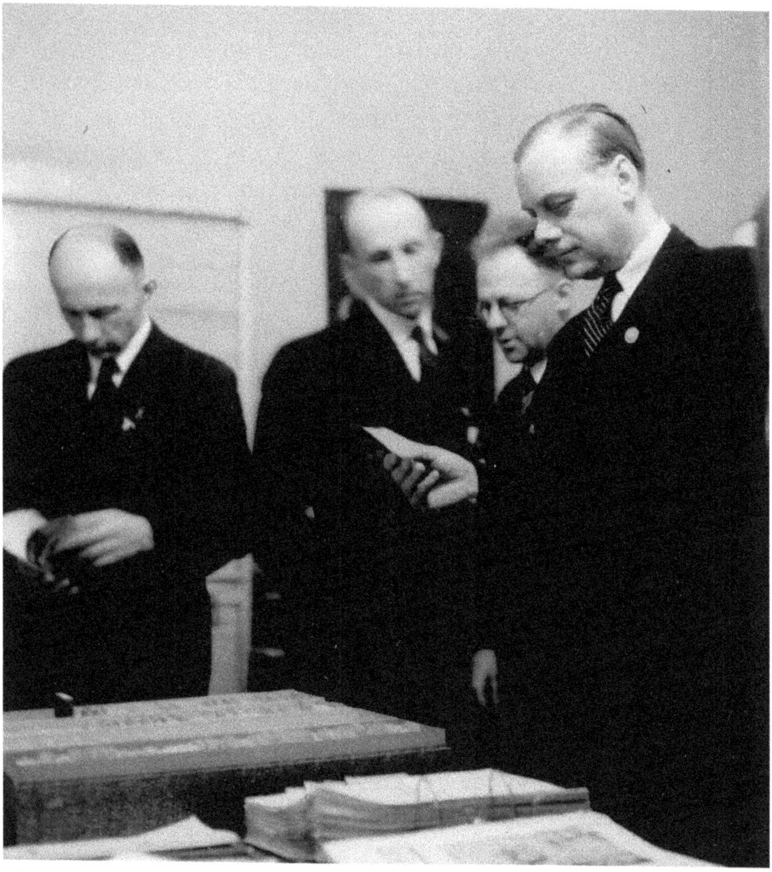

Fig. 1.12. Alfred Rosenberg examining a document at the head office of his 'Einsatzstab', the organisation that plundered Jewish collections in the name of 'enemy research'. © Yad Vashem.

France, Belgium and the Netherlands had been principal destinations for Jewish refugees fleeing the Reich.[137] There they hoped either to build a new life for themselves, or to prepare to move on to other countries that might be willing to welcome them – a process that became more difficult as the number of Jewish emigrants increased in line with the escalating persecution unfolding within the borders of Nazi Germany. Having lost so much in order to gain their German exit papers, they now faced further daunting obstacles in the form of the means-tested entry requirements imposed by states that did not want to accept large numbers of impoverished foreigners across their borders. The arrival of German troops dramatically worsened the situation as Jews were expelled from their apartments to make room for Nazi officers. Increasingly forced into hiding, these terrorised people fled to unoccupied areas where they were forced to eke out an existence on the margins. In these circumstances, every last possession had to be sold or bartered for survival. If those possessions had included a print, drawing or other artwork, they would often eventually filter into the art dealerships and collections of these transit countries.

In June 1941, Germany invaded the Soviet Union. Mere weeks prior to the attack, a representative of the State Museums in Berlin had visited Leningrad and Moscow, where he created an inventory of 300 artworks of interest held in the galleries of the Hermitage and the Pushkin Museum.[138] This list would have been of great interest to the familiar set of Nazi organisations following in the wake of the Wehrmacht with their dual goal of 'enemy research' and the seizure of cultural property. As 'Operation Barbarossa' surged into action, these operatives were now entering a country which the Nazis considered to be the embodiment and epicentre of 'Judaeo-Bolshevism'.[139] The author of the inventory had predicted that the task that lay ahead would be easier than ever before because, he said, the Soviets had already nationalised all significant artworks.[140]

Although the Soviets had been ambushed by the German attack, they were nevertheless able to evacuate significant collections to the interior of the country. Undaunted, the Nazis seized everything that they could still find; among those involved in the seizures was, once again, Alfred Rosenberg, now elevated to the position of Reich Minister for the Occupied Eastern Territories (Figure 1.13).[141] In Kyiv, arguably the largest cultural centre that came under German occupation, Rosenberg's Einsatzstab scoured archives and libraries for records and books that promised insight into the 'Jewish question'. In the process, they discovered 200 Torah scrolls that the Soviets had previously removed from local synagogues.[142] As in Poland, the museum landscape was destroyed and plans were drawn up to reorganise it in the service of the German occupiers, meaning that the collections would be used to legitimise German rule and simultaneously prevent any resurgence of local nationalism.[143]

The invasion of the Soviet Union marked the beginning of the systematic mass murder of the Jews within the Nazis' direct sphere of influence. During the first few months of the invasion, German death squads executed more than one million Jews.[144] Considering the unspeakable suffering of innocent men, women and children and the overall brutality of the German occupation in the East, it is difficult to talk about the fate of cultural property. But, as ever, persecution

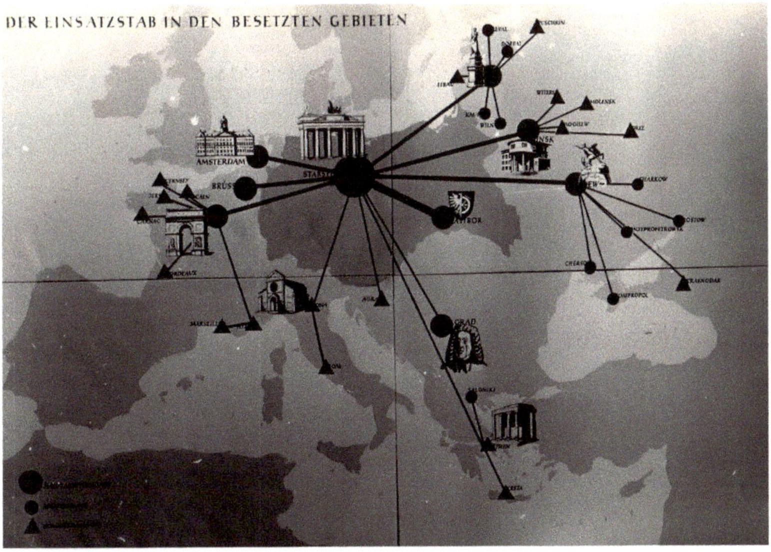

Fig. 1.13. A map showing the activities and vast scale of the Nazi-looting operation Einsatzstab Reichsleiter Rosenberg in German-occupied Europe. © Yad Vashem.

was always accompanied by dispossession. In October 1941, the Nazi regime began deporting Jews from within the greater Reich to the occupied eastern territories (Figure 1.14).[145] As the Jews, now forced to live together in overcrowded apartments, were told to pack a suitcase for an unknown destination, they were also instructed to complete one final inventory of everything they still owned after all these years of dispossession. Before they sealed the apartments, German officials checked these inventories against the contents and then marched their victims to the train station.[146] Within months, Nazi bureaucrats streamlined the process by issuing a new law which declared that the assets of anyone who moved away from the Reich automatically became state property.[147] This cynical legislation on the surface resembled an extreme version of the Reich Flight Tax, but in reality it was focused not on emigrants, but on defenceless victims who had been taken across the border to ghettoes and concentration camps, where they would soon be murdered.[148]

Once the deportation trains pulled out of the stations, the Nazi officials returned to the sealed apartments and began the task of 'liquidating' the contents. To streamline this grim process, they turned to trusted auctioneers who often set up shop in the apartments themselves

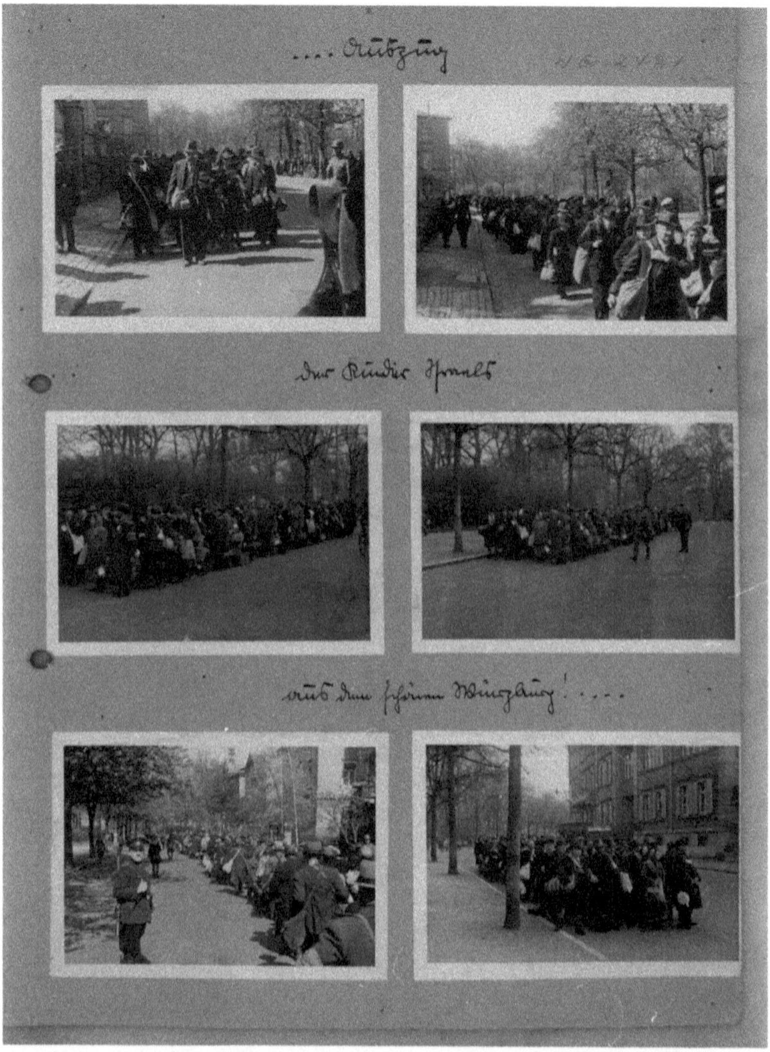

Fig. 1.14. Photo album created by the Würzburg Gestapo celebrating the deportation of the Jewish population in broad daylight. Note the caption: 'The exodus of the children of Israel from the beautiful city of Würzburg'. Public domain (Source: United States Holocaust Memorial Museum).

in order to sell off the material traces of the many lives that German society had now condemned to death.[149] As ever, museum directors and curators were brought in to determine whether the Nazi vultures had turned up any valuable items among the property left behind, before the rest was sold off to German citizens who queued around the block

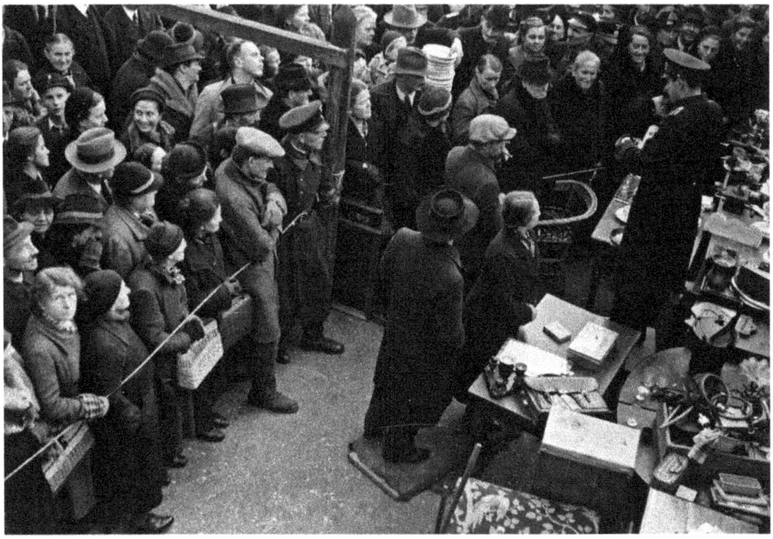

Fig. 1.15. Germans bidding at a public auction for the property of their Jewish neighbours, who had just been deported (Lörrach, Baden-Württemberg). © Stadtarchiv Lörrach.

in search of a bargain (Figure 1.15).[150] When the deportation trains started to roll out of the Western European countries as well, the ERR in France and the Benelux countries expanded its 'collecting' to include items of furniture. Rosenberg's men went to homes that now stood empty of life, seizing the furniture left behind by the Jewish inhabitants who were now on their way to the extermination camps in the East. If items were of insufficient importance to be processed at the Jeu de Paume, they were shipped to the Reich to be distributed to bombed-out German citizens: hence the name M-Aktion: Möbel (furniture).[151]

The last material traces of the Jewish lives torn apart by Nazi ideology would be seized at the point of extermination. The final dispossession took place in the extermination camps, where the victims' glasses, shoes, clothes, suitcases and even gold teeth were seized for the Nazi Reich.[152]

Conclusion

As the tide of war began to turn against the Reich, German museums prepared to evacuate their collections in order to protect them from the Allied bombers that would rapidly reduce German cities to rubble.[153]

Among the artworks crated up and taken to remote locations were many items that told the stories of the innocent people who had been persecuted, expelled and murdered in the name of the Nazis' racist ideology. The regime had banned Jews from visiting museums, but it had no qualms about enriching those same institutions with items taken from this shunned minority.[154]

In just a handful of years, German society had been transformed into a Nazi 'racial community' in which there was nothing extraordinary about auction catalogues that openly marked Jewish consignors with asterisks, or the Gestapo offloading crates emblazoned with the legend 'Jewish property' on the doorsteps of museums. Hidden within the provenance of these objects that now flooded the galleries were stories of careers destroyed, businesses stolen, families torn apart and brutal acts of violence and murder.

As new items were added to the museums in this way, the Nazi regime simultaneously tore objects out of the collections: those paintings and sculptures that were deemed 'degenerate'. Through their exhibitions, German museums became sites at which Nazi rule was actively promoted and legitimised, sharply distinguishing them from their counterparts in other countries. Nevertheless, museums abroad soon acquired items that – although they had often come through familiar sources on the international art market – were ultimately the spoils of Nazi policies. During the war, the Nazi regime applied its six years of experience in domestic persecution and dispossession to the occupied territories, confiscating Jewish collections in Western Europe, and assaulting cultural institutions in Poland and the Soviet Union with the same ruthless focus with which they had crushed their political enemies within the Reich. With the Red Army approaching from the East and the Allied landings in the West, the Nazi regime refused to abandon its cultural loot. In the chaos of retreat, Nazi operatives frantically loaded artworks onto the evacuation trains heading back into the heart of the crumbling Reich.[155]

Further reading and resources

Even in the 1960s professional historians were concerned that the scholarship on the Nazi period was so expansive that it was difficult to navigate and process. This scholarship has only continued to grow over the intervening decades. It is all too easy to feel overwhelmed and discouraged by this, but in truth this rich scholarship places us at a great advantage. No matter how obscure or unusual our investigations may be, there are almost always studies from which we can draw to understand and contextualise the stories behind the objects in our collections.

The best approach to the literature is to start with works that synthesise the scholarship and then to follow the footnotes to more specialised works. The historian Richard J. Evans (who serves on the UK Spoliation Advisory Panel) has provided us an ideal starting point with his magisterial Third Reich trilogy, which covers the entire period from multiple perspectives: *The Coming of the Third Reich* (London, 2003), *The Third Reich in Power* (London, 2005) and *The Third Reich at War* (London, 2008). Our research will often lead us to Jewish individuals whose lives were transformed or destroyed under the Nazis. Here, we can also turn to a book written by a leading historian who took a particular interest in the material traces left in our museum collections. David Cesarani (who served on the UK Spoliation Advisory Committee) wrote a comprehensive and deeply moving history of the Holocaust: *Final Solution: The fate of the Jews 1933–49* (London, 2016), which provides the best introduction and overview to Nazi policies and their impact. Dan Stone (a member of the UK Advisory Group on Spoliation Matters) recently published an important new overview: *The Holocaust: An unfinished history* (London, 2023), which incorporates the latest historiographical literature.

Works of art were of course only one element of the myriad items that were extorted and confiscated from the victims, which is why it is important to begin with an overview of the mechanisms of dispossession. These are explained with great clarity in Martin Dean's *Robbing the Jews: The confiscation of Jewish property in the Holocaust 1933–45* (Cambridge, 2008), which deals with the entire occupied continent. On Nazi looting and the art world during the Nazi period, the best starting points are the works of two historians who, due to their expertise, were the chosen speakers on these complex topics at the 1998 Washington Conference on Holocaust-Era Assets. These are: Jonathan Petropoulos's *Art as Politics in the Third Reich* (Chapel Hill, 1996) and *The Faustian Bargain: The art world in Nazi Germany* (London, 2000); and Lynn H. Nicholas's *The Rape of Europa: The fate of Europe's treasures in the Third Reich and the Second World War* (New York, 1995).

The vast literature on the Nazi regime is best navigated through historical bibliographies, such as the *Deutsche Historische Bibliografie* (historicum.net/metaopac), and the literature specifically about the dispossession of artworks through the *Central Registry* (lootedart.com) and the *Proveana* research database (proveana.de). We must not forget that museums have engaged this history in their galleries. The catalogues of two major exhibitions at the Jewish Museums in Berlin and New York also serve as an excellent overview: *Raub und Restitution: Kulturgut aus jüdischem Besitz von 1933 bis heute* (Berlin/Göttingen, 2008) and *Afterlives: Recovering the lost stories of looted art* (New York/New Haven, CT: 2021).

Notes

1 On the origins and key principles of Nazi ideology, see Burleigh and Wippermann 1991, 23–37.
2 Finkenberger 2008, 92.
3 von Leers 1933.
4 Leers spelled this out in more detail in: von Leers 1934.
5 von Leers 1933, 17.
6 On the Nazis' seizure of power and destruction of the left, see Evans 2003, 310–49.
7 'Decree of the Reich President for the Protection of Volk and State' (28 February 1933). In Rabinbach and Gilman 2013, 47. Here and below, wherever possible I provide references to English translations of Nazi laws.
8 Gritzbach 1939, 27.
9 On this terror campaign and the early concentration camps see Wachsmann 2015, 26–41.
10 See, for example, the case of the Communist Rudolf Renner, described in Strahl 2017, 13.
11 On these confiscations, see Dean 2008, 15–17; Friedenberger 2008, 52–5; Kuller 2013, 325–30; Ulbricht 2022, 61–110.
12 'Gesetz über die Einziehung kommunistischen Vermögens' (26 May 1933), *Reichsgesetzblatt* I: 293.
13 'Gesetz über die Einziehung volks- und staatsfeindlichen Vermögens' (14 July 1933), *Reichsgesetzblatt* I: 479.
14 Friedenberger 2008, 53. On the confiscation of works of art, see, for example, the case of a copy of the Delacroix painting 'Liberty Leading the People', which in 1933 was seized from the offices of the Social Democratic newspaper *Vorwärts*: Harry Wilke, affidavit of 20 January 1965, 2. B Rep. 025/06, Nr. 28/65. Landesarchiv Berlin.
15 On the Nazis' 'enemy research', see Botsch 2008; Wildt 2009, 137–40; Steinbach 2018; Steinweis 2008, 112–20.
16 On university libraries as recipients of confiscated works, see Conze and Reifenberg 2006.
17 Deinert 2011, 51.
18 On the distribution of confiscated books: Briel 2013, 161–77.
19 Deinert 2011, 52.
20 On the wave of terror against Jews in 1933, see Cesarani 2016, 37; Longerich 2010, 32–7.
21 Schilde et al. 1996, 54.
22 Steber and Gotto 2014, 6.
23 On the experiences of Jews in the face of this terror, see Kaplan 1998, 18–21.
24 Cesarani 2016, 38.
25 On the boycott, see Bajohr 2002, 28–35; Wildt 2012, 85–94.
26 Longerich 2010, 23. On Jewish responses: Cesarani 2016, 60–3.
27 'Law to Remedy the State of Emergency of Volk and Reich' (23 March 1933), 52. In Rabinbach and Gilman 2013, 52–3.
28 On the development and scope of this law, see Adam 2003, 40–9.
29 'Law for the Restoration of the Professional Civil Service' (7 April 1933). In Gruner 2019, 147–52.
30 'First Regulation on the Implementation of the Law for the Restoration of the Professional Civil Service' (11 April 1933), 155. In Gruner 2019, 155–6.

31 On the civil service in the Third Reich, see Mommsen 1966, 53.
32 Adam 2003, 48.
33 Elly Glaser, affidavit of 12 February 1963, 1. Reg. Nr. 52785. Entschädigungsbehörde des Landes Berlin, Berlin.
34 Maria Ash, affidavit of 22 December 1962, 2. Reg. Nr. 52785. Entschädigungsbehörde des Landes Berlin, Berlin.
35 On Curt Glaser's life and career, see the recent exhibition catalogue: Haidemann and Rauser 2022.
36 Adam 2003, 49–54.
37 Edward Hans Littmann, affidavit of 29 August 1960, 2. 22-1596/57. Bundesamt für zentrale Dienste und offene Vermögensfragen, Berlin.
38 Littmann, affidavit, 2.
39 Littmann, affidavit, 1.
40 Käthe Littmann, auction Mandate of 30 January 1935, 1. 22-1596/57. Bundesamt für zentrale Dienste und offene Vermögensfragen, Berlin.
41 On Ismar Littmann and his collection, see Heuss 2008b, 72–4.
42 On the emigration of Jews from Nazi Germany, see Wetzel 1993, 413–20; Kugelmann 2006.
43 On the history and application of these laws, see Dean 2008, 56–7; Friedenberger 2008, 68; Kuller 2013, 185–230.
44 'Vierte Verordnung des Reichspräsidenten zur Sicherung von Wirtschaft und Finanzen und zum Schutze des inneren Friedens' (8 December 1931), 731–5. *Reichsgesetzblatt* I: 699–745.
45 Friedenberger 2008, 129–30.
46 Kuller 2013, 208–17.
47 Dean 2008, 57.
48 Friedenberger 2008, 132.
49 On their role, see Meinl 2007.
50 Dean 2008, 58–9; Kuller 2013, 195–8.
51 Dean 2008, 58–9, 80; Friedenberger 2008, 81–2.
52 Friedenberger 2008, 134. On the German Gold Discount Bank, see Schoenmakers 2020.
53 Friedenberger 2008, 135.
54 Kuller 2013, 96.
55 Adam 2003, 64.
56 On the pressures faced by Jewish businesses, see Genschel 1980; Barkai 1988; Dean 2008, 25–33.
57 Friedländer 1998, 18.
58 Bajohr 2000.
59 Dean 2008, 47–8.
60 On the Nazi regime's 'cultural politics', see Steinweis 1993, 32–49; Brenner 1963, 35–62.
61 Osterloh 2000, 65; Petropoulos 2000.
62 Bajohr 2002.
63 Decision of 20 May 1953 with respect to the restitution claim brought by Siegmund Kaznelson against Horst Ritterhofer. B Rep. 025-05, Nr. 5122-50. Landesarchiv Berlin, Berlin, 143–9.
64 On the exhibition, see Benz 2010, 65–6.
65 Benz 2010, 89–95.
66 Benz 2010, 92–3.
67 Longerich 2010, 54–7.
68 Wildt 2012, 173–82.
69 'The Program of the German Workers' Party' (1925), 12. In Rabinbach and Gilman 2013, 12–14.
70 On the Nuremberg Laws, see Adam 2003, 89–94.
71 'First Regulation to the Reich Citizenship Law' (14 November 1935). In Gruner 2019, 550–2.
72 'Law for the Protection of German Blood and German Honour' (15 September 1935), 2019. In Gruner 2019, 520–1.
73 On the museum sector in Nazi Germany, see Petropoulos 2000, 13–61.

74 On how museums were transformed, see, for example, Müller-Kelwing 2020, 50–7.
75 On the art market, see, for example, Petropoulos 2000, 63–110; Enderlein 2006; Hopp 2012; Golenia et al. 2016, 92–105; Aktives Museum Faschismus und Widerstand in Berlin 2011.
76 'Verordnung gegen die Unterstützung der Tarnung jüdischer Gewerbebetriebe' (22 April 1938). *Reichsgesetzblatt* I: 404.
77 Löhr 2016, 31.
78 On this process, see Meinl and Zwilling 2005, 159.
79 See, for example, Kunsthalle Mannheim 2020, 107.
80 Meinl and Zwilling 2005, 159.
81 See, for example, Bach and Lange 2018.
82 See the informative overview and case studies in Deutsches Zentrum Kulturgutverluste 2019.
83 Schultze-Naumburg 1928, 151–61.
84 On Schultze-Naumburg and these ideas, see von Lüttichau 2014.
85 Schultze-Naumburg 1928, 106–15.
86 Zuschlag 1995, 178.
87 On this infamous exhibition, see Zuschlag 1995, 169–204; Peters 2014b.
88 Adolf Ziegler's speech at the opening of the Degenerate Art exhibition, delivered on 19 July 1937. In Rabinbach and Gilman 2013, 500–3.
89 Peters 2014b, 117. See also Hüneke and von Lüttichau 1998.
90 Adolf Hitler's speech at the opening of the Great German Art exhibition, delivered on 19 July 1937. In Rabinbach and Gilman 2013, 494–500.
91 On this second wave, see Zuschlag 1995, 205–21.
92 On the Nazi regime's sale of these works, see, for example, Jeuthe 2007; Hüneke 2007.
93 Paas 1983, 19.
94 See the exhibition catalogue Peters 2014a.
95 Stiftung Sächsische Gedenkstätten zur Erinnerung an die Opfer politischer Gewaltherrschaft 2000.
96 On Elfriede Lohse-Wächtler, see Reinhardt 1996.
97 On the mass murder of the mentally and physically disabled, see Burleigh 1995.
98 Ploil 2014; Benz 2010, 115–26.
99 Cesarani 2016, 148–50. See the shocking and moving accounts of witnesses to and victims of this violence in Safrian and Witek 2008, 23–38.
100 Schwarz 2018, 22.
101 Schwarz 2018, 31.
102 Schwarz 2018, 34.
103 Haupt 1999, 56.
104 Löhr 2016, 28–46.
105 Löhr 2016, 28–46.
106 Cesarani 2016, 157.
107 Arendt 1964, 74.
108 On the planning for the seizure of Jewish assets, see Dean 2008, 85–111; Safrian 2000.
109 On this crucial law, see Dean 2008, 88–9; Meinl and Zwilling 2005, 45–6.
110 'Regulation on the Registration of Jewish Assets' (26 April 1938). In Heim 2019, 141–3.
111 'Dritte Verordnung zum Reichsbürgergesetz' (14 June 1938), 627. *Reichsgesetzblatt* I: 627–8.
112 On the 1938 November pogrom, see Steinweis 2009.
113 Cesarani 2016, 183.
114 Longerich 2010, 112.
115 Weiler 2019, 145–6.
116 Hoppe 2002, 191.
117 'Regulation on the Atonement Fine for Jews of German Nationality' (12 November 1938). In Heim 2019, 406.
118 Longerich 2010, 112–16.
119 'Regulation on the Exclusion of Jews from German Economic Life' (12 November 1938). In Heim 2019, 407–8.
120 See, for example, Müller 2016, 82; Voigt 2018.

121 On the endless succession of discriminatory laws and directives, see, for example, the compilation Walk 1981, 253–300.
122 On this process see, for example, Daub 1999.
123 On Nazi Germany and the Second World War, see Evans 2008; Stargardt 2015.
124 On the dispossession in the occupied territories see Dean 2008, 173–313; Petropoulos 1996, 100–50; Nicholas 1995, 57–202. For the various institutions and agencies involved in the confiscations of cultural property in the Western and Eastern theatres of war, see Heuss 2000.
125 Mazower 2008, 63–95.
126 Dean 2008, 173–86.
127 Steinweis 1991, 474–80.
128 Nicholas 1995, 57–80; Petropoulos 1999, 100–10.
129 Benz 2010, 159–67.
130 On Rosenberg, see Piper 2005, 462–508; Löhr 2018, 20–31. On the Institute, see von Papen-Bodek 2004.
131 Löhr 2018, 33.
132 Löhr 2018, 84.
133 Löhr 2018, 82.
134 Löhr 2018, 83.
135 Löhr 2009, 41; Yeide 2009, 12–15.
136 Löhr 2018, 83.
137 On Jewish emigration, see Wetzel 1993, 479–83; Cesarani 2016, 437–45.
138 Heuss 2000, 67.
139 Herf 2009, 100.
140 Heuss 2000, 67.
141 Löhr 2018, 51–62.
142 Heuss 2000, 185.
143 Heuss 2000, 191.
144 Longerich 2010, 192–247.
145 Longerich 2010, 286–9.
146 On this process, see Dean 2008, 241–3; Meinl and Zwilling 2005, 141–76.
147 On the 'Eleventh Decree to the Reich Citizenship Law', see Dean 2008, 161–7.
148 Wachsmann 2015, 289–337.
149 Meinl and Zwilling 2005, 196–8.
150 See, for example, Stadtmuseum Düsseldorf 1998, 149–88.
151 Hemke 2018.
152 See, for example, Hördler 2020.
153 See, for example, Artinger 2020, 197–203.
154 Matthes and Ewald 2017.
155 Löhr 2018, 128–31.

2

After the war: Nazi-era provenance research today

Before we embark on our research into the Nazi-era provenance of museum objects, it is crucial that we have a clear understanding of the post-war provenance and restitution effort. Even before the regime was defeated, curators and art historians in the service of the Allies gathered huge amounts of information about Nazi looting, as they prepared for the recovery and return of looted artworks to the galleries and private collections from which they had been taken. In the ruins of the Third Reich, they catalogued objects and painstakingly attempted to establish where they had come from, resulting in the restitution of millions of artworks.

While this was a truly remarkable effort, museum collections were not subjected to the same scrutiny as the treasures recovered from Nazi institutions. This unexamined legacy continued to grow until, more than 50 years after the war's end, a major international conference in Washington, DC unexpectedly catapulted the issue back to the forefront of the art world. The 1998 Washington Conference on Holocaust-Era Assets galvanised research into the Nazi-era provenance of museum collections not just in Germany, Austria and the formerly occupied territories, but even in Britain and America. Not only did the Washington Conference transform the field of provenance research, it also fundamentally changed the expectations placed upon art museums, leading them to become places in which the Nazi past is actively engaged.

Foundations for the post-war restitution effort

After the outbreak of the Second World War, museum directors in the US received disturbing reports of the unprecedented looting of cultural property perpetrated by the Nazi state and its agents across the European continent (see Chapter 1). Despite the thousands of miles which separated them from these events, they nevertheless felt as though a direct assault was being made on their most cherished values: they could not help but feel a deep kinship with their colleagues whose institutions had been so ruthlessly pillaged. In November 1942, Francis H. Taylor, the Director of the Metropolitan Museum of Art in New York, penned a dramatic memorandum intended for the US President, Franklin D. Roosevelt (Figure 2.1). Taylor was not only the director of 'the largest and most comprehensive art museum in the United States', but also the President of the Association of Art Museum Directors, which gave his words considerable weight. In his memorandum, he described in vivid prose the 'wholesale looting and destruction of art property that is going on today in the occupied territories of Europe'.[1] He explained that Nazi leaders had 'acquired by conquest ... the greatest art collections of all times', which 'are considered part of the spiritual heritage and patrimony of these subjected peoples'.[2] Taylor wrote in the shadow of the Japanese attack on Pearl Harbor, which had prompted US museums on the West and East coasts to evacuate their most prized possession to the interior of the country. Indeed, the Nazi empire was at its peak: the swastika straddled the European continent from the outskirts of Leningrad to Brittany; even as the Americans entered the war in December 1941, German military defeat still seemed a distant possibility.

This climate of uncertainty did not stop the forceful Taylor from urging Roosevelt to plan for victory and make concrete plans for something many military leaders would, at best, consider an afterthought: the protection, recovery and restitution of works of art. In his words, 'This is not a matter which can wait until after the war but must be organized now so that there will be a body of experts ready to move in immediately behind the armies and salvage whatever is possible.'[3] To create this 'body of experts', Taylor naturally thought of individuals who were already 'competently trained', namely museum curators and art historians.[4] Their involvement would also ensure that, in the effort to drive back the Germans, the Allied troops would not inadvertently add to the destruction of cultural property. As Taylor put it, 'There must be some way of preserving and protecting works of art that lie in the way of our invading armies.'[5] Taylor emphasised that these museum professionals would be 'only too glad to serve the country in this way' – because 'everything for which the

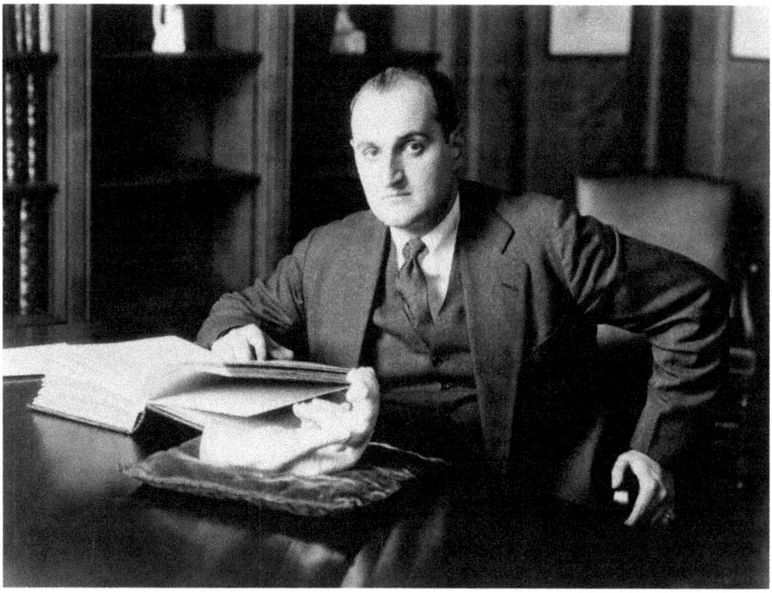

Fig. 2.1. Francis Henry Taylor, Director of the Metropolitan Museum of Art, who campaigned passionately for restitution even before German defeat seemed assured. © The Metropolitan Museum of Art, New York/ Scala Archives.

great museums of the United States stand … – both morally and intellectually – is at stake'.[6]

In order for his plea to reach the desk of the President, Taylor turned to Harlan Stone, the Chairman of the Board of the National Gallery in Washington. Stone was also the Chief Justice and could therefore be trusted to get the President's attention for an issue that in the grand scheme of things, and at that particular moment, did not possess the same self-evident importance as strategic military concerns. Stone certainly shared Taylor's vision, but was infinitely more diplomatic in his approach. To prepare the document for the President, he stripped away from Taylor's memorandum some of the more emotive statements, not least Taylor's fiery condemnation of the removal of the Parthenon Marbles to Britain, which would only have antagonised the US's closest ally. Stone transformed Taylor's memorandum into a detailed plan for the creation of a commission in order to gather information to protect cultural property during the war, and once this was over 'to aid in salvaging and returning to … the lawful owners … objects which have been appropriated by Axis powers'.[7]

The 1943 London Declaration

As he penned his memorandum, Taylor could not know that at the same moment Allied officials were putting the finishing touches to a document that would become known as the 'London Declaration'. In July 1942, at the Treasury in London, the Finance Ministers of countries under Nazi occupation had met to work on a document titled 'Inter-Allied Declaration against Acts of Dispossession Committed in Territories under Enemy Occupation or Control'.[8] Like Taylor, the Finance Ministers were deeply troubled by Nazi looting, but they were understandably less concerned by looted artworks than with the assets that were being stolen from their central banks. Their immediate aim, as British government officials put it, was to do something to 'frighten the neutrals' so that they would not become money launderers for the Nazi state's stolen booty.[9]

Although this document was thus primarily intended for 'propaganda purposes', like Taylor, these ministers also laid plans for what should happen once their countries had been liberated.[10] The Declaration stated that they 'reserve[d] all their rights to declare invalid' any transfers of property executed under Nazi occupation, irrespective of 'whether such transfers have taken the form of open looting and plunder', or if they were 'apparently legal in form, even when they purport to be voluntarily effected'.[11] As German troops faced their first major defeat in the ruins of Stalingrad, the 'London Declaration' was blasted over the airwaves across the neutral countries in January 1943, alerting listeners to the Allies' clear intent to unmake the Nazi order. While the word 'art' did not appear in the Declaration itself, the British added an introductory note to make it clear that this would be a truly comprehensive mission that would be 'extended to every sort of property – from works of art to stocks of commodities, from bullion and bank-notes to stocks and shares in business and financial undertakings'.[12] The spirit of Taylor's memorandum and the London Declaration, which were followed by a flurry of policy documents discussed at Allied conferences, would in time find its fullest expression in the largest provenance research and restitution effort in recorded history.[13]

Intelligence gathering

By June 1943, with the Wehrmacht's aura of invincibility shattered in the wake of Stalingrad, Roosevelt felt that the time had come to make plans for a post-war order. He established a commission tasked with making Taylor's vision a reality: the 'American Commission for the Protection and Salvage of Artistic and Historic Monuments in War Areas', chaired by Harlan Stone's colleague, Supreme Court Justice Owen J. Roberts (the 'Roberts Commission').[14] If Taylor's 'body of experts', which began to materialise in the form of the 'Monuments, Fine Arts, and Archives program', was to succeed in its work, it would be essential that they had reliable information. As part of the Roberts Commission, a committee was established at the National Gallery in Washington to 'compile, through the assistance of refugee historians of art and librarians, lists of property appropriated by the Axis invading forces, by representatives of Axis governments, and by private citizens of Axis governments'.[15] This was no small task: these were events that had taken place thousands of miles away over the course of several years. The reports they received could be outdated and incomplete, but in many cases the information they collected proved surprisingly accurate, which is a testament to the courage and skill of the resistance networks which, for years, had smuggled this information out of a continent surrounded by walls and barbed wire.[16]

From the outset, the Americans recognised that their aims could be achieved only through international cooperation and therefore urged the creation of similar commissions across the Allied coalition. These were established in rapid succession, soon forming a vast international research network that gathered, collated and circulated information received from each member's respective intelligence networks. The British counterpart of the Roberts Commission was the Macmillan Committee, dedicated to 'the Preservation and Restitution of Works of Art, Archives and Other Material in Enemy Hands', whose Chair was a Trustee of the British Museum and who, in coordinating this work, naturally drew on the expertise of the country's museum directors, including the Victoria & Albert Museum's Director, Eric Maclagan.[17] Together, these bodies hoped to generate a comprehensive inventory of looted art which the museum curators and art historians, who would become known as the 'Monuments Men', could check against the collections they hoped to liberate.

As D-Day drew closer, London became the epicentre of this intelligence-gathering operation. Various governments-in-exile had made their home in the British capital, making the city the ideal clearing house for intelligence related to Nazi looting. In 1944, the 'Inter-Allied Commission for the Protection and Restitution of Cultural Material' (the 'Vaucher Commission') was established, which drew up restitution policies and became a hub for 'the collection and organization of information relating to looting'.[18] At the same time, the CIA's predecessor (the 'Office of Strategic Services') recruited curators and art historians to form the Art Looting Investigation Unit (ALIU). These officers set up shop in rooms vacated by the curators of the V&A, creating index cards mapping the agents and institutions involved in Nazi plunder. While the aim of the various commissions was to protect, recover and restitute, these ALIU officers were at this stage more concerned to prevent the Nazis from potentially using works of art to finance a guerrilla war against Allied occupying forces.[19]

Recovery: cataloguing looted art and its restitution to the countries of origin

At the beginning of 1945, museum curators and art historians donned military uniforms and followed the Allied armies deep into the crumbling Reich. Picking their way through the rubble and destruction, they searched for the hidden sites to which the Nazis had evacuated 'their' art collections. The British members of the team would not be surprised to discover that many of these treasures had been hidden away in salt mines, tunnel networks and remote castles – the same types of hiding place to which the collections of the V&A and other British institutions were removed for the duration of the war. Among the ruins, they uncovered hundreds of hiding places stuffed with Europe's greatest art treasures (Figure 2.2). As the war raged on around them, the Monuments Men secured these sites as best they could: guards were posted, and the locations were placed behind barbed wire.[20]

When Germany finally capitulated in May 1945, it at last became possible to tackle the issue of restitution in earnest. The first step was to create centres at which the recovered artworks could be centrally gathered and systematically examined and identified. In June, Officer Craig Hugh Smyth was driven to Munich to establish the first of these 'collecting points'.[21] Munich was the obvious choice: several large caches of art had just been recovered from major Nazi institutions in the vicinity. As his military Jeep rattled through the ruins of the former Reich, Smyth contemplated how best to tackle this daunting task. Drawing upon his training at the National Gallery in Washington, he decided to approach it as a systematic cataloguing exercise, just as he and his fellow curators would do at any large museum.[22] He

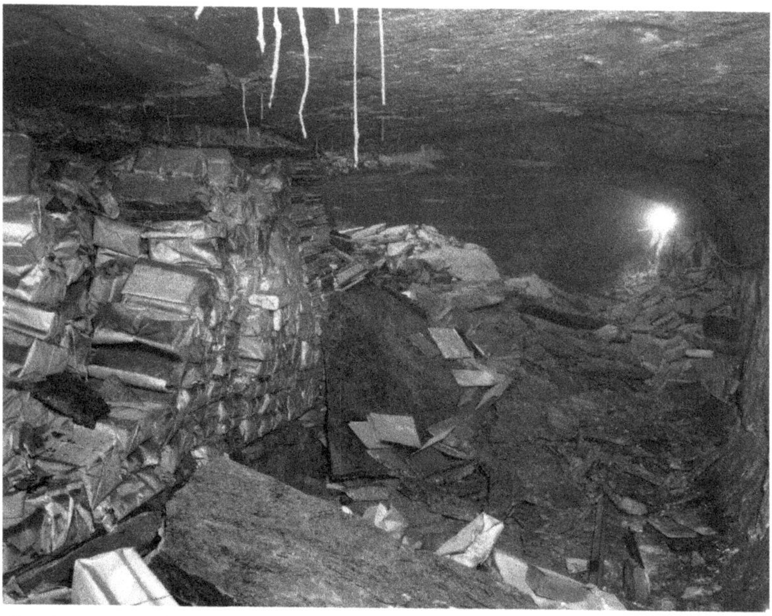

Fig. 2.2. Looted Jewish books stacked in the cellar of Alfred Rosenberg's 'Institute for Research into the Jewish Question' in Frankfurt am Main. Public domain (Source: United States Holocaust Memorial Museum).

would first have to strongarm the American military commander, who considered Smyth's mission of negligible importance compared to his own primary mission to secure the occupation of the birthplace of the Nazi movement.[23] It is a remarkable sign of Smyth's tenacity and determination that he was able to secure the former Nazi Party headquarters as the base for his operation. At first, the only artworks held in the building were Hitler portraits defaced by the Allied troops, but within a matter of weeks a succession of trucks would deliver hundreds of crates, crammed with myriad cultural treasures (Figure 2.3).[24]

As Smyth's officers made their way through the crates, they meticulously documented each object on index cards, recording the name of the artist or maker, the titles and dimensions of the pieces, as well as any other information which they hoped could help identify the object's country of origin (Figure 2.4).[25] Next they compared this information to the inventories of looted art compiled prior to the Allied invasion. These inventories continued to grow in breadth and depth as the compilers added information captured from the defeated Nazi state – not least the very similar index cards created by the Einsatzstab Reichsleiter Rosenberg (ERR; see Chapter 1).[26] At the

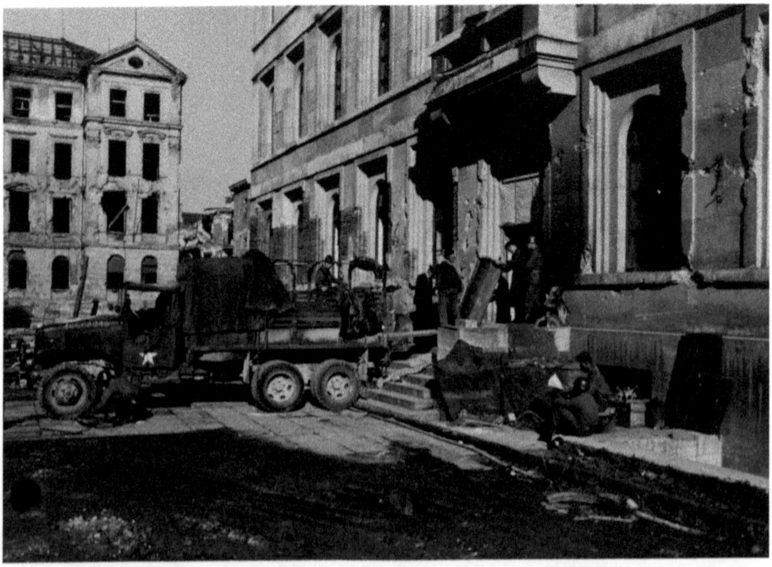

Fig. 2.3. An American military truck filled with crates of artworks recovered from the Nazi regime. Workers unload this bounty, carrying it into the Munich Central Collecting Point for processing.

same time, the ALIU was hunting down Nazi agents and extracting crucial information from them, not only about the mechanisms of Nazi looting, but also about specific artworks that had fallen victim to this campaign.[27] Following the Munich model, further collecting points were established, such as the Wiesbaden Collecting Point in the Landesmuseum Wiesbaden, which first had to be cleared of the displaced persons who had sought refuge in the building.[28] The Collecting Point in Offenbach received 1.5 million books and Jewish ritual objects liberated from Alfred Rosenberg's Institute for Research into the Jewish Question.[29]

Once established, these collecting points effectively became bustling international research centres, with representatives of all the countries affected by Nazi looting rushing in and out; Soviets were rubbing shoulders with Italians, Norwegians with Dutch (Figure 2.5).[30] The principal goal of these centres was to return the liberated artworks to their countries of origin. To achieve this aim, when the restitution officers were able to match an object against an inventory, they took it to a room allocated to a specific country. Soon, these collecting points took on the appearance of a museum, with galleries dedicated

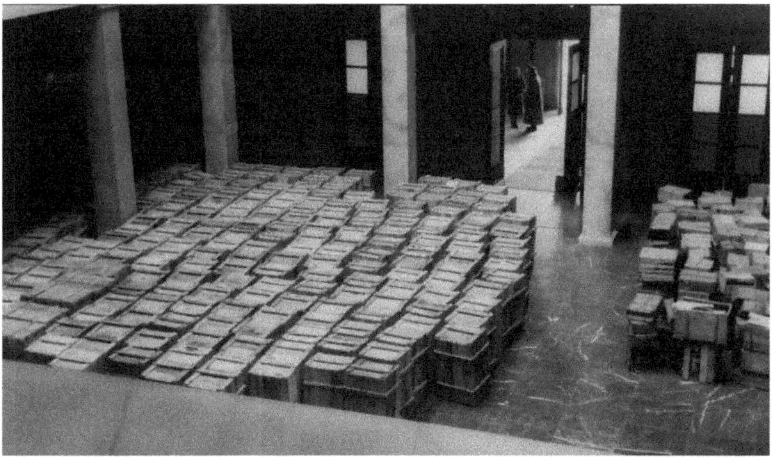

Fig. 2.4. Crates of artworks at the Munich Central Collecting Point, where they would be organised by country of origin. © J. Paul Getty Trust.

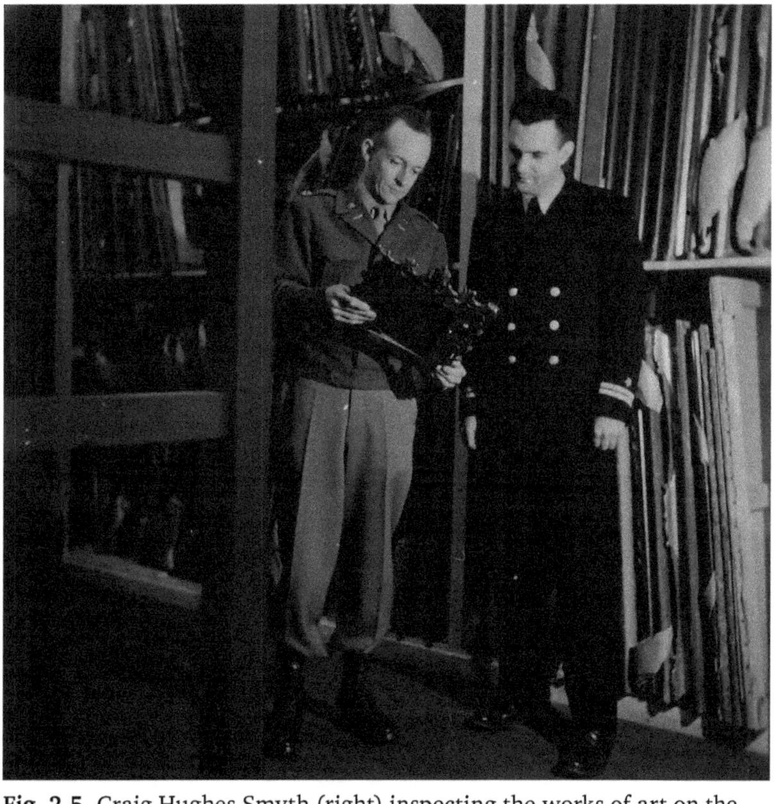

Fig. 2.5. Craig Hughes Smyth (right) inspecting the works of art on the shelves of the Munich Central Collecting Point. © J. Paul Getty Trust.

to particular countries; but these were museums whose only visitors were restitution officials who came to arrange the transport of these treasures back to their 'homelands'.

In other words, the aim of this post-war provenance research was first and foremost to identify the countries of origin. Once the items had been returned, it became the responsibility of the country in question to restore the artworks to the galleries and private collections from which they had been taken. The first item restituted from the Munich Collecting Point was the Ghent Altarpiece; this fifteenth-century masterpiece would be the first of tens of thousands of items restored to their countries of origin.[31]

'Internal restitution'

As objects began to leave for their countries of origin, the Allied officers at the collecting points were increasingly reminded that the Nazi regime had waged a war of extermination and conquest not only abroad, but also against a large number of their own citizens. To address this unprecedented campaign of persecution, dispossession and mass murder (for which existing international law provided no remedy), in 1947 the Americans passed Military Law 59, which made it possible for individual victims of the Nazis to file restitution claims 'for reasons of race, religion, nationality, ideology or political opposition to National Socialism'.[32] Similar laws were issued in the British and French zones of occupation; there was no equivalent in the Soviet zone, where concepts of private property were very different.[33]

The laws in the Western zones of occupation opened the door to what became known as 'internal restitution'.[34] However, for the survivors and the families of the victims, this would prove an extremely difficult process – not least because the Allies tasked German officials with administering this process. At a time when they were struggling to rebuild their shattered lives, victims were expected to navigate a profoundly confusing bureaucratic process filled with moving deadlines, complex forms and, considering these victims had often fled or lived in hiding for several years, often unrealistic expectations of formal evidence. To embark on this process also required a willingness to re-confront trauma and loss.[35] If, under the Nazis, they had been forced to fill in lengthy documents detailing their possessions so that these could be taken away from them, they now had to

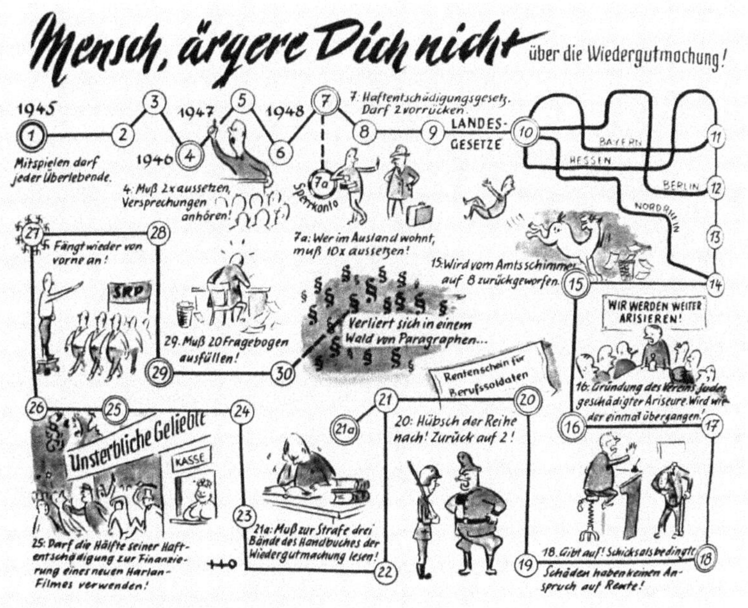

Fig. 2.6. Caricature in a Jewish newspaper (Allgemeine Wochenzeitung der Juden in Deutschland) highlighting the obstacles involved in the post-war compensation/restitution process, comparing it to the notoriously frustrating German board game 'Man, don't get angry'. © Deutscher Koordinierungsrat der Gesellschaften für Christlich-Jüdische Zusammenarbeit.

fill in very similar documents in the hope of having them restored. Even with the greatest degree of persistence, success was far from guaranteed (Figure 2.6).[36]

If the artworks had been confiscated from the victims' homes, they could have ended up anywhere; passing through a network of art dealers, an object that once belonged to a Jewish family in Germany could even have found its way to a museum on a different continent by 1945. Others had been destroyed by Allied bombs. Therefore, the only realistic chance of recovery was if an Allied officer working for a collecting point had noted a Jewish name on an item's label or in the paperwork, or if the victims knew exactly into which collection the artwork had been sold (for example, if they had been forced to sell it to a museum in the 1930s).[37] Nobody knows how many confiscated or extorted artworks still rest in museum collections around the world today.

'Return to normal'

Once the American and British curators and art historians returned to their own countries of origin, we might have expected them to apply their in-depth knowledge of Nazi looting, and the provenance research skills they had developed in Germany, to their own collections.

But this was not the case. Their first priority was to reopen their museums and, as far as possible, to return to normal. The moment that Luftwaffe bombers and German rockets no longer posed a threat, the curators of, for example, the V&A eagerly restored to their galleries the objects that had been sheltered in secure hiding places. The curators, the majority of whom had served in the war effort, were above all eager to return to their familiar everyday duties and to the projects they had been forced to abandon during the war. This return to a pre-war normality also extended to the way in which provenance was recorded; no new standards were implemented to account for the dramatic dislocation of cultural property perpetrated by the Nazis.[38]

This remained the case even when, in 1947, the V&A's curators were joined by the art historian John Hayward, who had been directly responsible for recovering and restituting the Jewish libraries that the Nazis had confiscated across Europe.[39] Even with this expert now on staff, the museum did not scrutinise its own collections, nor did it ask in-depth questions about the provenance of new acquisitions, nor of the objects that had entered the collections since 1933. In part, this situation is simply a testament to the inertia of large institutions. But just as important was the understandable perception that the restitution effort had largely been successful, and that any matters that remained outstanding were being addressed by restitution officers on the continent. If curators had asked questions about the provenance of new acquisitions, they could have turned to various publications detailing lost artworks, such as *Le Répertoire des biens spoliés en France durant la guerre 1939–1945* published by the French government between 1947 and 1949, or the Polish government-in-exile's *Poland's Cultural Losses: An index of Polish cultural losses during the German occupation 1939–1944*.[40] But these publications were always fragmentary and incomplete, which is no surprise in itself, given the vast extent of the Nazis' campaign. Although British and American museums had been instrumental in laying the foundations for the post-war restitution effort, at war's end this matter quickly faded from their minds.

In the formerly occupied countries, museums were delighted to receive back the items that the Germans had removed from their galleries. But they, too, did not interrogate their own collections which, in Western Europe, had often grown during the pre-war years of Nazi rule, when desperate refugees fleeing the Reich had sold off their collections. Perhaps they were also particularly eager to move on in order to avoid uncomfortable questions about the often thin line between adaptation and complicity under Nazi occupation.[41]

In Germany, on the other hand, many directors and curators who had served under, and worked closely with, the Nazi state remained in post after 1945. It comes as no surprise that here they were entirely unwilling to confront the consequences of their actions. Instead, they busily reinvented themselves as heroic defenders of culture against Nazi incursions.[42]

If museums, for a variety of reasons, quickly left the Nazi past behind them, this was never a possibility for the survivors, whose lives had been irrevocably damaged and transformed. While it is certainly true that some could not bear to talk about what had happened to them (often even to their own children), in the post-war decades countless others embarked on the lonely and emotionally fraught journey to recover their possessions. This meant entering a bureaucratic labyrinth with little chance of support or even compassion from the museums which, over the years, had come to view all items in their galleries as legally and morally their own.

The 1998 Washington Conference on Holocaust-Era Assets

The Munich Collecting Point closed its doors in 1951, at which time any artworks whose precise origins had not been established were transferred to Bavarian museums for safekeeping – in much the same way that French and Dutch officials transferred such items to their own state collections. In the decades that followed, the scale of the unexamined Nazi-era provenance in museum collections only continued to grow. By the late 1980s, the V&A alone had added almost 250,000 new items to its collections, the provenance of which had never been examined in light of the Nazi past.[43]

The fall of the Iron Curtain ushered in a new political order, opening the doors for a reassessment of the post-war restitution effort which, as far as private property was concerned, had stopped at the Soviet checkpoints. In 1996, Bill Clinton tasked the US State Department with investigating assets that had not been recovered and restituted after the war. Led by the US diplomat Stuart Eizenstat, this effort initially focused on real property in Eastern Europe and expanded to include financial assets, such as dormant accounts held by Swiss banks and insurance policies belonging to victims of the Holocaust.[44] This time, art became part of the investigation, not because American museum directors campaigned for it, but because newspaper reports increasingly highlighted that artworks belonging to victims of the Nazis had found their way into the galleries of American museums, such as a 1997 *New York Times* report on the provenance of the Egon Schiele painting Portrait of Wally.[45] These revelations sent shockwaves through the American museum world and, because the curators and directors had long felt proud of their active role in the post-war restitution effort, they were immediately put on the defensive.

In the 1940s, a Director of the Metropolitan Museum had written a memorandum to persuade the US government to take active steps to reverse Nazi looting across the European continent; now, more than 50 years after the war, the Met's new director, Philippe de Montebello, was dragged before a House Committee to explain, as the Chairman of the Association of Art Museum Directors' Task Force, how it was possible that American museums could have become the unwitting beneficiaries of Nazi looting (Figure 2.7). De Montebello, who as a child had lived under Nazi occupation in Paris, explained that there is 'a major difference between museums which display, publish and invite dialogue on their collections, and other kinds of institutions, such as banks, which recently have been shown to have hoarded, for half a century, the spoils of war and genocide – not in the open, as with works of art, but in the darkness of total secrecy'.[46] Despite his combative stance, he had to admit that the Nazi past had been a genuine blind spot for American museums and promised that they would now, belatedly, take concrete steps to address this omission. If this was an issue for museums in the US, then there was no reason to assume it would not also be a problem for Britain's museums – and indeed for any other museum, no matter where it was located, that had expanded its collections after the Nazi seizure of power.

In 1997, the newly established Holocaust Educational Trust alerted the British Secretary of State for Culture that 'some of the major art galleries in Britain may also hold artworks which were looted under the Nazis'.[47] While de Montebello led the American museums' response, in Britain this task fell to the V&A's Director, Alan Borg, who was the Chairman of the National Museum Directors' Council (NMDC). More than half a century after the war, a renewed alliance emerged

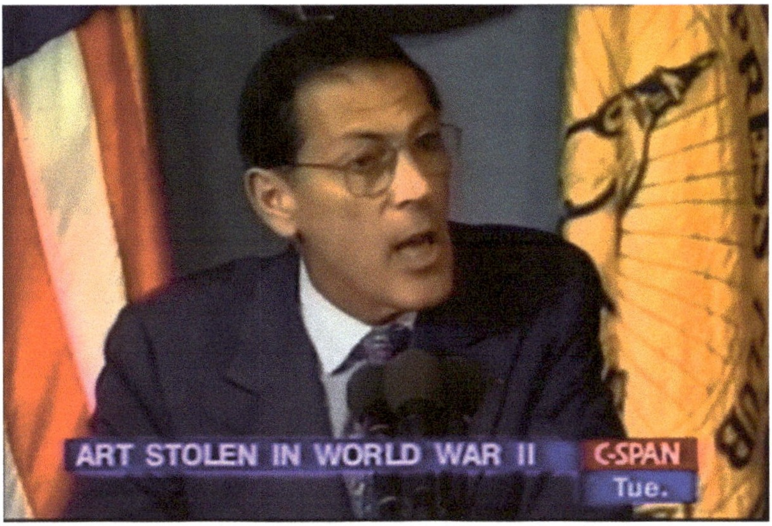

Fig. 2.7. Philippe de Montebello, Director of the Metropolitan Museum of Art, speaking at a press conference in July 1998 about the steps taken by American museums to confront the Nazi-era provenance of their collections. © C-SPAN.

between the American and British museums and their Dutch and French counterparts in order to address the elephant in their galleries and storerooms. This matter became increasingly urgent when it was announced that the US State Department was planning a major international conference in Washington on Holocaust-era assets which would not only touch upon insurance policies and real property, but would also directly address looted works of art. In the run-up to the conference, American and British museums both issued policy statements that committed their members to carry out provenance research with respect to the Nazi past. Similar statements were soon released by museums in other countries, changing museum practices forever.[48]

On 30 November 1998, the Washington Conference's opening ceremony was held at the new US Holocaust Memorial Museum, a location powerfully resonant of the importance of the issues at hand (Figure 2.8). This location was itself a manifestation of the growing public awareness of the persecution and dispossession of the Jews, an interest that was only increased by the release of Holocaust-focused memoirs and films such as *Schindler's List* (1993). In the Hall of Witnesses, the conference delegates, representing 44 countries and 13 non-governmental organisations, listened to deeply moving speeches

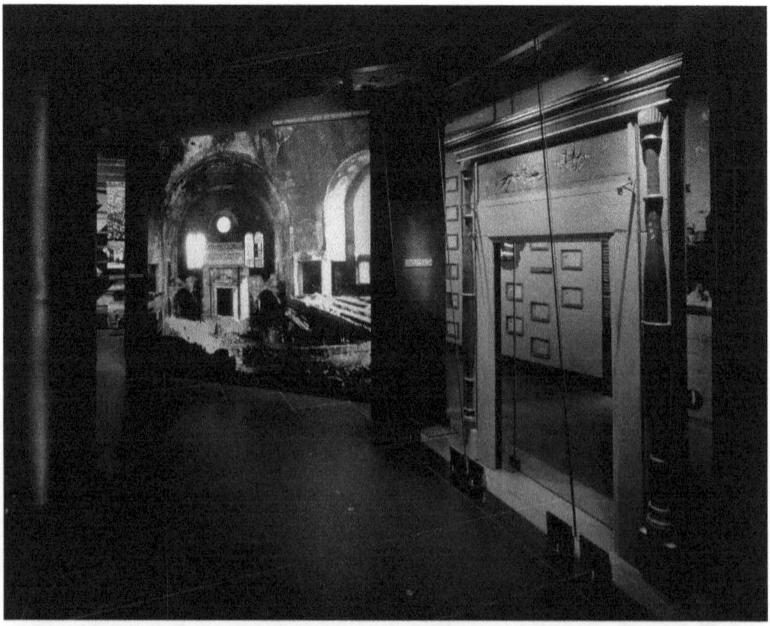

Fig. 2.8. Scene from the Kristallnacht gallery at the United States Holocaust Memorial Museum, the site of the 1998 Washington Conference on Holocaust-Era Assets. © United States Holocaust Memorial Museum.

about the enormous suffering of the Jews under the Nazis. The delegates were reminded by Holocaust survivor and Nobel Laureate Elie Wiesel that time was running out for many Holocaust survivors and that this conference could well be the last chance some would have to see justice done.[49] After the speeches, delegates explored the museum's exhibitions, which recounted in detail the harrowing experiences of Jews during the Nazi period.[50]

The setting for the next day of the conference would emphasise the gravitas and overt political dimension of the proceedings. The delegates made their way into the heart of the State Department, where no less a figure than the US Secretary of State, Madeleine Albright, gave the keynote address. Albright, whose family had fled to Britain due to Nazi persecution, declared: 'We're here to chart a course for finishing the job of returning or providing compensation for stolen Holocaust assets to survivors and the families of Holocaust victims.'[51] She emphasised that this was a task of great urgency, as the 'remaining Holocaust survivors have reached an advanced stage in life. More than five decades have passed since the Nazis perpetrated their thefts and murders.'[52]

The conference considered many different Holocaust-era assets, but it was the session on looted art that would change everything for the museum world. As Nazi looting was an issue that many of the museum professionals in attendance had never seriously considered, it was only natural that the session included speeches from two expert historians who outlined Nazi policies and the history of post-war restitution efforts. Lynn Nicholas addressed directly the understandable but misplaced impression that this matter had been dealt with after the war: 'After the great bulk of objects had been returned, and as the number of claims declined, both interest and funding diminished, leaving a quantity of works in the hands of European government agencies and museums, where many still remain.'[53] She highlighted that the art which was not recovered posed an enormous challenge, 'for we do not know where or exactly what it is until it suddenly appears in a museum or on the market and is recognised'.[54] Nicholas explained that, even with an awareness of these issues, there was no simple solution to the problem: 'There is, at [the] present time, still no easy way for the layman to check the status of a work about which he has suspicions' because the records pertaining to claims and confiscations 'for the most part [had] been relegated to storage and were in disorder'.[55] Jonathan Petropoulos expressed the view that museums were still a 'largely untapped' resource which, if re-examined with questions of Nazi-era provenance in mind, could help achieve justice at this crucial moment.[56]

Washington was not the first conference to address issues of Nazi-looted art, but unlike academic conferences it did far more than provide a mere forum for discussion. The aim of the Washington Conference was to pave the way for direct action. Its outcome, the Washington Principles, was an 11-point statement, carefully drafted by Stuart Eizenstat, that would set the agenda for museums for years to come (Figure 2.9). The question of provenance was directly addressed by the first principle, which stated: 'Art that had been confiscated by the Nazis and not subsequently restituted should be identified.' The ninth principle set out the aim for this research, namely to achieve 'just and fair solutions'. The other principles effectively supported the vision outlined in principles 1 and 9, by, for example, calling for archives to be opened and setting up commissions 'to assist in addressing ownership issues'.[57] In his concluding remarks, Eizenstat left no doubt that the 11 principles endorsed by the delegates would not remain a merely academic document, but would directly and swiftly transform museum practice in the field of provenance. As he summed up, 'The art world

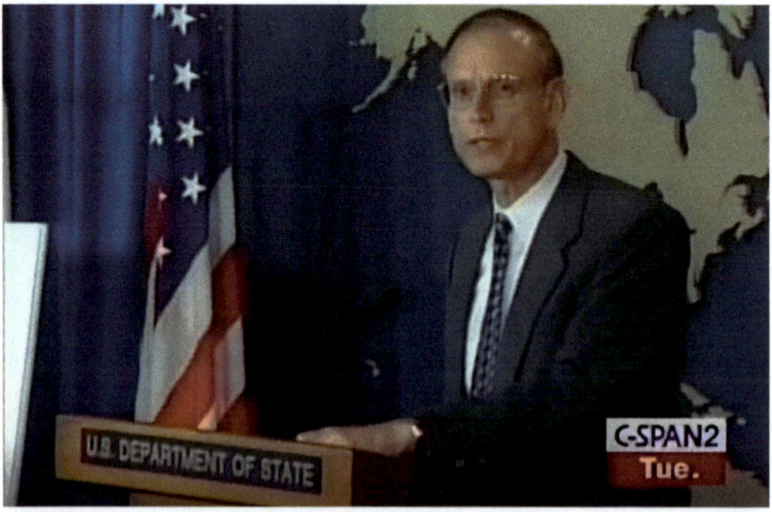

Fig. 2.9. Stuart Eizenstat, the driving force behind the 1998 Washington Conference, presenting a report at a press conference on unrecovered Nazi-looted assets (July 1998). © C-SPAN.

will never be the same in the way it deals with Nazi-confiscated art. From now on, the sale, purchase, exchange, and display of art from this period will be addressed with greater sensitivity and a higher international standard of responsibility.'[58]

In the 1940s, the Allied governments could draft curators into new units to restitute works of art, but in the 1990s all they could do was appeal to curators' moral conscience and encourage them to do so. Nevertheless, for all its inevitable faults and shortcomings, the Washington Conference redefined the very idea of what provenance was for, transforming it into a forensic-style tool designed to address historical injustices. Even if the Washington Principles were most comprehensively implemented only in countries that had already played a major role in the post-war restitution drive, they nevertheless represented a powerful moral yardstick against which all museums would now be judged.[59]

Research into the Nazi-era provenance of museum collections

The momentum generated by the Washington Conference ignited research efforts into an area previously considered peripheral to museum practice.[60] As with the Monuments Men, the task fell primarily to curators, but with the crucial difference that this time they were turning the spotlight on their own collections. Despite their best intentions as laid out in museum policy statements and the Washington Principles, curators and researchers in Britain and America soon came to the realisation that the faith they had placed in their own records had been misguided. Giulia Bartrum of the British Museum described the realities that the curators encountered as they began to investigate their archival records: 'Although British Museum acquisition registers will always record from whom and usually where an object was purchased, it is very rare to find any note of earlier ownership. Purchase invoices were never retained in the archive, and correspondence was heavily weeded.'[61] While the specifics varied from institution to institution, the curators soon realised that to reconstruct the provenance trail and make connections with the Nazi past would require them to go far beyond their own archives. When British and American curators talked to their German colleagues, they learned that the situation in the former Reich was quite different. The acquisition books often contained the names of the Jewish collections from which objects had been taken; all that was really required was the willingness to look for them. By contrast, all that curators in Britain could usually establish was that objects contained significant gaps in their provenance.

Another way of approaching this research task was to examine the resources built up by the Allies during the war and in the immediate post-war period, such as the 'red flag' lists of names compiled by Allied intelligence officers, or publications about lost works of art, which could then be compared to the museum's catalogue.

One of the most immediate impacts of the Washington Conference was that it galvanised efforts to make such resources digitally available to researchers, who therefore no longer had to travel to archives to consult, for example, the index cards created by the ERR (see Chapter 3). At the same time, there was a recognition that new resources had to be created to enable the registration of objects that had been confiscated and extorted from the victims and that were now considered lost. The hope was that by creating such lost art databases, researchers working in museums would be able to check them without even having to leave their desks. Today, the largest and most comprehensive database is the one maintained by the German Lost Art Foundation, which was originally set up so that German museums could register their own post-war losses. In the decades that followed, after the Washington Conference had helped to throw open the doors of the archives, this research has vastly expanded in scope, resulting in in-depth and careful reconstructions of the fate of individuals whose lives were torn apart by the Nazis.

Provenance research and restitution

The Washington Conference defined as the clear purpose of this research the restitution of artworks that had fallen through the cracks of the post-war restitution effort.[62] The eighth principle stated:

> If the pre-War owners of art that is found to have been confiscated by the Nazis and not subsequently restituted, or their heirs, can be identified, steps should be taken expeditiously to achieve a just and fair solution, recognizing this may vary according to the facts and circumstances surrounding a specific case.[63]

Upon close inspection, the seemingly straightforward formulation 'just and fair solutions' raises many questions. The reason for using this turn of phrase, instead of simply 'restitution', was hinted at in the preamble, which noted that serious legal questions always loomed in the background. The 'conference recognises that among participating nations there are differing legal systems and that countries act within the context of their own laws'.[64] This vague statement glosses over an enormously complex legal situation in many countries by using the term 'rightful owners', as opposed to 'legal owners'. These complexities largely revolved around statutes of limitations; laws concerning museum collections; deadlines for post-war restitution claims that had long since elapsed; and the recognition that many countries were unwilling to overturn their respective ownership laws in order to facilitate a new wave of restitution.[65] The vagueness of what 'just and fair' meant in practice ensured a wide buy-in from the participants, but was inevitably interpreted quite differently in different countries. Nevertheless, whatever the legal situation may be in a given country, provenance research is always absolutely vital for finding 'just and fair solutions', whatever their concrete nature.

Britain was forced to consider its own particular legal complexities in 2002, when the British Museum received a restitution claim with respect to four drawings which the Gestapo had seized in 1939 from the Jewish collector Arthur Feldmann and that, after the war, resurfaced on the art market in England.[66] This shone a powerful spotlight onto the laws governing the collections of Britain's national museums, a topic usually of interest only to a small number of museum lawyers. These laws prohibited national museums such as the British Museum and the V&A from deaccessioning items from their collections outside a set of narrowly defined exceptions, none of which applied to the items in question. In 2000, the British government had established an independent panel of experts to issue recommendations with respect to items carrying a problematic, Nazi-era provenance, but the panel found that they could not recommend what the Washington Conference had promised to deliver, namely the restitution of these items.[67] This was the beginning of a long process in which Britain's museum directors would push for legal reform in order to make restitution possible.[68]

Eventually, in 2009, the Holocaust Act was passed, which finally enabled the British Museum and other national museums to restitute items if so recommended by the Spoliation Advisory Panel.[69] As a result, Britain now has a very efficient system that serves claimants and museums, both of whom can rest assured that each case will be scrutinised by an independent body of experts.[70] Curators can therefore continue to focus on researching provenance and communicating what they know to the public, while the often complex decisions regarding what should happen on the basis of their research are 'outsourced' to independent experts. This is a particularly positive aspect of the restitution mechanism because these experts, unlike the museums, have no direct connection to the objects and therefore cannot be accused of bias.

The panel publishes its recommendations, a vital step in ensuring transparency around these proceedings, but also representing an incredibly important resource for researchers seeking to understand how and why particular decisions have been made. Similar committees exist in Germany, Austria, the Netherlands and France, and are currently under discussion in Sweden and Switzerland.[71] Interestingly, no such body exists in the country where the Washington Conference took place, because in the United States, most museums are not state institutions. As a result, decisions either remain in the hands of the individual museums, or must be contested in the courts.[72]

Following the Washington Conference, thousands of items have been restituted to their rightful owners. The majority of these artworks came from German and Austrian institutions, with only a small number of restitution cases emerging in the UK.[73]

Despite the fact that museums can now turn to official guidance, many often still feel a great deal of anxiety and uncertainty when they receive a formal restitution request, or when their own research determines that an item in the collections was confiscated or extorted from victims of the Nazis but was not restituted after the war.[74] In some cases, curators may simply be embarrassed to admit publicly how little the museum knows about particular items in its collections; in others, they may instinctively rush to protect the museum's reputation or particular items that play a crucial role in their galleries. It is certainly disappointing that some museums still think that restitution should be approached as an antagonistic and legalistic exercise, rather than taking it as the opportunity to embark on a collaborative research project that can clarify the status of an object and determine its best possible place. While museums are normally eager to share their thinking about the objects in their care, they have often been very reluctant to draw back the curtain on how the restitution process works in practice.

Restitution claims often concern objects that curators had never before considered in this light, and therefore spark intensive research activity behind the scenes. This was the case in 2010, when the V&A received a request for the return of a Meissen piece from the Emma Budge Collection, which was forcibly sold at auction in Nazi Germany in 1937.[75] The ceramics curator Hilary Young turned to the acquisition records for this item, which showed that it was acquired in the 1980s and that the Emma Budge provenance was not seen as a concern at the time. Young also examined the object itself and discovered that it carried the collector's mark 'H. E. B.', which stood for 'Henry and Emma Budge'. This discovery enabled him to locate two other items bearing the same mark, which had not been part of the original claim. With the objects identified and their authenticity confirmed, the museum tasked a German-speaking curator with researching the circumstances of the 1937 Berlin auction where the Budge Collection was dispersed.[76]

Heike Zech found that the objects had come to the museum via a complicated path, through an English collector living in Rome, who had in turn acquired them from a Russian art dealer living in Paris.[77] Compared to many items in museum collections, this is in fact a relatively simple provenance trail, highlighting the wide-ranging international journeys which many objects take prior to their arrival in a museum collection. When Zech reviewed the acquisition files, she was also struck by the extent to which provenance practices have changed since the 1980s. Today, it would be impossible for an item that had been sold at auction in 1930s Germany not to raise serious questions. In contrast to the acquiring curators in the 1980s, Zech could draw from research that had recently been carried out into the circumstances of this sale, which left no doubt in her mind that the objects had been forcibly sold and that the morally correct thing for the museum to do would be to support their restitution.[78] The museum trustees shared her view, and when they were asked by the Spoliation Advisory Panel to submit a formal response, they echoed Zech's sentiment, wholeheartedly endorsing the restitution of the three Meissen pieces. As always, the panel's report included a summary of the legal and policy background established as a result of the Washington Conference, before undertaking a forensic examination of the case, resulting in the recommendation that the objects should be restituted.[79] Consequently, the items, after more than 75 years, were finally returned to the descendants of this Jewish art collector.

In Britain and other countries, most in-depth provenance research has been carried out in response to specific restitution claims. Despite the fact that formal restitution proceedings are intended as an alternative to litigation, they have often taken on the form of tense legal proceedings, which divorced this research from normal curatorial practice. As a result, the detailed research reports produced in such cases have rarely been shared beyond the offices of a museum's lawyers, although this is slowly starting to change. Museums were established to share with the public the knowledge that they hold about the objects in their care. Items that are the subject of restitution claims should clearly be no different. If we want the public to appreciate the importance of provenance research, to understand how the objects entered museum collections and the complexities of the restitution process, we must share the fruits of this research as widely as possible.

Due diligence for acquisitions and incoming loans

With their existing collections now under scrutiny in the wake of the Washington Conference, museums were understandably eager not to add to the scale of the unexamined legacy within their collections. Long before the Washington Conference, in 1986 the International Council of Museums had issued a code of ethics that urged museums to scrutinise new acquisitions or loans, but this had focused on cultural property that was illegally exported from their countries of origin, reminding us again of the Nazi-era blind spot in museum practice.[80] Even before the Washington Conference, the American and British museum community had made a clear commitment to Nazi-era provenance as part of their due diligence for new acquisitions and loans.[81] With the Washington Principles in place, and the prospect of restitution becoming a legal possibility, this research has become incredibly important for museums as it aims to ensure that no item with a problematic Nazi-era provenance is added to the collections. Over time, the requirement to conduct Nazi-era provenance research has been written into the collecting and acquisition policies of museums around the world.[82]

Although this new standard of due diligence has been widely adopted, it remains extremely challenging. Research into an existing collection is complex and time consuming, but when considering potential acquisitions it becomes infinitely more challenging. The crucial factor here is time pressure. When a curator spots an object with gaps in its provenance at an upcoming auction, they have very little time to research it before the object may be sold to a private collector who is under no obligation to follow due diligence protocols. The stakes for museums are high, not only in a moral and reputational sense, but also financially. If they acquire an item that then turns out to be problematic, they risk losing the object, the money that they spent on it and their reputation as a diligent institution in the process.[83]

Faced with this time pressure, most museums rely on simple checks of the Lost Art database (www.lostart.de) which, although the largest and most comprehensive database of its kind, with c. 120,000 entries, can provide only a small snapshot of the artworks that may have been tainted by the Nazi past (see Chapter 3).

Loans can be equally difficult. For an exhibition, a curator may request hundreds of items from dozens of different international lenders. The most immediate source of concern here is not so much public lenders, and especially not those whose collections have been published online for many years, but rather private collections, the contents of which may not be publicly known, and which feature objects that may never have been publicly displayed. Less experienced private collectors are frequently taken aback by questions about the Nazi-era provenance of their collections, whereas experienced collectors know that they must be able to provide in-depth provenance information in order to see their item in the gallery of a prestigious museum.

Like the restitution-focused research, the painstaking work required for due diligence protocols rarely sees the light of the galleries. From a museum perspective, this research is designed to eliminate risks, but not to share the fruits of this research can deprive museum visitors of the opportunity to learn more about the personal histories behind the objects. For example, if due diligence checks revealed that an item once belonged to a Jewish collector persecuted under the Nazis but was then restituted after the war, this would provide a perfect opportunity for a museum to share a moving and important chapter of history with the public.

Curating Nazi-era provenance in art museums

Art museums were created not only to showcase objects but also to contextualise and interpret them. Historically, this meant that they would share with visitors information about the artistic qualities of the artworks on display and, at least sometimes, would mention their provenance. However, the provenance was usually only communicated if the museum believed that this would help to unlock a better understanding and appreciation of the objects themselves, or because it was particularly illustrious.[84] This distinguished these institutions from history museums, which generally selected the objects not because of their artistic qualities, but because they provided tangible evidence of a time, a place or a people.[85] In a museum or memorial dedicated to educating visitors about the Nazis and the suffering of their victims, we may encounter, for example, the desk on which a specific order was signed, alongside an empty suitcase, or a pair of shoes that belonged to one of the millions of victims who were murdered as a result of that order.[86] This is not to say that artworks do not feature in such museums, but they usually do so in order to celebrate the resolve of the victims in the face of Nazi terror – for example, through sketches detailing the everyday horror of the concentration camp system, or the attempts of artists to commemorate these unspeakable events after the war.

By contrast, art museums have always struggled with difficult histories, a factor that may be due in no small part to them often having understood themselves as places where people could go to forget about their problems and concerns, and instead lose themselves in the artworks. After the war, museums were acutely conscious of this desire as they threw open their doors to visitors who had just spent years in bomb shelters, or who had fought directly in the war. This pattern was reflected across the world, not least in Germany, where many felt a profound desire to draw a line under the Nazi past.[87]

In the wake of the Washington Conference, Nazi-era provenance issues became a topic that museums could no longer ignore. The research that followed into the material legacies of the Nazi past increasingly trickled down to the galleries themselves, resulting in hundreds of provenance exhibitions and displays, and changes made to labels in the permanent galleries.[88] If German museums had been reluctant to address this issue in the decades following the Second World War, they were now the ones leading the charge. This was part of a much wider transformational process called 'Vergangenheitsbewältigung' (which describes the process of coming to terms with, or mastering, the past), in which a kind of social redemption ritual is performed.[89]

Usually prompted by external pressures, German institutions called in researchers to document the truth about their history under the Nazis. The aim was not to whitewash their history, but to acknowledge its darkest chapters and thereby enable the current generation to move forward. Museums in Germany felt very acutely that if they were to retain their status as respected members of the international museum community, they would have to confront the Nazi past and publicly own up to it. This they did directly in the arena in which they were most familiar: their galleries. But this was not just a calculated public relations exercise; it created a favourable environment for conscientious provenance researchers who, as a result, were given the opportunity to share their research with the public, thereby ensuring that the work carried out in the wake of the Washington Conference was not reduced to a mere box-ticking exercise concealed behind closed doors. And while they did not feel the same pressure to confront the Nazi past as the museums in the country of the perpetrators, it is only natural that the Nazi past also became a topic for museums in countries that had been occupied. Certainly, their initial efforts were limited to sharing their own institutions' experiences under Nazi occupation, but there have since been increasing numbers of more nuanced exhibitions which directly address the Nazi-era provenance of items within their collections that were acquired both during the Nazi period and in the decades after the war.[90]

American and British museums were ideally placed to create similar exhibitions, but due to their close involvement in the initial post-war restitution efforts, they would not have felt the same kind of pressure to confront their own collections. Nevertheless, there has been a growing number of such exhibitions, including the display 'Provenance: A Forensic History of Art' at the Krannert Art Museum, the 'Discriminating Thieves' display at the Nelson-Atkins Museum of Art and the 'Concealed Histories' display at the V&A – as well as numerous changes made to the labels in the permanent galleries in museums as far apart as Los Angeles and Oxford.[91] It is wrong to assume that the paucity of provenance exhibitions is simply a sign of resistance or an unwillingness to engage: in most cases, the reason is simply that museums lack the confidence and courage to rethink their practice. Researching Nazi-era provenance requires a skillset that goes beyond traditional provenance research, and it is therefore no surprise that we have seen more exhibitions of this kind in countries where governments have made funding available to support this specialised research, particularly in Germany.

If the aim of provenance research is to recover the stories behind the objects, then the aim of any exhibition or intervention in the galleries is to share this knowledge with the visitors. But how this should best be done often raises a lot of questions. Even 25 years after the Washington Conference, curators at some institutions are still faced with the misplaced objection from their directors that to address this topic in the galleries could reflect badly on the museum – as if any museum has ever been criticised for thoroughly researching the Nazi-era provenance of its collections and sharing this research in a transparent, sensitive and thoughtful manner. Similarly, the same curators might hear that to address the Nazi past within the galleries would distract from the core mission of the museum – as if information about the aesthetic qualities of the object could not be balanced with information about its provenance, and as if addressing familiar objects in a new light would not bring audiences to the galleries. Another, more complex objection to communicating the Nazi-era stories of certain items is due to the research being so closely linked to restitution. This association often leads to the assumption that, if an object does not need to be restituted then to talk about its Nazi past is unnecessary or could lead to misunderstandings; or, on the other hand, if an object is in the process of being restituted or has already left the institution, there is no clear way to talk about this in the galleries. The reality is, of course, that museums have found creative ways for curating 'absence', such as the use of empty display cases, or alternative objects that provide crucial context for why an object is no longer there.[92]

Another issue standing in the way of open communication is that, in some cases, question marks remain over certain objects which have not yet been resolved, and perhaps never will be. Museums may be reluctant to display these items because they feel that such question marks must first be resolved, and that to display the object would somehow taint it, when in fact displaying them could actually lead to the discovery of new information, not least from interested visitors. Indeed, time and again, provenance exhibitions have demonstrated

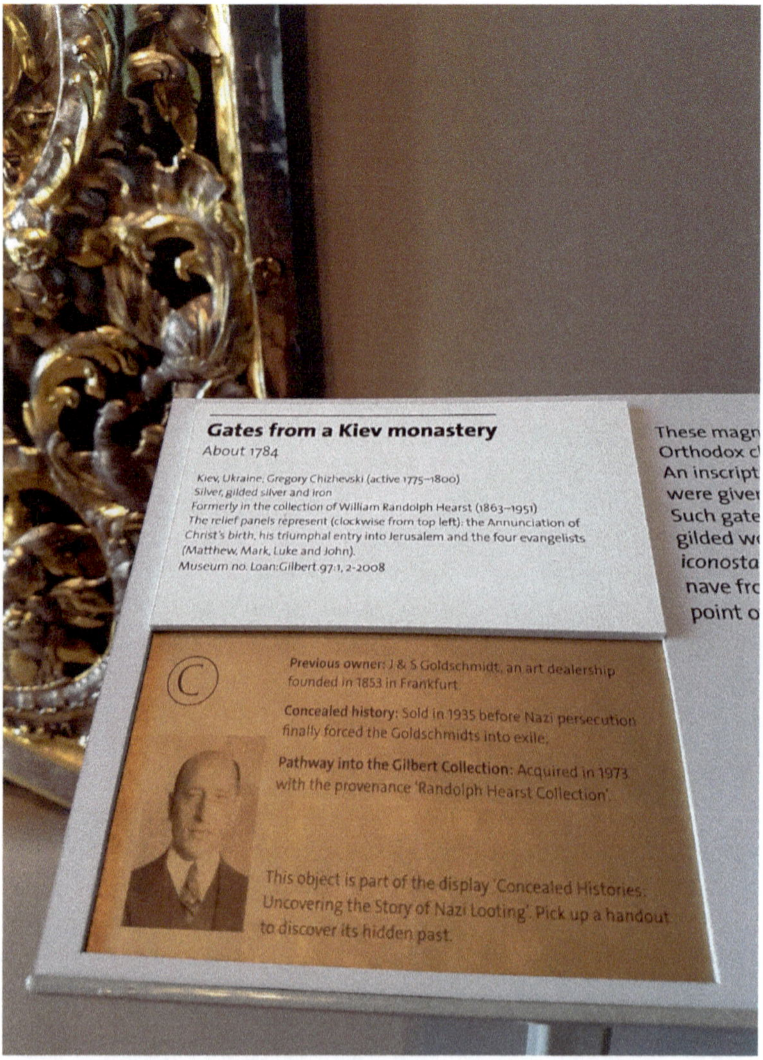

Fig. 2.10. Scene from the special provenance display, 'Concealed Histories: Uncovering the Story of Nazi Looting' at the Victoria & Albert Museum, London. © Jacques Schuhmacher

that museum visitors are very interested in the Nazi past and are quite fascinated by the 'detective work' that goes into provenance research, even in countries that were not directly touched by Nazi rule.[93] Any reservations on the part of museums regarding such exhibitions should have long been allayed by the facts on the ground.

The way in which Nazi-era provenance is curated naturally always depends on the institution, the collection and the specific questions raised by research. When curators at the V&A started in 2019 to work on a display based on their provenance research efforts into a collection of works of decorative art, their principal aim was to use the fruits of their research in order to bring to life the stories of the objects' previous owners (Figure 2.10). The research had discovered that items in the collection had belonged to Jewish victims of the Nazis, but which were restituted after the war, while other items had belonged to Jewish collectors during the 1930s and had a significant gap (sometimes of decades) in their provenance. This collection was built by Arthur Gilbert from the 1960s onwards; as a Jewish collector, Gilbert was acutely aware of the horrors of the Holocaust, but like most collectors of his time, he did not ask in-depth questions about the provenance of the objects he acquired – which highlights once again that the stories of Nazi-era provenance are never simple.[94]

The curators were faced with two options. They could place all the items they had identified in a single display case, which would prompt an increased focus on Nazi-era provenance research, but would also divorce the subject from the rest of the collection. The curators decided instead to integrate the items into the existing galleries, in order to emphasise the wider context in which they were acquired, and to give visitors the opportunity not only to discover the personal stories behind the objects, but also to develop an appreciation for their artistic qualities, in line with the existing gallery narrative. The curators wanted to be mindful of the fact that these galleries have a long history of attracting visitors interested in the objects and who may never have considered issues of Nazi-era provenance. To cater to this audience, they chose to retain the original label, but added a new one alongside it, carrying a photograph and additional information about the previous Jewish owner. A survey conducted at the start of the exhibition revealed that while many international visitors were profoundly interested in artworks with a connection to the Nazi past, their understanding of what had happened between 1933 and 1945 was, at best, fragmentary. In light of this, the curators recognised the need to provide information beyond what can be contained within a traditional museum label (which usually allows for only some 50 words of description). For this reason, they decided to produce an additional brochure that would provide more information and allow the moving stories of the victims to be told with much greater detail and sensitivity. The resulting 'Concealed Histories: Uncovering the Story of Nazi

Looting' display demonstrated that even a relatively small display can draw significant attention and prompt new and important conversations about the objects in the galleries which would otherwise never have happened.[95]

Online catalogues

At the time of the Washington Conference, only a small number of museums listed their collections online, which explains the rapid drive to create websites on which museums could post information specifically about items with a Nazi-era provenance gap, such as the American Alliance of Museums' *Nazi-Era Provenance Internet Portal* (www.nepip.org) or the Collections Trust's *Spoliation Records* in the UK (collectionstrust.org.uk/cultural-property-advice/spoliation-research-by-uk-museums-for-1933-45/).[96] A lot has changed since then. Today, all major museums have their own online collections catalogues, as do an ever-increasing number of smaller museums. It is easy to assume that these catalogues are consulted primarily by specialist researchers, but in reality these databases often attract substantially more visitors than the museum galleries themselves – simply because they can be easily discovered and accessed by anyone.[97]

These databases share the common aim of placing information online that was previously recorded only in local acquisition books and index cards. Unlike the labels in the galleries or the pages of a printed catalogue, the provenance fields of these online catalogues are not constrained by word limits. Therefore online databases have become a platform on which museums share information about what they know, and do not yet know, about the provenance of their collections. The way in which this information is presented varies considerably from museum to museum, ranging from lists of names, dates and modes of transfer, to narrative essays that unpack the stories behind a simple statement such as 'Budge sale, Graupe, Berlin, lot 852'.[98]

In provenance research, precision and transparency are always crucial, and Nazi-era provenance is no exception. This is why museums are increasingly adding references to the provenance fields, allowing visitors to clearly understand where the museums' information comes from, and enabling researchers to pick up the provenance trail in the literature and archives.[99] As they can be easily updated (and corrected), these online records have the character of living and breathing research documents. By sharing their knowledge about the provenance of their collections in this way, museums in turn can benefit from the research carried out by others, who can now easily discover with a simple web search, for instance, that an item from a particular collection ended up in several museums, which can often mark the beginning of fruitful research exchanges and collaborations.

Conclusion

As the Washington Principles were presented to the world, Stuart Eizenstat famously said that 'the art world will never be the same again'.[100] While a lot of work remains to be done, what in 1998 was merely a hopeful prediction has become increasingly true. If Taylor's memorandum and the London Declaration helped to usher in the provenance and restitution effort of the post-war period, then the Washington Conference spread a clear awareness that, despite this remarkable effort, the Nazi past was still very much 'alive' in museums around the world – even in the galleries and storerooms of the institutions whose curators had been actively involved in this important post-war work.

The aim of the conference was as simple as it was morally urgent: to finish the job begun by the Monuments Men and Women. It is no coincidence that the first Washington Principle highlighted the importance of provenance research, for this was nothing less than the crucial precondition for achieving 'just and fair' solutions. As a result, it transformed provenance research from a minor and often neglected discipline into a forensic-style tool for addressing past injustices. It galvanised research into the provenance of museum collections and threw open the door for restitution, albeit only in a much smaller number of countries than Eizenstat would have hoped.[101] Nevertheless, the core message of the conference – that we should not let the Nazi past live on unexamined and unchallenged – has fundamentally reshaped expectations of the role and moral responsibility of museums around the world. Crucially, it helped transform art museums into places where visitors can hope to learn not only about the aesthetic qualities of the items on display, but also about the moving human realities behind them.

Further reading and resources

The Nazi regime was in power for 12 years. By contrast, the efforts sparked by the Washington Conference to address the legacies Nazism left in museum collections have now lasted for more than 25 years – and continue to this day. There is no end in sight. Nevertheless, compared to the vast scholarship on the Nazi period, it is relatively straightforward to gain an overview of the literature about provenance research and restitution efforts.

For the Allied restitution effort in the immediate post-war period, the best starting points are the relevant chapters in Lynn H. Nicholas's *The Rape of Europa: The fate of Europe's treasures in the Third Reich and the Second World War* (New York, 1995) and Iris Lauterbach's *The Central Collecting Point in Munich: A new beginning for the restitution and protection of art* (Los Angeles, 2018), which incorporates much recent scholarship. The Monuments Men and Women Foundation, whose founder Robert M. Edsel is the author of *Monuments Men: Allied heroes, Nazi thieves and the greatest treasure hunt in history* (New York, 2009), maintains an ever-expanding online *Bibliography on the Looting and Protecting of Cultural Heritage* (monumentsmenandwomenfnd.org/bibliography).

It is impossible to overstate the profound transformational impact of the Washington Conference on Holocaust-Era Assets on the field of provenance research and the museum sector. It therefore may come as a surprise that no book has been written about this landmark conference. Thankfully, the US State Department has published the *Proceedings of the Washington Conference on Holocaust-Era Assets* (Washington, DC, 1999), which represents the best starting point for an engagement with the issues raised. Twenty years on, in 2018, the German Lost Art Foundation hosted an international conference in Berlin to mark the anniversary of the Washington Principles and to provide space for reflection and to chart the way forwards. The informative presentations at this conference titled '20 Years Washington Principles: Roadmap for the Future' were recorded and are available online at *kulturgutverluste.de/en/eventdocumentation/specialist-conference-20-years-washington-principles-roadmap-future*.

The best overview of the restitution landscape in the wake of the Washington Conference is the incredibly rich volume edited by Ruth Redmond-Cooper: *Museums and the Holocaust: Second edition* (Builth Wells, 2021), which brings together chapters dealing with key themes and different countries and thus provides the ideal entry point to the more specialised and often legal literature. The best ways to stay abreast of the developments in this dynamic field are the *Newsletter of the Network of European Restitution Committees*, which is published quarterly by alternating national committees, as well as the newsletter published by the *Central Registry of Information on Looted Cultural Property 1933–1945*, which provides an indispensable weekly round-up of newspaper articles about restitution cases, conferences, publications and exhibitions (lootedart.com/subscribe).

Notes

1 Francis H. Taylor, draft memorandum of 24 November 1942 for submission to the President of the United States. RG 239, Roll 56. National Archives at College Park, Maryland. On Taylor and his colleagues' campaign, see: Nicholas 1995, 209–13.
2 Taylor, draft memorandum, 1–2, 3.
3 Taylor, draft memorandum, 4.
4 Taylor, draft memorandum, 2.
5 Taylor, draft memorandum, 2.
6 Taylor, draft memorandum, 4.
7 Harlan F. Stone, letter of 8 December 1942 to Franklin D. Roosevelt, 1. RG 239, Roll 58. National Archives at College Park, Maryland 1942.
8 Foreign Office memo of 21 September 1942 with respect to the Proposed Inter-Allied Declaration against Axis Looting in the Occupied Territories, pp. 1–2. FO 371/32221/4. National Archives, London, 1–2.
9 Foreign Office memo of 21 September 1942, 1.
10 Foreign Office memo of 21 September 1942, 1.
11 On this declaration, see Palmer 2000, 60–1; Fiedler 2000, 200–3.
12 'Inter-Allied Declaration against Acts of Dispossession Committed in Territories under Enemy Occupation or Control, 5 January 1943', 318. In Redmond-Cooper 2021, 318–19.
13 On the Allied discussions regarding the restitution of cultural property, see, for example, Kurtz 2006, 60–121.
14 On the Roberts Commission, see the comprehensive report: American Commission for the Protection and Salvage of Artistic and Historic Monuments in War Areas 1946, 1–5.
15 American Commission for the Protection and Salvage of Artistic and Historic Monuments in War Areas 1946, 2.
16 Lauterbach 2018, 22–3; American Commission for the Protection and Salvage of Artistic and Historic Monuments in War Areas 1946, 44–6.
17 On the Macmillan Committee, see: American Commission for the Protection and Salvage of Artistic and Historic Monuments in War Areas 1946, 60–1; Bevins 1999, 505–6; Commission for Looted Art in Europe 2011, 11.
18 On the Vaucher Commission, see: American Commission for the Protection and Salvage of Artistic and Historic Monuments in War Areas 1946, 27–8; Nicholas 1995, 277; Kurtz 2006, 70–2.
19 On the ALIU, see: Nicholas 1995, 282; Bernsau 2016; National Archives 2016.
20 On the discovery of these caches, see American Commission for the Protection and Salvage of Artistic and Historic Monuments in War Areas 1946, 126–34. For first-hand accounts, see Howe 1946; Rorimer 1950.
21 Smyth 1988, 29. On the history of the Munich Central Collecting Point, see Lauterbach 2018, 52–105.
22 Smyth 1988, 29.
23 Smyth 1988, 31.
24 Lauterbach 2018, 94–105.
25 Lauterbach 2018, 95–100.
26 Smyth 1988, 57.
27 The ALIU's Reports are available at https://www.fold3.com/publication/631/wwii-oss-art-looting-investigation-reports# (accessed 6 December 2023).
28 Farmer 2000, 29. On the Wiesbaden Collecting Point, see: Bernsau 2013, 179–255.

29 On the Offenbach Collecting Point, see Hoogewoud 1992, 167–73; Waite 2002, 215–24; Geschichtswerkstatt Offenbach 2011.
30 Lauterbach 2018, 106–49.
31 Lauterbach 2018, 128.
32 'United States: Military Government, United States Area of Control, Germany; Law No. 59; Restitution of Identifiable Property', *American Journal of International Law* 42, no. 1 (1948): 11–45.
33 Lillteicher 2007b, 101–4.
34 Goschler 2007.
35 See, for example, Pross 2001; Nietzel 2020, 272–7.
36 On the restitution process, see Lillteicher 2007a, 85–134.
37 Lauterbach 2018, 169–71.
38 Schuhmacher 2021a, 35–6.
39 Schuhmacher 2021a, 36.
40 Bureau Central des Restitutions 1947–9; Estreicher 1944. For a bibliography of similar publications concerning other countries, see: monumentsmenandwomenfnd.org/bibliography (accessed 21 November 2023).
41 On this sensitive and complex topic, see, for example, Perschke 2016, 333–4.
42 On German museums and the Nazi past, see Baensch 2016, 11–12.
43 V&A acquisitions between 1945 and 1989, information provided by Pamela Young on 11 March 2023.
44 Eizenstat 1997, i.
45 O'Donnell 2021, 239–40.
46 Philippe de Montebello's testimony before the House Banking and Financial Services Committee, 12 February 1998, V&A Archive, 1998/943.
47 Lord Janner of Braunstone, letter of 19 February 1998 to Chris Smith. 2000/722. Victoria & Albert Museum Archive, London.
48 Association of Art Museum Directors 1998. National Museum Directors' Council statement of principles and proposed actions, 1998, available online at: https://www.nationalmuseums.org.uk/what-we-do/contributing-sector/cultural-property/spoliation/spoliation_statement/ (accessed 6 December 2023).
49 Wiesel 1999.
50 Sharon Page, Report of 15 December 1998 to NMDC Working Party: Washington Conference on Holocaust-Era Assets. 2000/722. Victoria & Albert Museum Archives, London.
51 Albright 1999, 29.
52 Albright 1999, 31.
53 Nicholas 1999, 450.
54 Nicholas 1999, 451.
55 Nicholas 1999, 451.
56 Petropoulos 1999, 447.
57 US Department of State 1999, 971–2. The Washington Principles on Nazi-Confiscated Art are available online at: https://www.state.gov/washington-conference-principles-on-nazi-confiscated-art (accessed 21 November 2023).
58 Eizenstat 1999, 127.
59 Fisher and Weinberger 2014.
60 On this wave of research in America and Britain, see Wechsler 2005; Mixon 2005.
61 Giulia Bartrum, Interim Report to the Advisory Committee from the British Museum on the Progress Made and Difficulties Met. 2000/722. Victoria & Albert Museum Archive, London.
62 On 'restitution', see Herman 2021.
63 US Department of State 1999, 972.
64 US Department of State 1999, 971.
65 On the Washington Principles as a compromise, see Eizenstat 2003, 197–9.
66 Spoliation Advisory Panel 2006, 3. On Arthur Feldman, his collection and his persecution, see Eßl 2015, 9–10.
67 Woodhead 2021, 54.
68 Schuhmacher 2021a, 46.
69 Woodhead 2021, 68–9.

70 Jenkins 2015.
71 On the different panels, see Marck and Muller 2015; Network of European Restitution Committees 2019. On the UK Spoliation Advisory Panel, see Woodhead 2021, 54–72.
72 O'Donnell 2021, 230–8; Davidson 2015, 100–1.
73 See the UK Spoliation Advisory Panel's reports at: https://www.gov.uk/government/collections/reports-of-the-spoliation-advisory-panel (accessed 21 November 2023).
74 For England, see Arts Council England 2022. For Germany, see the comprehensive guide: Heidt 2017.
75 Letter of 10 August 2010 from Lothar Fremy to V&A, V&A Archive, External Liaison File, Restitution Claim, Emma Budge, Pt 1, September 2010–.
76 On the forced sale of the Emma Budge collection, see Michels 2021, 93–112; Heuss 2008a.
77 Heike Zech, Budge Collection: Claim to the Spoliation Advisory Panel. Case notes, 2. External Liaison File, Restitution Claim, Emma Budge, Pt. 1 September 2010–. Victoria & Albert Museum Archives, London.
78 Zech, Case notes, 7.
79 Spoliation Advisory Panel 2014.
80 International Council of Museums Code of Ethics, revised 2004, https://icom.museum/wp-content/uploads/2018/07/ICOM-code-En-web.pdf. (accessed 6 December 2023). On the ICOM Code, see Lewis 2016.
81 Association of Art Museum Directors 1998; National Museum Directors' Council 1998.
82 See, for example: Metropolitan Museum of Art 2023, 7–8; Victoria & Albert Museum 2019, 6.
83 On due diligence in the museum context, see the case study Reed 2013.
84 On the traditional function of provenance, see, for example Masurovsky 2020, 140.
85 Alexander and Alexander 2008, 113–38.
86 See, for example, Paver 2018.
87 See the interesting reflections in Fuhrmeister and Hopp 2019, 214.
88 The German Lost Art Foundation maintains an ever-expanding list of provenance exhibitions around the world: https://www.kulturgutverluste.de/Webs/DE/Recherche/AusstellungenProvenienzforschung/Index.html (accessed 21 November 2023).
89 On 'Vergangenheitsbewältigung', see Fischer and Lorenz 2015.
90 See, for example, Langfeld et al. 2015; Le Masne de Chermont and Sigal-Klagsbald 2008; Museum Boijmans Van Beuningen 2018; Krejčová 2019.
91 Karrels 2019; Mallon 2022; Schuhmacher 2021b.
92 Liebighaus Skulpturensammlung 2017, 19–20; Reininghaus 2009; Schwärzler 2000, 58–63.
93 Milosch and Hull 2019, 39. On provenance exhibitions, see the thought-provoking contributions to Andratschke and Jachens 2020.
94 Schuhmacher 2021b.
95 The exhibition texts are available online at https://www.vam.ac.uk/articles/about-the-concealed-histories-display (accessed 5 December 2023).
96 On the American *Nazi-Era Provenance Internet Portal*, see Wechsler and Ledbetter 2004.
97 Lejeune 2007, 89.
98 https://collections.mfa.org/objects/466173/figure-of--harlequin (accessed 5 December 2023).
99 On provenance documentation standards, see: Yeide et al. 2001, 33–4; Arbeitskreis Provenienzforschung 2018, 4–8.
100 Eizenstat 1999, 127.
101 See the overview in Fisher and Weinberger 2014.

3

Research strategies and resources: uncovering the stories behind museum objects

Today, many traces of the Nazis' reign of terror can still be discovered in museum collections across the world. Through provenance research, these objects can speak to us about the lives of people who were tormented, expelled and murdered – and about the Nazis' efforts to reshape the museum landscapes under their control in the image of 'racial purity'. Without provenance research, these objects remain silent witnesses to one of the most traumatic periods in history; to restore these voices to the historical record and to our understanding of our shared cultural inheritance, we must discover and dispel the hidden shadows that lie within our galleries and storerooms.

This is a daunting task: not only can the size of museum collections and archives feel overwhelming and intimidating, but many likely reflect the full range of Nazi policies. Over 12 long years, first in Germany and then encompassing so much of the European continent, the Nazis engaged in the largest campaign of persecution and dispossession the world has ever seen. The mechanisms of dispossession and the racist logic behind them were applied to millions of victims and came in many forms (see Chapter 1).

As provenance researchers, we must always keep this big picture in mind, not least because it allows us to question the accounts provided in documents created by the perpetrators, but also to make sense of the experiences of the victims. This chapter aims to provide a map of the territory, while acknowledging that each provenance researcher's journey and the stories they will discover will inevitably be unique. To be useful for as many different scenarios and collections as possible, this part of the book aims to showcase how, through careful detective work and the triangulation of different types of sources, we can embark on research that aims at nothing less than to ensure that the Nazis' attempts to disconnect these objects from their previous owners do not live on in the heart of our own civic institutions.

Researching the Nazi-era provenance of a museum collection

Initial survey

The size and nature of a museum collection varies enormously from institution to institution. For example, since its foundation in 1852, the size of the Victoria & Albert Museum's collection has grown to more than 2.8 million objects, encompassing not only diverse artworks but also objects of everyday use, and a staggering number of books and manuscripts.[1] Other collections will be much smaller, yet even small regional museums may contain holdings running to hundreds of items. Whatever the scale of the collection before us, it is essential to begin our provenance work with a systematic survey in order to focus our efforts.

It may be disorienting to realise that there is not always an obvious place to start. While Marxist literature or a Torah crown may immediately draw our interest because they are so obviously associated with groups the Nazis victimised, it is crucial to remember that Jewish collectors appreciated every conceivable form of art, ranging from Christian icons to East Asian vessels, modernist paintings to archaeological finds and classical antiquities.[2] Likewise, Social Democrats and Communists were perfectly capable of owning objects representative of societies and histories that they wanted to overthrow and overcome.[3] This means that we should never exclude objects based on who made them, or where they originated. To do so would be to underestimate the agency and interests of collectors, and the dynamic flows of the networks of collecting and the international art market in the first half of the twentieth century.

Nevertheless, because our aim is to make objects speak about the Nazi past, we can confidently exclude all items *created* after 1945. For all other items, we must carefully determine the years in which they entered our collections. To do so, it may be possible simply to run an automated search script on a collections database to create a list of all objects that came into the collection within a certain time period. In other cases, we may have to manually search through acquisition books and index cards to find the same information. We can exclude works of art that entered the collections before Hitler was appointed Reich Chancellor in 1933. However, we cannot become fixated on the Nazi period of 1933–45. It may be tempting to think that the fall of the Third Reich can mark a clear cut-off point for our investigations, but we must remember that many relevant objects entered museum collections decades after the war, right up to the present day.

Even if we exclude all pieces created after 1945 and those that entered the collections prior to 1933, we are still potentially left with a huge number of objects. In order to make this more manageable, we can now prioritise objects from this selection which have obvious gaps in their provenance, contain enigmatic references to 'private collectors' which require further clarification, or point to a transfer of ownership in Germany or in Nazi-occupied territories. In constructing this shortlist, we must not forget that provenance records may have been manipulated by art dealers or collectors to avoid tainting the objects with unwanted associations, or that they may have never been questioned before. A sound opening strategy is therefore to choose a number of objects whose provenance records, taken together, represent a broad cross-section of the often uneven base of evidence before us. This means that we should take an object with a seemingly complete and substantiated provenance; an object that has obvious gaps in its past; an object that has no meaningful provenance information at all; and an object that raises our suspicions because, for example, its record contains a name we may recognise as Jewish. Taking this approach increases our understanding of the collection and gradually hones our intuition for what we should prioritise.

Examining the museum records

Once we have selected an object or group of objects from the collection to investigate, it is logical to begin with the museum's own records. However, before we embark on this process, it is important to consider by whom and for what purpose these documents were created. It can be tempting to assume that a museum's records would provide us with a full, unbiased account of the objects' provenance, or even that, being the authority on the objects under its care, a museum would surely have the most complete information available. Unfortunately, this is often not the case.

Historically, when a museum acquired an object, curators would usually record information about it in an acquisition book or card index. The purpose of these records was not to create detailed object biographies, but merely to catalogue the objects for administrative and practical purposes. In most cases, museums traditionally recorded from whom an object was received, while curators gladly added more, if further information was available and seemed relevant to art-historical understandings of the item. Historically, curators did not aim to create an unbroken, complete provenance chain in order to identify potential problems; much like a résumé, they were more interested in emphasising the 'career highlights' of an object in order to burnish its reputation and further justify its inclusion in the collections. As with any standard form, the extent of the information added depended significantly on the personality and interest of the curator involved. Some only recorded the bare necessities and clearly rushed the entries, while others used beautiful handwriting to describe the object, and also cited scholarly publications as they strove to provide as comprehensive a record as possible.

Our first step is to get a clear sense of the extent of the information contained in the relevant acquisition books or card indexes.[4] In some cases, this might provide us with the name of a Jewish collector, enabling us to move directly to the archives to research their fate under the Nazis. In others, it may provide us with the name of an individual who owned the object prior to the Nazis' seizure of power; if so, we can pick up the trail from that point in time and attempt to trace the object's path through the dark years of 1933–45. Conversely, if the object was acquired more recently – for example, from an art dealer or auction house – we can use this information to trace the object backwards through time (these strategies are described in more detail below).

It is also crucial to review the museum records for any more subtle provenance clues. We should verify that our records provide an accurate description of the object, bearing in mind that artist attributions and titles may have changed over time, and that objects may have been measured with or without frames or plinths, or may have been significantly restored, altering their appearance. In other words, before we can turn to the relevant online databases to pick up the historical trail, we need to be sure that our sense of the object is flexible enough to take into account the different ways it may have been perceived in the past.

In all areas of provenance research, we need to pause and think carefully about where an object may have left traces in the archival record, and it is always important to apply this same reflective approach to our own museum archives. We must keep in mind that the acquisition records are not necessarily the only records our museums may possess about the object. When curators were considering the acquisition of a new item, they often corresponded with art dealers and collectors, and while they sometimes added these exchanges to the acquisition records, these documents (which often provide important clues about complex provenance histories) were often filed separately in the archives. For example, if an index card mentions the name of a specific dealer, it is always worth checking if the museum archive holds a separate correspondence file for that dealer, or if there are research papers produced by the curator in charge of the acquisition, in which they would often have needed to present in-depth materials to directors, committees or municipal and state authorities.

We should not forget to examine seemingly bureaucratic documents such as invoices or export licences, and sometimes even insurance documents, because between the lines of these transactional papers, we can frequently learn very specific details about the physical and cultural significance of an artwork.

A simple look at a museum's acquisition book can mark the beginning of a research process that allows us to see the objects in a new, but often darker, light. A Louis XVI chest of drawers from the State Museum Oldenburg's collections is a perfect example (Figure 3.1). When provenance researcher Marcus Kenzler opened the museum's acquisition book, he could not have anticipated that the simple line 'auction through Heimsath, Oldenburg' would lead to the revelation that the museum was only able to acquire the object because, in 1940, the Nazi authorities had terrorised an 80-year-old-Jewish woman, Rosa Israels, into selling it along with the rest of her possessions (Figure 3.2).[5] The auction proceeds were earmarked to pay for her deportation to Theresienstadt, where she 'perished' in 1942 – a word that is often used when we do not know the precise circumstances of death.[6] After he examined the acquisition book, Kenzler knew only the name of the auctioneer and the year of the sale. There was no printed auction catalogue for him to consult. Undaunted, his research took him to the City Archives in Oldenburg where he unearthed numerous relevant documents, including a form filed by the auctioneer revealing the name of the 'consignor': 'Rosa Sara Israels'.[7] Her last name (and indeed the middle name, Sara, which the regime had forced Jewish women to carry to mark them out) made it immediately clear that the 1940 sale had been one of the infamous 'Jewish auctions' (see Chapter 1).

The first goal of provenance research is always to arrive at a name, which then allows us to research the fate of a previous owner in greater detail. With his archival discoveries, Marcus Kenzler was

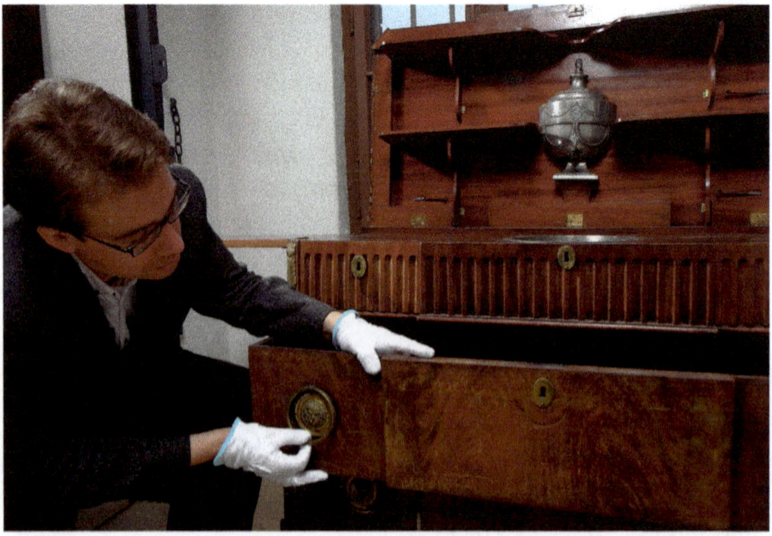

Fig. 3.1. Provenance researcher Marcus Kenzler examining the chest of drawers, which carried no signs that it had formerly belonged to Rosa Israels. © Landesmuseum für Kunst und Kulturgeschichte Oldenburg. Photo: Sven Adelaide.

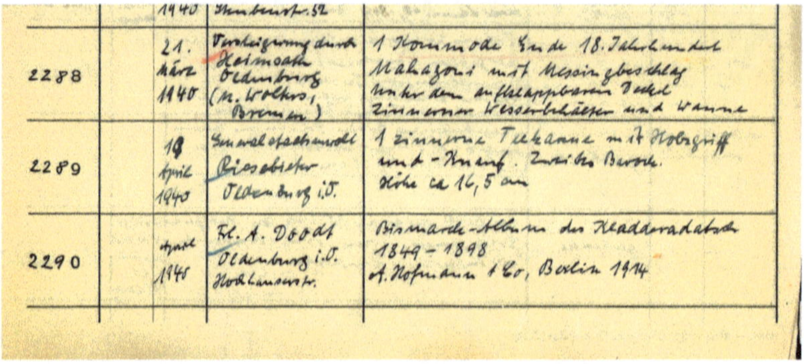

2288	21. März 1940	Versteigerung durch Heimsath Oldenburg (M. Wolkers, Bremen)	1 Kommode Ende 18. Jahrhundert Mahagoni mit Messingbeschlag unter dem aufklappbaren Deckel Zinnerner Wasserbehälter und Wanne
2289	18 April 1940	Juwelengeschäft Riesebieter Oldenburg i.O.	1 zinnerne Teekanne mit Holzgriff und -Knauf. [illegible] Höhe ca 16,5 cm
2290	April 1940	Frl. A. Doods Oldenburg i.O. [illegible]	Bismarck-Album des Kladderadatsch 1849–1898 A. Hofmann & Co, Berlin 1914

Fig. 3.2. Entry in the acquisition book for the chest of drawers, which became the starting point for Marcus Kenzler's research (acquisition book V, 1938–51). © Landesmuseum für Kunst und Kulturgeschichte Oldenburg.

now able to piece together the details of Rosa Israels's life under the Nazis. When the Nazis seized power, Rosa was 73 years old, widowed and living alone in the East Frisian town of Weener. In the subsequent years, she helplessly witnessed how the lives of her children and grandchildren were destroyed in the name of the Nazis' ideology.[8]

During the night of 9–10 November 1938, stormtroopers informed the local police that they intended to set the synagogue in Weener ablaze. Armed with gasoline, hastily pre-ordered at a local petrol station, the stormtroopers broke into the synagogue. As the building went up in flames, the fire brigade ensured that the fire did not spread to the buildings next door. The Nazi mob then turned their hatred upon the Jewish population.[9] They invaded and ransacked Rosa's home and confiscated various valuables. The family business had already been 'aryanised', or it would otherwise have been destroyed like the other local Jewish businesses.[10] The stormtroopers rounded up the Jewish population and locked them in the police station. On the next day, Rosa's son Ivo and the other Jewish men from Weener were corralled at the local slaughterhouse before being transferred to Sachsenhausen concentration camp. From the moment of their arrival, they were brutally mistreated.[11] In February 1940, the Nazis expelled the last remaining Jews from Weener, including the elderly Rosa, who was forced to move to Oldenburg. The house she left behind was turned into a Nazi kindergarten.

On the same day that a Weener newspaper published a triumphalist report announcing that 'the last Jew has left the soil of our hometown', the State Museum Oldenburg spotted an advert for the auction of Rosa's property.[12] The museum director, Walter Müller-Wulckow, was well aware why such a collection would appear at auction; he served as an 'expert for the liquidation of items of jewellery and art from Jewish property'.[13] At this auction, Müller-Wulckow, or one of his assistants, acquired the chest of drawers for 250 Reichsmarks.[14] It goes without saying that Rosa never saw any of this money, and while the chest was being catalogued by the museum, Rosa was expelled once again – this time from Oldenburg to Berlin. Her tragic odyssey, which had begun in Weener, finally concluded in 1942 in Theresienstadt, where her death was recorded a few months later.[15] Her death was just one chapter of a larger family tragedy: her son Ivo died in 1940 as a result of the violence that the guards inflicted on him in Sachsenhausen; German soldiers shot Rosa's son Arnold in 1940 as he tried to flee to the Netherlands; his wife and their two children were murdered in 1943 in the Sobibor extermination camp; Rosa's daughter Helene was murdered alongside two of her children in Auschwitz between 1942 and 1944.[16] As Marcus Kenzler wrote: 'The case of Rosalie Israels is not least a vivid example of the fact that seemingly harmless entries in museum inventory books … can conceal harrowing fates and blatant injustice.'[17]

When we consider the acquisition books of museums outside Germany, we discover that the links to Nazi history are often less direct. In these cases, we often only find the name of an art dealer who was, for instance, based in London, and who sold an item to the V&A. In such cases, there is always the possibility that these items have a connection to the Nazi past, and we therefore need to apply the same determination displayed by Kenzler and make every effort to establish who owned these items during the period 1933–45.

Examining the objects

It is easy to forget that the objects themselves may often carry subtle yet informative clues about the hands through which they passed before coming to rest in our collections today. When these objects arrived in museums, curators would naturally have examined them carefully, but we should not assume that they would consider every detail worth recording in the acquisition files. Indeed, there are many cases in which the written provenance record omits information about previous owners that is readily apparent if one looks at the surface of the object. For curators, these outward signs were self-evident and did not necessarily interest them.

For librarians, an 'ex libris' stamp or name on the first page of a book mattered little for cataloguing purposes: they were interested in the author, the title and the date and place of publication. Provenance marks of this kind come in many forms: labels applied to the back of paintings or the base of sculptures, attached by proud collectors or by curators and art dealers for internal cataloguing purposes.[18] Sometimes even the numbers scrawled on the works by Nazi officials, bent on the confiscation or suppression of the objects, provide us with clues about the twisted paths these artworks took over the years.[19]

Examining the objects may not be as easy as it sounds. While they are often on public display in the galleries, to get to this information we often have to remove them from cases, frames or atmospherically controlled environments. This process always requires great care and might not always be feasible, but this should be attempted if at all possible, because we might otherwise miss important clues without which our research may grind to a halt. Such provenance marks will never tell the full story; they provide starting points or evidence for further triangulation, but they can often arm us with circumstantial information that can greatly improve our chances of success in the voluminous holdings of the archives.

When Julia Eßl, provenance researcher at the Albertina in Vienna, examined the provenance of a drawing by Rudolf Friedrich Wasmann depicting 'a young woman with a distaff', she was first able to establish from the acquisition records that the Viennese museum had acquired it in 1939 from the C. G. Boerner auction house in Germany (Figure 3.3).[20] She therefore turned to the auction catalogue (accessible online), in the hope that it would provide information about who had consigned the drawing to the auction that took place in April 1939 in Leipzig – six months after the November pogrom. However, to her disappointment, the auction catalogue abbreviated the names of the consignors, leaving Eßl with no other clue to work with than the enigmatic letter 'H'.[21] She therefore turned to the object itself. When she examined the reverse of the drawing, she immediately discovered stamps of the initials 'CH' and 'WSK', the presence of which had not been noted in the museum's written records.[22] This directly highlights how important it can be to examine the object itself and that we should not assume that previous generations of researchers have catalogued the objects exhaustively. To decode these acronyms, Eßl turned to the indispensable encyclopaedia of provenance marks: *Les Marques de Collections de Dessins & d'Estampes*. First published in 1921, this crucial research tool has become synonymous with the name of its first editor, Frits Lugt – and has been made available online (marquesdecollections.fr).[23] With the 'Lugt', Eßl was able to decode 'CH' as 'Carl Heumann' and 'WSK' as 'Wilhelm Koenig'. In combination with the auction catalogue, which had abbreviated the name of the consignor of the Wasmann drawing with 'H', Eßl focused her research on the collector whose surname began with this letter: Carl Heumann, who, as the 'Lugt' had informed her, lived in the German city of Chemnitz.[24]

This information enabled Eßl to begin archival research that would eventually reveal the true story behind the object. She sent an enquiry to the State Archives in Saxony (the region in which Heumann lived), which unearthed documents that allowed her to piece together Carl Heumann's story. Born in 1886 in Cologne, Heumann was a banker, collector and philanthropist of the arts (Figure 3.4). Just before the outbreak of the First World War, he converted from Judaism to Protestantism, which counted for nothing when the Nazis seized power.[25] The records in the Leipzig archives reveal an all too familiar story: because of his Jewish heritage, Heumann was driven from his profession and subjected to an onslaught of discriminatory measures. He had to surrender his passport to the Nazi authorities and was in its place given a 'Jewish Identification Card' with the name Carl 'Israel'

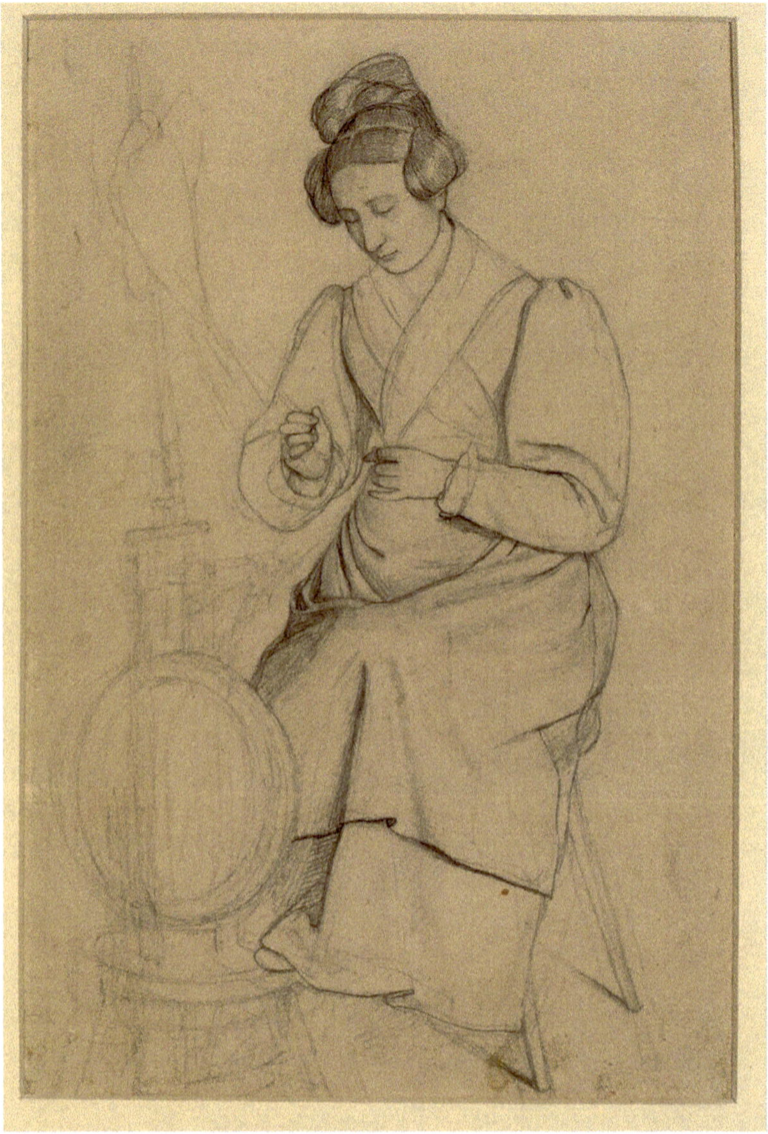

Fig. 3.3. Rudolf Friedrich Wasmann (1805–1886) drawing which, on its reverse, carried the enigmatic collector's mark 'CH'. Public domain (Source: Albertina).

Heumann. The Currency Office blocked his bank accounts and confiscated the contents of his bank safes. After the November pogrom, Carl Heumann was, like all Jews, forced to pay 'compensation' for the damage caused by Nazi thugs in Leipzig and across the Reich.[26] In the

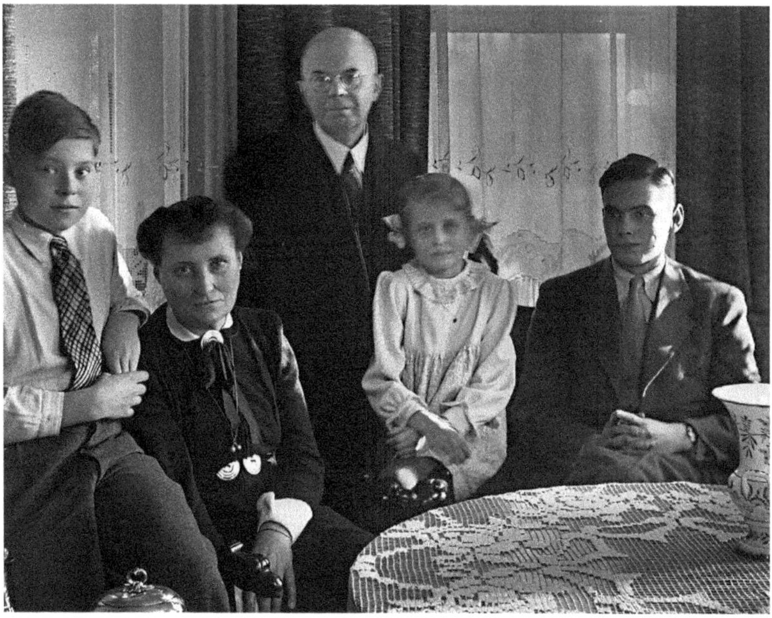

Fig. 3.4. Carl Heumann with his family. © Carol Heumann Snider.

eyes of the Nazis, Carl's wife Irmgard was an 'Aryan', and the fact that he lived in a 'mixed marriage' afforded him a small but only temporary degree of protection. With this small reprieve in mind, Carl placed his art collection in his wife's name, hoping that this would shield it from further Nazi incursions.[27]

By turning to the object itself, Eßl had managed to discover that a two-letter abbreviation carried a troubling history. Irmgard died in 1944, and the next year Carl, who would have been forced by this time to live in an overcrowded 'Jew house', was tragically killed by the same Allied bombs designed to put an end to the Nazi regime that had tormented him and so many others for almost a decade.[28]

Examining the literature

As we have seen, careful examination of museum records and the objects themselves can reveal important provenance clues that enable us to uncover the hitherto unknown stories of their previous owners – and to tell their stories for the first time in a museum context. Nevertheless, these success stories should not blind us to the reality that very often the museum's resources remain silent, or are too limited to provide us a map with which to continue our research. Even if the museum's records do provide us with plentiful information, until we expand our knowledge of the object and its history, we have no clear sense of what we do not know.

To broaden our perspective and increase our knowledge, we must consult the scholarly literature and review it with our specific research questions in mind.[29] We should therefore cast our net as widely as possible in order to capture all the relevant publications. If we are investigating, for instance, European paintings, prints, drawings and sculptures, the immediate starting points are the International Foundation for Art Research's *Catalogues Raisonnés* database (www.ifar.org/cat_rais.php), the *Bibliography of the History of Art* and *Répertoire international de la littérature de l'art* (primo.getty.edu/primo-explore/search?vid=BHA) and the *International Bibliography of Art* (about.proquest.com/en/products-services/iba/). As we review the publications we have identified, we can deepen our reading further by closely examining the footnotes; this simple yet often overlooked strategy frequently leads us on to works highly relevant to our research that we would otherwise have missed, often simply because the title did not contain the keywords we were searching for. They can also connect us with so-called 'grey literature', such as museum brochures or private publications, that are often not reliably catalogued on the relevant scholarly databases. It is also vital that we consult *WorldCat*, the largest online library catalogue, which aims to cover every library in the world, including those of specialised art-historical libraries such as the V&A's National Art Library, the Warburg Institute in London or the Frick Art Reference Library in New York (www.worldcat.org). We will also want to find out if the object has appeared at previous auctions, whose catalogues can hold valuable provenance clues, in which case we can turn to historical auction house catalogues, such as *Art Sales Catalogues Online* (which provides access to scanned auction catalogues from 1600 to 1900 at primarysources.brillonline.com/browse/art-sales-catalogues-online), and databases that register more recent sales, such as the *Art Price* and *Artnet* databases (featuring entries dating back to the mid-1980s at www.artprice.com and www.artnet.com, respectively).

We can see the different ways in which researching the literature can lead us to a name if we consider the complex case of a snuffbox crafted by the renowned maker Johann Christian Neuber (Figure 3.5). In 1987, a London-based art dealer sold the snuffbox to the private collector Arthur Gilbert, whose collection is now on display at the V&A. When the box came to the museum, it was accompanied

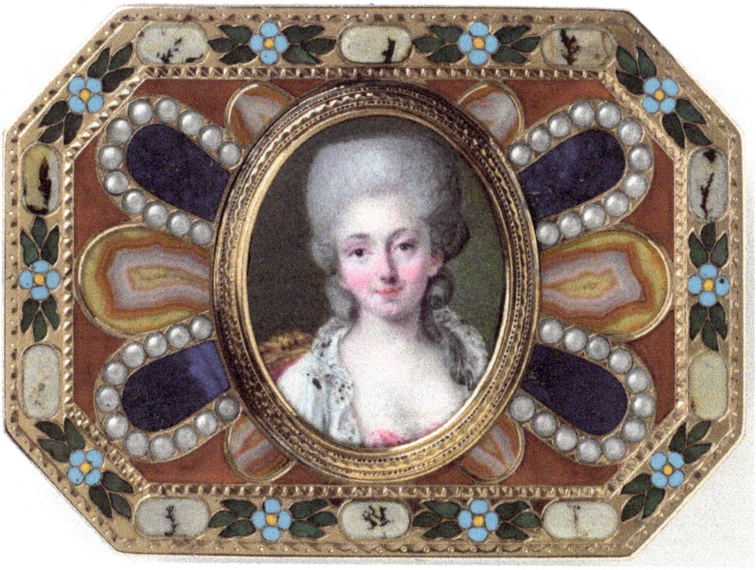

Fig. 3.5. Johann Christian Neuber snuffbox, now on display at the V&A as part of the Gilbert Collection. © The Rosalinde and Arthur Gilbert Collection on loan to the Victoria & Albert Museum, London.

by a file that included Arthur's correspondence with the dealer. The documents in this file provide plentiful information about the famous maker and the snuffbox, created in c. 1775, but they do not provide any information about its provenance, leaving us with a gap of more than 200 years.[30] The trail was cold in the museum archives, but there are different strategies that we can adopt when researching the literature. The first step is always to review the literature about the collection in question; in this case, that would lead us to the catalogue of Arthur's gold boxes. As the catalogue's author drew from the archival documents, it is no surprise that here we only find in the provenance field the name of the dealer who sold it to Arthur Gilbert.[31] However, in the literature section, we discover a reference to a book which enables us to go further.

The book concerns the maker and was published in 1935. In it, we not only find a photograph of a box that looks identical to the one in the Gilbert Collection, but we also learn that it once formed part of the 'Sammlung Guthmann in Berlin'.[32] Now we have surname and a city as the starting point for our research. But this is still not the kind of breakthrough we might hope for. During this time period, the spelling of names was very flexible, and unless we experiment

(a)

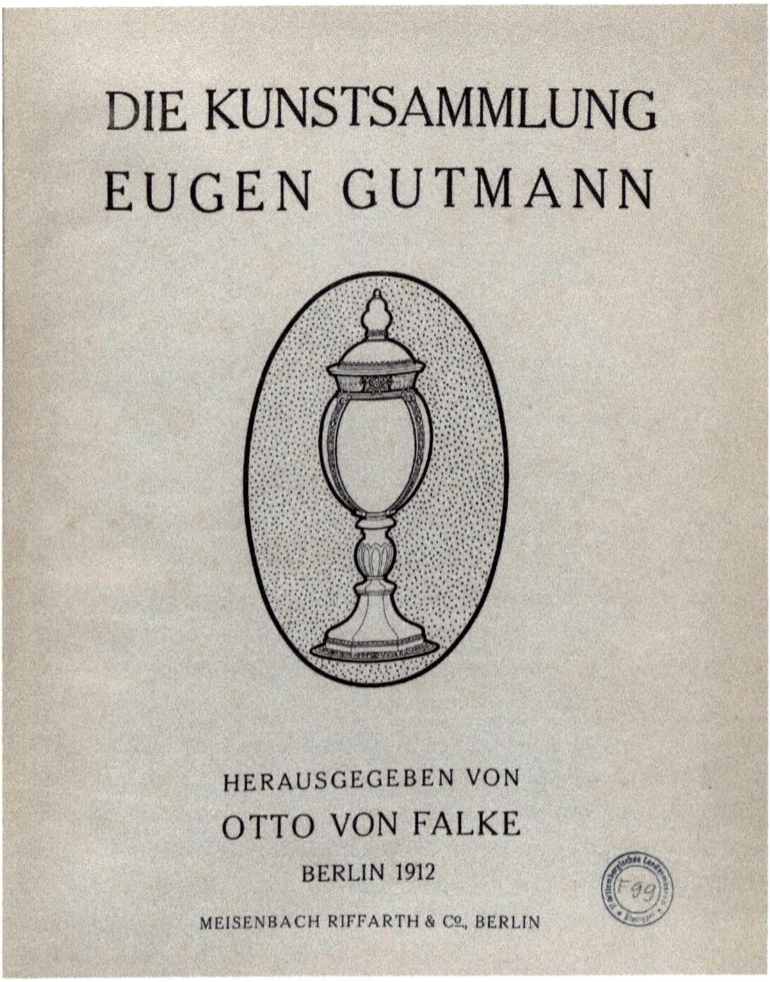

Fig. 3.6. Catalogue of the Eugen Gutmann Collection, 1912, (above) cover and (on p. 97) page featuring a detailed description and photograph of the snuffbox now at the V&A. Public domain.

with different variations of 'Guthmann' and search for 'Gutmann', it is difficult to discover that there is a 1912 catalogue for the collection: *Die Kunstsammlung Eugen Gutmann*, which provides us with a detailed description and photograph of the box (Figure 3.6).[33]

Another way to get to the same catalogue would be, instead of beginning our search with the literature about the Gilbert Collection, to start with publications about the maker. If we search for 'Johann Neuber', we not only immediately find the 1935 book, but also a 2012

(b)

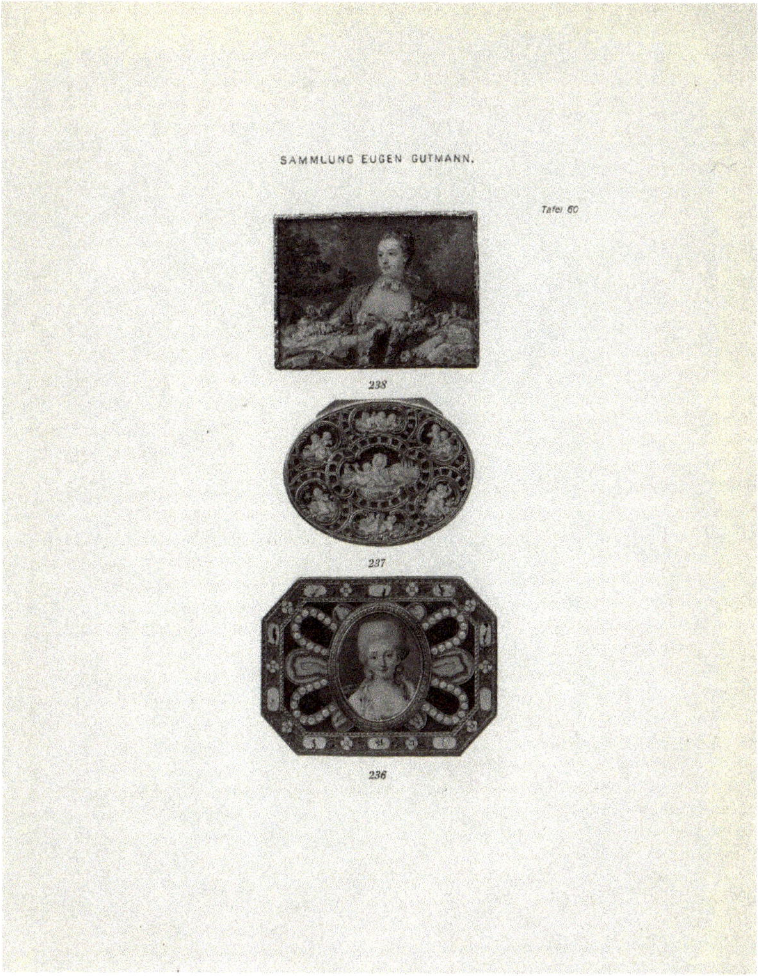

catalogue titled *Gold, Jasper and Carnelian: Johann Christian Neuber at the Saxon court*, which contains an entry for the box, featuring the provenance information 'Collection Eugen Gutmann, c. 1912', with a reference to the 1912 catalogue.[34]

Once we have discovered a name using either of these methods, we can now research the individual behind the collection. While the 1912 catalogue provides a great panorama of Eugen's collection, it does not tell us who he was outside of his collecting life. When we search for

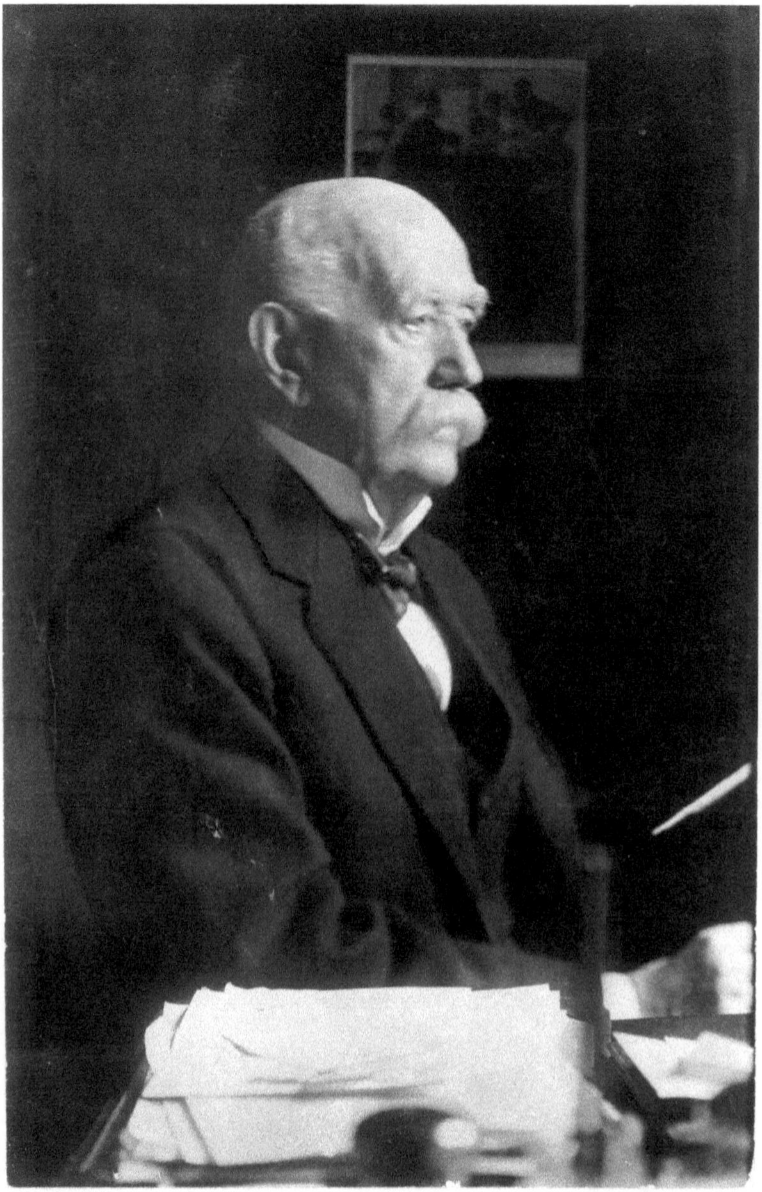

Fig. 3.7. Portrait of Eugen Gutmann, taken in 1922, when he could look back on a highly successful, decades-long career as a banker and art collector in Germany. © Bundesarchiv, Bild 183-L1108-500/CC-BY-SA 3.0 (Source: Wikimedia Commons, https://bit.ly/3FDAU4b).

his name in library catalogues, we are quickly able to piece together the image of a successful banker who, in 1872, founded the Dresdner Bank, which he ran for some 40 years (Figure 3.7). We also learn that he was born into a Jewish family and converted to Protestantism at the end of the nineteenth century, which becomes crucial as we begin to think about what happened to his collection after his death in 1925. In the Nazi worldview, it did not matter if someone had been baptised if 'Jewish blood' continued to run through their veins (see Chapter 1). This immediately raises the prospect that, if the box stayed in his family, it may have been lost due to antisemitic persecution.

In his book, Simon Goodman, Eugen's great-grandson, has movingly reconstructed the persecution of his family at the hands of the Nazis, and their quest to receive at least material compensation after the war. When the Nazis seized power, Eugen's son Friedrich, who, like his father, was an art collector, was living in the Netherlands, where he also kept the collection he and his siblings had inherited. [35] In the summer of 1939, Friedrich transferred some of his most treasured artworks to Paris in the belief that they would be safer there, but after France had been overrun by German troops, the artworks were confiscated by German forces and catalogued by the Einsatzstab Reichsleiter Rosenberg.[36] It did not take long before art dealers in the service of Nazi leaders appeared on Friedrich's doorstep and forcefully indicated their interest in his father's collection.

In 1942, Karl Haberstock and the Munich art dealer Julius Böhler inventoried 218 items from this collection and took them to Munich.[37] Their inventory numbers correspond to those we find in the 1912 catalogue, but the inventory did not mention the snuffbox we are investigating.[38] In contrast to the records of state institutions, there is no obligation for private companies to preserve their archival documents or to make them accessible to researchers. This is often a challenge for provenance researchers to overcome. In this case, however, the Bavarian Economic Archive holds records for the Julius Böhler art dealership. There we discover that in April 1943, the dealership wrote to the director of the Schlossmuseum in Berlin to give him the opportunity to earmark certain items from this collection, but the dealership also lamented the fact that several of the objects mentioned in the 1912 catalogue, including the snuffbox, were no longer available.[39] It seems, therefore, that the snuffbox and certain other objects had already left the collection at some point between 1912 and 1943. A month after this letter was sent, Friedrich Gutmann and his wife Louise were deported to Theresienstadt.

In April 1944, Friedrich was murdered there. Louise was murdered in Auschwitz in May 1944.[40]

Our research has successfully filled in hundreds of years of the object's history, but although we can now make a connection between the snuffbox and Eugen Gutmann, there remains a significant gap in the provenance between 1912, when the catalogue was published, and the 1980s, when the box resurfaced on the art market.[41] As a result, we will probably only be able to resolve this complex case when the auction house opens its archives for this time period to researchers, which will be possible when the relevant privacy and data protection laws allow. Until that time, the full history of this object will remain unclear.

Red flags

After completing our review of the object, its records and the scholarly literature, it is important that we integrate all this information. Armed with this foundation, we should next turn to resources that have been compiled specifically to facilitate research into acts of dispossession. We are in the fortunate position that we can now draw on resources created even before the war was over, and from the immediate post-war period, both of which captured information that would otherwise have been lost.

As the conflict in Europe raged on, Allied intelligence officers set up shop in the halls of the Victoria and Albert Museum in London, where they worked night and day to establish a clear picture of the Nazis' campaign of art dispossession. The collections of the V&A, as of many British museums, had been spirited away to secret locations to ensure that they would not fall into Nazi hands or be destroyed by the Luftwaffe's bombs. Surrounded by empty display cases, the intelligence officers would have been acutely aware of what was at stake. Their research efforts focused primarily on works of art removed from countries occupied by the Nazis. At the same time, the officers tried to produce a comprehensive picture of the Nazi organisations, German art dealers and museum officials who had been involved in this campaign of plunder (Figure 3.8).

It is important to remember that the Allied effort relied on the partial information they received from secret intelligence networks operating in the anti-Nazi underground. While the lists they compiled are a remarkable achievement, the contents were often based on what refugees could recall of the situation in Germany in the early 1930s. After the Allies landed in France in 1944, and pushed on to capture

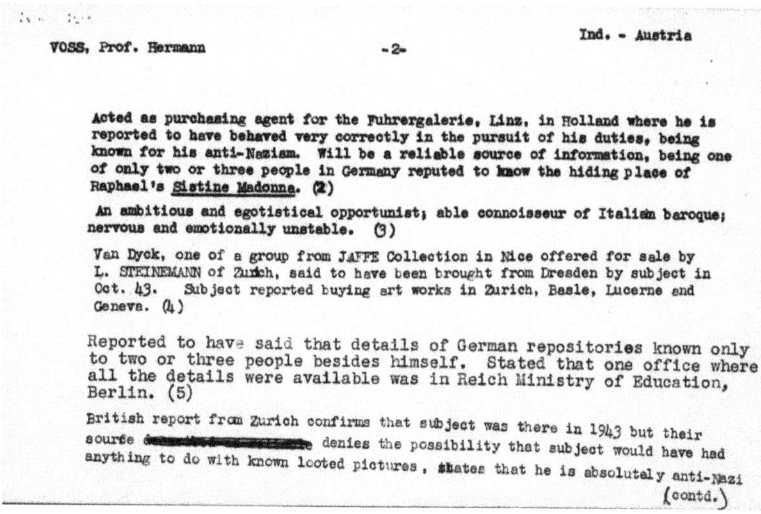

VOSS, Prof. Hermann -2- Ind. - Austria

Acted as purchasing agent for the Fuhrergalerie, Linz, in Holland where he is reported to have behaved very correctly in the pursuit of his duties, being known for his anti-Nazism. Will be a reliable source of information, being one of only two or three people in Germany reputed to know the hiding place of Raphael's Sistine Madonna. (2)

An ambitious and egotistical opportunist; able connoisseur of Italian baroque; nervous and emotionally unstable. (3)

Van Dyck, one of a group from JAFFE Collection in Nice offered for sale by L. STEINEMANN of Zurich, said to have been brought from Dresden by subject in Oct. 43. Subject reported buying art works in Zurich, Basle, Lucerne and Geneva. (4)

Reported to have said that details of German repositories known only to two or three people besides himself. Stated that one office where all the details were available was in Reich Ministry of Education, Berlin. (5)

British report from Zurich confirms that subject was there in 1943 but their source [illegible] denies the possibility that subject would have had anything to do with known looted pictures, states that he is absolutely anti-Nazi (contd.)

Fig. 3.8. Allied intelligence index card consolidating reports on Hermann Voss, the man in charge of making acquisitions for Hitler's museum project in Linz. Public domain (Source: National Archives and Records Administration, Washington, DC).

the Reich, they were able to interrogate many of the individuals who had featured so prominently in their documents. This allowed them to add new names and institutions to their ever-expanding registers (See Chapter 2).

The lists and resources created by these Allied intelligence officers are now frequently used and commonly referred to as 'red flags' for provenance researchers; the name index is available online at www.lootedart.com/MVI3RM469661.[42] However, it is important to keep in mind when using these resources that the intelligence officers sought to craft a black-and-white picture of the individuals and institutions involved in the art and museum world, classifying them as either Nazi or anti-Nazi. After decades of research, which continues to complicate and add nuance to our understanding of the Nazi period, we now know that this binary does not do justice to the complexity of the dispossession. When we use these resources, it is therefore crucial that we do not unintentionally fall into the self-serving narrative generated in post-war Germany, which claimed that only a select number of high-ranking Nazi officials, the Gestapo and the stormtroopers were culpable for the dispossession of the Reich's enemies.

There have also been more recent attempts to follow in the footsteps of the Allied intelligence officers to compile similar 'red flag' lists, which are equally important for today's researchers. For example, the German Lost Art Foundation has created a list of auctions in which it was established that Jewish property was sold, and lists with the names of prominent Jewish art collectors (www.proveana.de). Nevertheless, even a list of thousands of names would scarcely scratch the surface: we must not forget that when the Nazis seized power, there were more than half a million Jews living in Germany, and as the Reich expanded its racist influence across the continent, millions more came under direct German control and were systematically dispossessed. Moreover, it would be foolish to assume that just because a name does not appear on one of these lists, an object's provenance is therefore unproblematic. This would be to assume that absence of evidence is the same as evidence of absence. Regrettably, this can be a shortcoming of contemporary provenance research, which is sometimes performed as a box-ticking exercise and therefore robs us of the opportunity to dig deeper and to uncover the complex history of an object and its past owners.

Unfortunately, the absence of a red flag is potentially meaningless – after all, it is difficult to imagine anything more likely to have been obscured or omitted from the documentary trail than a Nazi-era provenance. The provenance record may contain the names of many people actively involved in the process of dispossession, but for whatever reason did not make it onto the Allied or post-war 'red flag' lists. A clear example are German museum curators whose institutions had become the direct beneficiaries of Nazi looting, but who were now classified as 'anti-Nazi' and found themselves working shoulder to shoulder with the 'Monuments Men'.[43]

Taking stock

By this point, we will have dramatically improved our understanding of the collections and the objects in question. At the end of this initial survey, we may have identified objects that were outside Germany or the occupied territories during the period of 1933–45 and which can therefore be safely excluded (provided that the provenance information has been verified). We may have identified objects that provide clues that immediately catapult us into the Nazi period, such as the name of a Jewish collector living in Germany or the occupied territories, or perhaps a sale that took place there. Or we may be confronted with objects with a gap in their provenance which we must attempt to fill. This may indeed reveal that there is no problem with the object's provenance, or it may lead us to discover that this gap conceals connections to the Nazi past.

Online databases

After the initial survey has been completed, it is time to turn to online databases, which often allow us to move far beyond the limitations of museum records, and indeed any information carried by the objects themselves. More importantly, they allow the modern provenance researcher to potentially sidestep years of fruitless searching in archival holdings, and at the touch of a button may provide a wealth of information that sets us off in a clear direction. It is therefore important at this point that we consult these databases before moving forwards, especially because this may help us to identify objects in the collections whose museum records and physical provenance marks did not contain any information that singled them out for research.

There are essentially four different kinds of object databases: (1) databases of looted art; (2) databases of digitised auction catalogues; (3) databases of records created under the Nazis; (4) databases of records created during the Allied restitution effort. Depending on the size of the collection before us, it may be possible to check the entirety of the collection against these databases.

Lost art databases

Our museum records may provide no meaningful provenance information, but even if they do, it is always essential that we check for any information available in the databases of items confiscated or extorted under the Nazis. The Lost Art Database (www.lostart.de) is the largest of its kind and, like other databases in the field of Nazi-era provenance research, it may enable us to establish connections between the objects under investigation and the Nazi past that would otherwise be impossible to establish. The history of the Lost Art Database is fascinating in its own right, highlighting the shifting attitudes towards the Nazi past. It is run by the state-sponsored German Lost Art Foundation, whose predecessor was established not to enable the identification of items that once belonged to the Nazis' victims, but to achieve the restitution of German museum collections removed during the Soviet occupation of East Germany.[44]

After the Washington Conference, this body's focus shifted from the losses of German institutions to the darker corners of their own collections. As there was no consolidated 'master list' of all the items confiscated or extorted under the Nazis, it was crucial to create a space where such objects could be listed in order to cross-reference them against the catalogues of museum collections. The Lost Art Database was launched in 2001; since then, it has grown to almost 130,000 entries. Although it is administered by a German foundation, the scope of this database is certainly not limited to Germany, but provides information about objects that were lost across the European continent.

Loosely speaking, this database resembles a 'lost and found' noticeboard, in which victims and their families share as much information as possible about artworks with which they hope to be reunited. Entries on the database resemble museum collections databases, in that they provide a description and sometimes a photograph of the object, along with information about previous owners.

Although the Lost Art Database contains a huge amount of information, like any historical resource it carries certain limitations. It cannot provide us with a complete record, and many of the entries remind us that a lot of information concerning the objects has been lost over time. The descriptions can be short and superficial; they may reflect knowledge about the object that has now been superseded by scholarly research; attributions to artists may be inaccurate, as can the piece's dimensions; and sometimes entries may even lack the title (something that often changes across the years) or a description sufficient to our purposes. In spite of these undeniable drawbacks, this and similar databases nevertheless can enable researchers to overcome the limitations of their object records, and are therefore a crucial tool for reconnecting objects to their often deeply affecting histories.[45]

The great value of the Lost Art Database becomes immediately apparent when we consider the fascinating provenance research story of a painting that entered the galleries of Hesse's Museum Wiesbaden in 1987 (Figure 3.9). At first glance, the painting did not appear to have a problematic history because a local art association had acquired it from a private collector who said that she had purchased it long before the Nazis seized power.[46] However, provenance expert Miriam Olivia Merz was determined to be as thorough as possible in her research. Her investigation began with a simple step: she entered the name of the artist – Adolf Hölzel – into the search field of the Lost Art Database. This immediately returned an entry for a painting that fitted the description of the piece she was investigating, but it carried a slightly different title.[47]

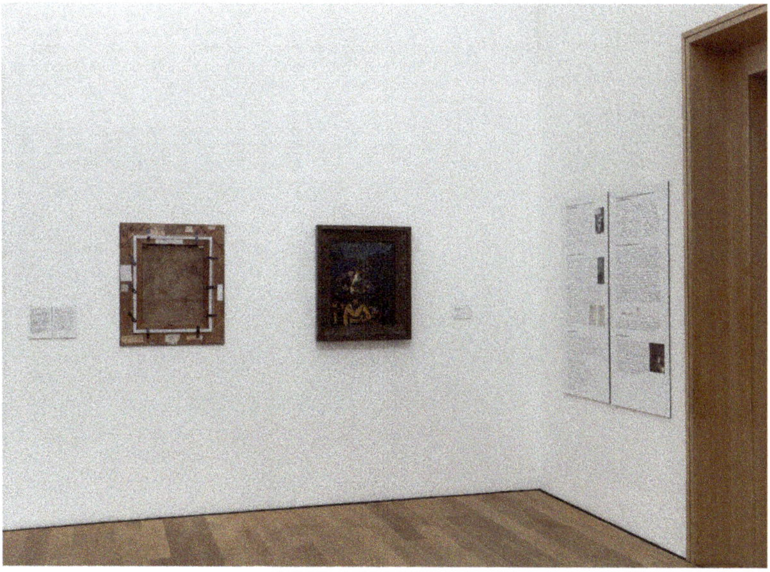

Fig. 3.9. The Hölzel painting hanging in the Museum Wiesbaden, prior to its restitution to the heirs of Ernst Flersheim. © Museum Wiesbaden/ Bernd Fickert.

The database entry had been submitted by the descendants of the daughter of Ernst and Gertrud Flersheim, who were murdered in 1944 (Figure 3.10). After the war, the victims' daughter had filed a compensation claim, which compressed her family's traumatic experiences into the fields of a standardised form.[48] From 1934 onwards, Ernst Flersheim had found himself in the crosshairs of the Nazi authorities. They carried out multiple investigations into his import business in Frankfurt, which traded in valuable commodities, including ivory. These investigations would be the prelude to Ernst's removal from the company.[49] Under mounting pressure and the fear of imminent arrest, Ernst made the difficult decision to flee Germany.[50] In so doing, he was following in the footsteps of his two daughters who, early on, had realised there was no future for them in Hitler's Reich. His wife Gertrud stayed behind, finding it hard to believe that she was in as much danger as her husband – and in order to oversee the sale of their material assets.

In May 1937, Gertrud sold their art collection through the Hugo Helbing auction house, which itself became a victim of 'Aryanisation'.[51] A few months after the sale was completed, the Gestapo wrote to the Currency Office to inform them that they planned to deliver yet

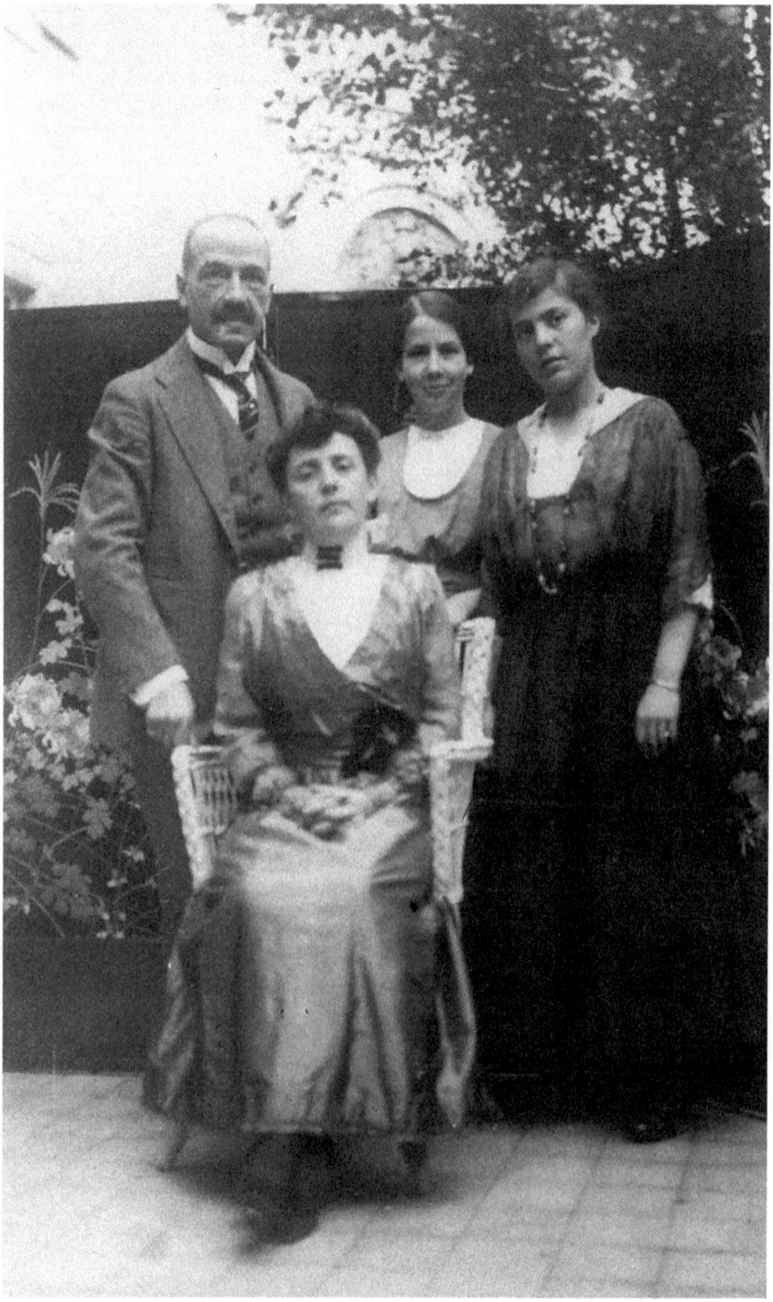

Fig. 3.10. Ernst and Gertrud Flersheim with their daughters Edith and Margarete. Public domain (Source: Wikimedia Commons, https://bit.ly/3tVtIOk).

another blow to the Flersheims, and effectively asked the tax officials for evidence of any legal violations that they could cite in order to fulfil their ideologically driven aims. The language they used betrayed that this was not a normal investigation. They asked 'whether violations of the Currency Laws existed', but they were clearly far more interested in tangible information on whatever assets the Flersheims possessed in order to seize these for the Reich.[52] In June, Ernst had to learn from the pages of the *Reich Tax Gazette* that he had been stripped of his citizenship and that all his assets would now be confiscated. In response, he wrote a measured yet clearly distraught letter, stating that 'I have no idea what I am supposed to have done to justify this measure', adding, 'My wife and I have always been good Germans' – as if this could have changed the minds of Nazi officials tasked with implementing racist policies.[53]

Even in 1938, the Flersheims were still in limbo: they stayed temporarily in Belgium and France, but had not yet decided where to permanently settle outside Germany, wanting to wait until their daughter, who was paralysed from multiple sclerosis, had found a safe haven so that they could join and care for her there. They eventually settled in the Netherlands in 1940, taking up residence in a small apartment in Amsterdam.[54]

The confiscation of Ernst's remaining assets in Germany included the entire contents of his home. In desperate need of financial support, not least to pay for his daughter's medical treatments, Ernst pleaded with the Nazi authorities to at least leave him these household goods so that he could sell them off.[55] But these entreaties fell on predictably deaf ears. The last time we hear the living voices of the Flersheims in the historical record is in a letter they wrote in 1943 to a nephew in Switzerland. In it, Ernst wrote that he and Gertrud 'had been through a lot', only hinting at what must have been a desperate struggle for survival.[56] We know that shortly afterwards they were taken to the Westerbork concentration camp, and in February 1944 they were transferred to Bergen-Belsen, where they were murdered.[57]

All this crucial information, which enables us to reconstruct the human realities behind the painting hanging in the Wiesbaden Museum, was stored only two kilometres away from Miriam Olivia Merz's desk. The Main State Archives in Hesse hold the compensation and restitution claims filed after the war by survivors and the families of the victims, including that filed by Ernst and Gertrud's daughter. The size of these archival holdings provides a clear sense of the vast extent of Nazi persecution: there are more than 90,000 records, all of which are catalogued by name. These names can be searched via an online database, but regrettably not even brief descriptions of the files' contents are available via this portal (arcinsys.hessen.de). Without the Lost Art Database, which enabled Merz to connect the painting to the name of a specific family, it would have been impossible to find any trace of the painting's provenance without manually searching through all 90,000 records, which together span more than half a kilometre of shelf space. By using the Lost Art Database, Merz was able to identify the specific files that provided insight into the fate of the Flersheim family under the Nazis, and the daughter's post-war struggle for compensation and restitution.

As effective as it was this time, it is important to remember that any database is only ever as useful as the information it contains. The Flersheims' name could only be found in the Lost Art Database because their descendants had added it in the hope of finding the lost painting. Had they not done so, Merz would have had to take a different, more laborious approach. She would have had to turn to auction catalogues, which thankfully have been digitised and made available online (see below), in order to seek out the 1937 sale of Ernst and Gertrud's collection.[58]

In search of more substantial evidence, a search of online auction catalogues was also the next step in Merz's investigation. But in this catalogue, the name of the consignor was only given as the enigmatic abbreviation 'FL'.[59] Because in 1937 it had not yet become compulsory for Jewish consignors to be explicitly identified, the forced nature of this sale would not have been immediately obvious. Indeed, it was only because Merz discovered the entry in the Lost Art Database that she was able to establish a connection to the Flersheim family.

Merz now had to determine whether the painting in the Museum Wiesbaden was indeed identical to the one in the 1937 sale. A museum catalogue featuring the painting stated only that the artwork had been in the possession of a private collector from the 1920s onwards, and had remained with that collector until it was placed on loan to the Wiesbaden Museum in the 1980s. Merz faced a very difficult task: neither the Lost Art Database, nor the auction catalogue, nor even the Flersheim compensation records contained a picture of the painting itself. She therefore wisely turned to the object, on the back of which she discovered a label which stated that the painting had been on loan to an exhibition at the Stuttgart State Gallery in 1953. Following this lead, Merz contacted the gallery, whose provenance researchers found a letter buried in their archives, stating that the private collector had in fact not acquired the painting in the 1920s, but rather in the 1930s in Frankfurt, where the Flersheim collection had been dispersed.[60]

Having painstakingly gathered all this evidence, which still remained tantalisingly circumstantial, Merz reached out to Ernst and Gertrud's descendants in search of further information. It turned out that they had another annotated copy of the auction catalogue in their possession, which featured the names of the buyers at the 1937 sale scribbled in the margins. This annotated catalogue confirmed that the same private collector was the buyer at the 1937 sale of the Flersheim collection, which provided the crucial piece of evidence needed to solve the case.[61] Sixty-eight years after Gertrud and Ernst's daughter had filed her restitution claim, the painting had been found and was finally reunited with the family in 2020.[62]

This story does not only reveal how crucial it is to keep an open mind and to question the sometimes deceptive authority of museum records when investigating the provenance of an object. It also shows us how a simple search on the Lost Art Database can set in motion complex research that enables us to reach the truth about objects in our collections, and of the fate of their previous owners under the Nazis.

Because of its size and international scope, the Lost Art Database has undoubtedly become the most important database in this field and is essential to any Nazi-era provenance investigation. But it is not the only one. A thorough provenance investigation should also include searches of Lootedart.com (which contains 25,000 object entries) – and the various online databases set up in formerly Nazi-occupied countries, such as the Belgian (lootedart.belgium.be), Dutch (herkomstgezocht.nl – in the category 'missing'), Polish (lootedart.gov.pl/en) and Russian (lostart.ru) databases which document the seizure of property under the Nazis. Searchable PDFs of the French *Répertoire des biens spoliés* are also accessible online.[63]

Database of 'degenerate art'

When we examine the paintings, sculptures, prints and drawings in our collections, it is important to check if they were affected by the Nazis' campaign against so-called 'degenerate art', so that we can find out whether they owe their presence in the galleries to this vicious ideological campaign (see Chapter 1). From 1937 onwards, the Nazi regime confiscated more than 16,000 works of art from public collections across the country which they considered a corrupting influence on the German 'racial spirit' (see Chapter 1). A selection of the objects seized was shown at the infamous 'Degenerate Art' exhibition, which opened in Munich and subsequently toured the Reich. The objects which had been removed from German galleries were liquidated by the regime: they were sold through the regime's trusted art dealers, exchanged for 'racially acceptable' artworks, while the remaining items suffered the same fate as the books heaped onto bonfires in 1933. Research into the surviving objects, many of which ended up in museum collections around the world, can often be much easier than the investigation of pieces that belonged to individual victims. The purge and mocking exhibition of 'degenerate art' was openly publicised; for museum directors in other countries, who learned that these items were now up for sale, this became an opportunity to rescue many works and to expand their own collections. Acquisition files frequently noted that such pieces had been excommunicated by the Nazis, often from prestigious German museums.

Nevertheless, it is important to realise that, in many cases, this information was lost along the way as these objects passed through various art dealerships, auction houses and private collections before they found their way into museums. This is one of the rare occasions when we can turn to a single document that genuinely attempted to provide a full record of a Nazi campaign (Figure 3.11). Created at the heart of the regime by Joseph Goebbels' Ministry of Propaganda, this 'master list' provides information on the artworks, the galleries from which they were taken and their immediate fate.

While this inventory allows us to determine the origins of the artworks, the document's own provenance remains a mystery. The only known complete copy of this important document came to rest not in a German institution, but at the V&A in London. In 1996, it was donated to the museum by the widow of Harry Fischer, a famous London art dealer. Fischer was Jewish and had come to London in 1938 after escaping Nazi terror in Vienna. It is unknown how he came to possess a copy of this remarkable document, which lay bundled together with dozens of auction catalogues and books on modernist art that arrived at the V&A as part of Elfriede Fischer's donation. The V&A's curators were stunned to discover this document and immediately contacted the German historian Andreas Hüneke, who had long worked on the Nazis' campaign against 'degenerate art'.[64] In 1973, he had worked with a partial copy of the inventory in the State Archives of East Germany, and had always regretted the fact that the second half of this 'master list' had seemingly vanished from history. The V&A's discovery at last allowed him and other researchers to fill in the blanks.

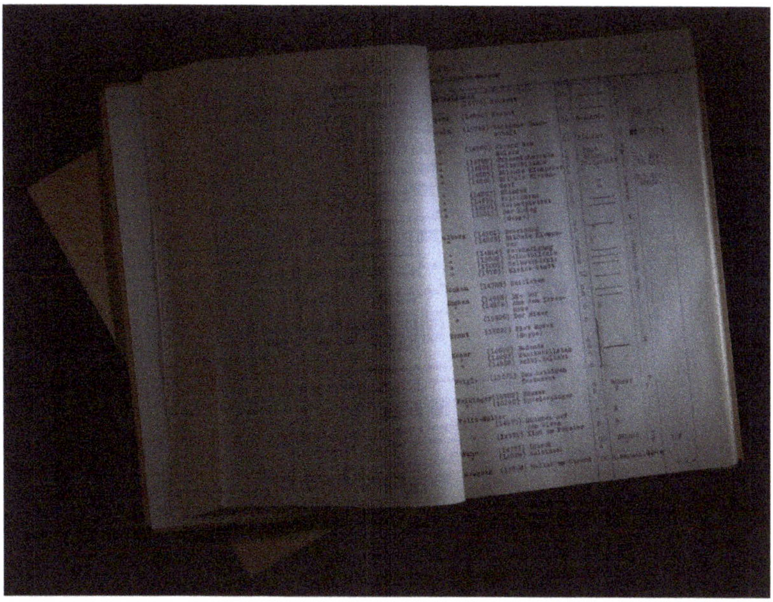

Fig. 3.11. The only known complete copy of the inventory of so-called 'degenerate' art, which came to the V&A through the Jewish refugee art dealer Harry Fischer (now commonly known as 'the Fischer List'). © Victoria & Albert Museum, London.

Hüneke developed a comprehensive spreadsheet of this material which eventually became an online database, now available to us via the website of the Berlin Free University's 'Degenerate Art' Research Centre (www.geschkult.fu-berlin.de/e/db_entart_kunst/datenbank/).

The pages of the printed inventory (available on the V&A website at www.vam.ac.uk/articles/entartete-kunst-the-nazis-inventory-of-degenerate-art) may be the ideal starting point for researchers wanting to reconstruct which works of art were confiscated in a specific city from a particular gallery, and whether these works were subsequently sold, exchanged or destroyed. If our research begins with a specific object, on the other hand, we would be best served by consulting the online database, which provides much more information about the objects than originally recorded by the Nazi officials tasked with compiling the inventory. In many cases, this includes photographs of the works in question, alongside additional information gleaned from the scholarly literature and from German museum archives. Crucially, the scholars behind the database have been able to find information on works that did not appear in the inventory but which – according to museum records – were in fact confiscated, as well as revelations that other works supposedly destroyed in Nazi bonfires in fact survived and subsequently found a new home.

The V&A's digitised inventory and the Free University's online database are the tools that enable museums like Tate to research and communicate the full story behind the objects in their galleries. To take just one example, these resources were able to confirm that a striking Edvard Munch painting, The Sick Child, had been taken from the Dresden State Gallery, and in 1941 was sold at a Swiss auction, where it was acquired first by a Norwegian art dealer before it finally entered the collections of the Tate Gallery in the 1950s, where it remains to this day.[65] The painting now prompts us to consider not only the difficult life of Edvard Munch, but also the danger and upheaval faced by so many precious cultural artefacts under the Nazi regime.

Digitised auction catalogues

Miriam Olivia Merz's successful research strategy reminds us that today's provenance researchers can call upon the information in digitised auction catalogues to illuminate object histories. It is of course important to remember that not all objects that changed hands in the 1930s–40s passed through an auction house that issued a detailed and richly illustrated catalogue; but hundreds of thousands of objects did.

In the past, researchers would have had to manually leaf through thousands of these catalogues, hoping they would recognise 'their' object in the descriptions or the photographs. To address this issue, in 2011 the Getty Research Institute, together with Heidelberg University Library and the Berlin Art Library, embarked on a massive project that aimed to digitise all German sales catalogues for 1930–45. These documentary traces had hitherto been scattered across Germany, Switzerland and Austria. As the first step, researchers travelled to 36 libraries, where they registered more than 3,200 catalogues that were subsequently scanned and made available online.[66] Although some catalogues are missing, it is difficult to overstate the enormous contribution that this project has made, opening up the disparate knowledge contained in auction catalogues to the widest possible audience (and it now includes catalogues going back to 1900).[67] The German sales catalogues can be accessed via the Getty Provenance Index (getty.edu/research/tools/provenance) and the Heidelberg University Library (digi.ub.uni-heidelberg.de/en/sammlungen/artsales.html).

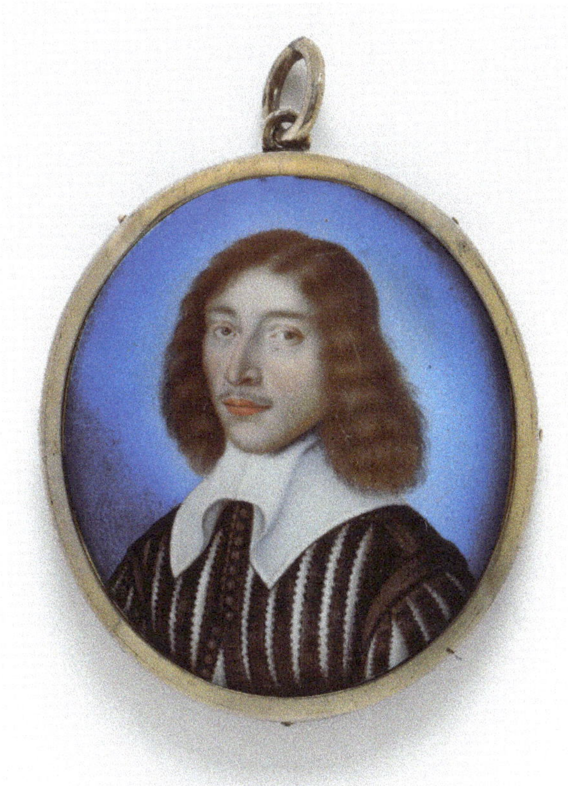

Fig. 3.12. Portrait miniature of a gentleman (Paul Prieur, Paris, 1645–50), formerly in the collection of Adolphe List and now on display at the V&A as part of the Gilbert Collection. © The Rosalinde and Arthur Gilbert Collection on loan to the Victoria & Albert Museum, London.

To find an item in an auction catalogue represents a first step. As provenance researchers, we want to know the identity of the consignor and who purchased the item – information that has often been scribbled in the margins of the catalogues. Unfortunately, the Getty project did not always scan annotated versions of the auction catalogues, particularly in cases where the unmarked copy was of overall superior quality. Thankfully, the researchers have provided an online list of the alternative copies which informs us where these volumes reside and whether they were annotated. This enables us to request scans of the specific pages from the relevant library.[68]

We can appreciate the great value of these digitised auction catalogues if we consider the example of a seventeenth-century portrait

(a)

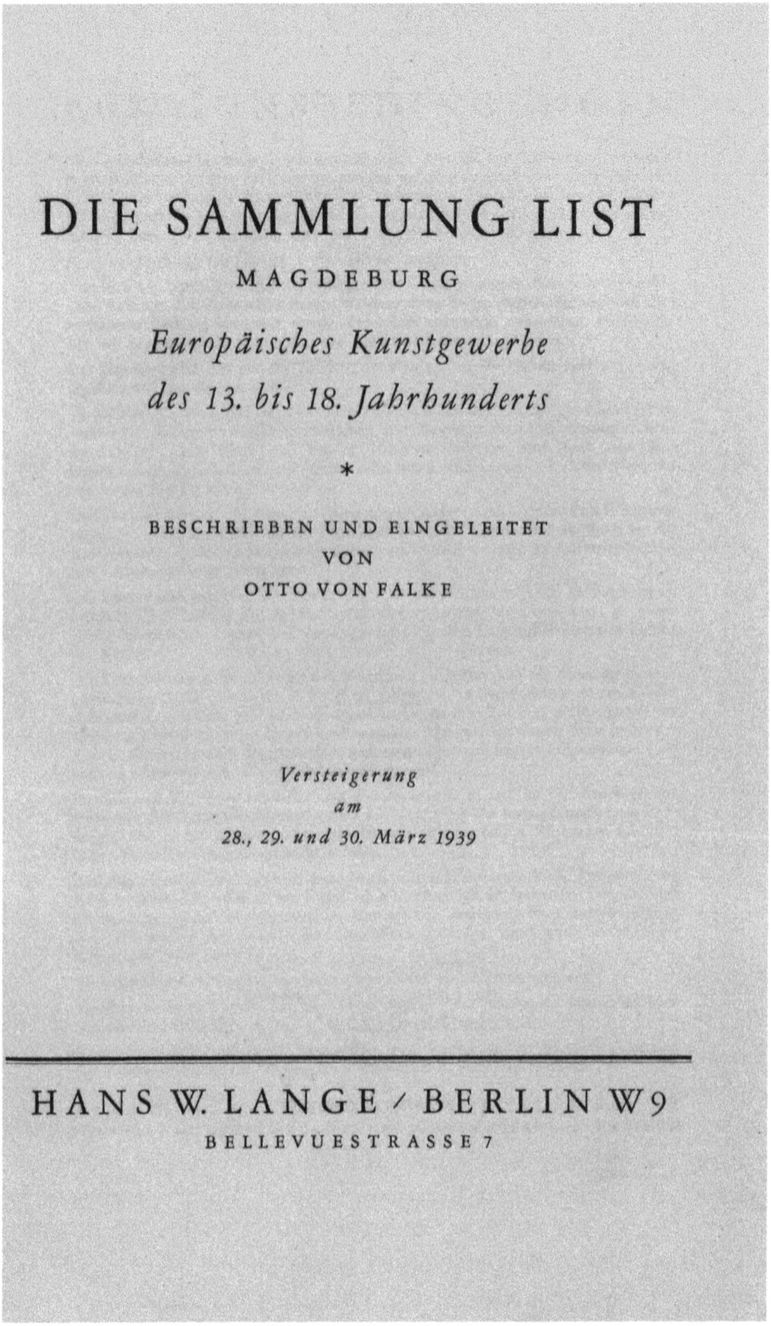

DIE SAMMLUNG LIST

MAGDEBURG

Europäisches Kunstgewerbe des 13. bis 18. Jahrhunderts

*

BESCHRIEBEN UND EINGELEITET
VON
OTTO VON FALKE

Versteigerung am 28., 29. und 30. März 1939

HANS W. LANGE / BERLIN W9

BELLEVUESTRASSE 7

Fig. 3.13. 1939 auction catalogue of the Adolph List collection, (a) cover and (b) page featuring a photograph of the portrait miniature now at the V&A (centre right).

(b)

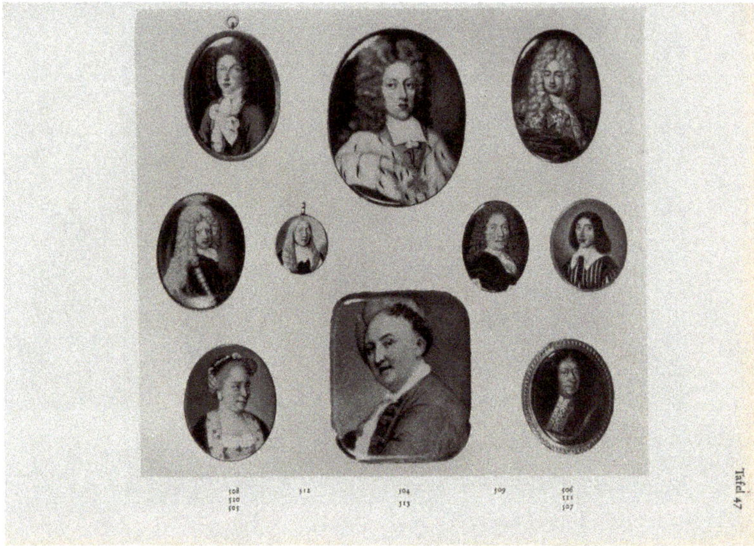

miniature from the Gilbert Collection at the V&A, depicting an unknown 'gentleman' (Figure 3.12). When it was acquired, it was attributed to Jean Petitot.[69] A simple search for the name of the maker revealed that it was part of a 1939 auction in Nazi Germany (Figure 3.13).[70] The catalogue contained a detailed description which, on its own, would not have been sufficient to confirm this was the same piece, but the accompanying photograph confirmed this was indeed the same object.

This approach allowed us to short-circuit a laborious research process that would otherwise have led deep into the V&A's National Art Library, which holds the largest collection of auction catalogues in the world, amounting to more than 140,000 volumes. To reach the same information provided by the database would have required the examination of every single catalogue – a task that could feasibly have taken years. The consignor's name – Adolph List – was mentioned in the catalogue, which made it possible to approach the archive in the city he called home. An enquiry to the State Archives in Magdeburg unearthed a story that once again reminds us that, in the Nazi worldview, race determined everything.

Adolph List came from a Jewish family that, like so many others, had converted to Protestantism in the nineteenth century. He studied chemistry in Leipzig and went on to co-found a saccharin factory in Magdeburg, the Fahlberg-List AG (Figure 3.14). In 1937, the board of directors received an anonymous postcard that denounced Adolph as a

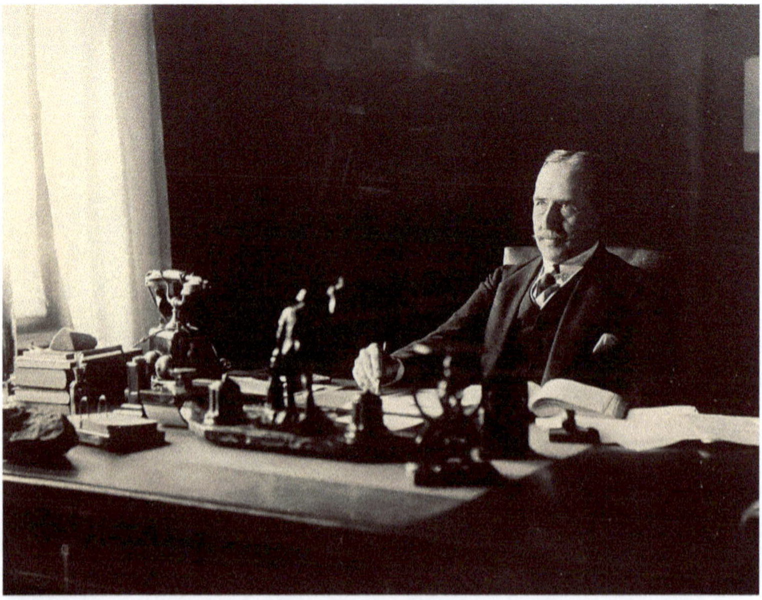

Fig. 3.14. Adolph Moritz List at his workplace. Public domain (Source: Wikimedia Commons, https://bit.ly/3Mnukmn).

'Volljude' (in essence, a 'full-blooded Jew').[71] It was signed by a concerned 'shareholder' who explained that 'this could be very damaging to a company, which has to count on state orders' and demanded that Adolph was removed from his post.[72] The board of directors wrote to the supervisory board and said that 'we cannot risk our company being regarded as non-Aryan!' and, therefore, the board thought that Adolph should be swiftly dismissed.[73] With everyone now arrayed against him, this is precisely what happened. A few days later, the company informed the local Nazi party that List had 'left' the company.[74] Exiled from the company he had founded, Adolph died the following year – supposedly of 'natural causes', if we can allow the stress and humiliation of his ousting to be considered 'natural'.[75]

In the meantime, the company had been informed that not only Adolph was Jewish, but so was his widow, Helene. This provided the company with an excuse to stop paying her pension; they therefore wrote to Helene to announce their intentions.[76] In contrast to Adolph, Helene was able to refute the allegations against her. She had obtained a certificate from the Reich Office for Genealogical Research (Reichsstelle für Sippenforschung) which confirmed that she was of 'German or related blood according to the first ordinance of the Reich Citizenship

Law of 14 November 1935'.[77] With this document in hand, her lawyer successfully argued that the antisemitic laws cited by the company to deny her pension could not apply.[78] Having secured her status in the Nazi Reich, Helene consigned her late husband's collection to the 'Aryanised' incarnation of the Paul Graupe auction house, which now carried the name H. W. Lange. Because she was an 'Aryan' in the eyes of the regime, Helene would have had full control over the auction and its proceeds; had her husband sold the same items, the sale would only have enriched the state.[79]

The auction catalogues of countries outside Germany can be as important and it is a reassuring sign that there have been increasing efforts to digitise these as well, such as the French Institut National d'Histoire de l'Art's online collection of scanned auction catalogues (bibliotheque-numerique.inha.fr/collection-toutes) and the Wildenstein Plattner Institute's database of auction catalogues (digitalprojects.wpi.art/auctions).

Databases of Nazi records

Although motivated by radically different interests to ours, the Nazi regime itself has left us vital documentary records, some of which have also now been digitised. It is understandable that the greatest progress in this area has been made with respect to the records created by those Nazi operations that were specifically set up to confiscate and absorb artworks belonging to the regime's victims.

When, in March 1938, German troops swept into Austria, a curator from the Kunsthistorisches Museum masterminded an operation that inventoried and catalogued the artworks which had been confiscated from Jewish collectors (see Chapter 1). The inventories and index cards created in this 'Central Depot for Seized Collections' were previously only accessible in the archive of the Kunsthistorisches Museum and the archive of the Austrian Federal Monuments Authority in Vienna, but they are now fully searchable online at www.zdk-online.org. The depot in Vienna was visited by Hans Posse, who had been given orders by Hitler to build up the collection for the Führermuseum in Linz. A database hosted by the German Historical Museum in Berlin makes it possible to research the works he selected from the loot at the Central Depot, as well as those the Sonderauftrag Linz acquired through other channels (www.dhm.de/datenbank/linzdb). This includes, for example, artworks from elsewhere in Europe that Posse and his successor acquired either themselves, or through their network of art dealers, including Karl Haberstock, on an open art market awash with extorted works (see Chapter 1).

Following the German occupation of France in 1940, Alfred Rosenberg became a key player in the myriad institutions dedicated to confiscating property belonging to Jewish people and others whom the regime considered 'enemies'. Just as the art collections of Jewish collectors from Vienna were catalogued in the Neue Burg, the same process was applied in Paris, where the loot was catalogued in the Jeu de Paume. The inventories and the tens of thousands of index cards they created in this Nazi 'collecting point' have been digitised and are now accessible online at www.errproject.org. The loot piling up in Paris quickly aroused the interest of the powerful Nazi leader Herman Göring who, like Adolf Hitler, had a passion for collecting. At the Jeu de Paume, he 'selected' more than 700 paintings for his private collection, the records of which are also accessible on the German Historical Museum website (www.dhm.de/datenbank/goering/dhm_goering.php).

As with the artworks that the regime removed from German public collections during the 'degenerate art' campaign, there was a constant flow of objects in and out of these operations in the effort to secure the best pieces for the Reich. If this could be achieved by exchanging or selling confiscated works, so much the better, and this was all diligently recorded in the relevant records. These works are of particular interest for provenance researchers because they could ultimately have ended up in any museum collection. They were not kept and stored by the regime's agents in one of many castles or monasteries, ultimately to be discovered by Allied troops at war's end. After they had been seized from their owners or removed from 'abandoned' apartments, these works only passed briefly through the hands of the regime's agents, before they disappeared into the international art market. As a result, a painting that was confiscated from a Jewish apartment in Paris could, over time, pass through many hands before it might come to rest in, for example, a British museum collection.

These databases allow us to break through the silence and reconnect the objects to their past. Their advantage becomes immediately obvious when we consider the example of Sven Haase's provenance research into a Picasso painting depicting 'a nude woman cleaning her feet', now in the collection of the Prussian Heritage Foundation. When he examined the reverse of the painting, Haase deciphered the handwritten text 'Rosenberg-Bernstein Bordeaux 12'.[80] The name, in combination with a city, provided Haase with a valuable starting point in his mission to discover the full provenance of the artwork. He went on to make a connection to the prolific Parisian art dealer Paul Rosenberg, who assembled works by artists including Cézanne, Monet, Renoir and Matisse, and who, from 1918, represented Picasso.[81]

Faced with the prospect of having his life's work destroyed by the Germans, in early 1940 Rosenberg retreated to Bordeaux and stored his art collection in various depots across the country, hoping that this would save them from destruction and seizure.[82] When Nazi troops marched into France, Rosenberg managed to flee to New York, leaving his artworks behind. Although he escaped, the possessions he was forced to abandon were quickly seized by Gestapo and Criminal Police officers in the service of the Wehrmacht's Secret Field Police. They invaded his Parisian gallery and apartment, seizing not only the 1,000 volumes in his library, but also every work of art they could find.[83]

Before he fled, Rosenberg had instructed a shipping company to take the Picasso painting and 74 other works of art to Lisbon. But instead the company passed on his list to the occupying forces, who promptly confiscated the haul at Floriac. From there, the Picasso was whisked back to Paris, where the ERR catalogued and photographed it, giving it the inventory code 'Rosenberg-Bernstein-Bordeaux 12' (Figure 3.15).[84] To find the relevant index card and photograph, we can now simply search for 'Picasso' on the ERR project database.[85]

Only three years prior, in 1937, more than 20 Picasso works in German collections had fallen victim to the 'degenerate art' campaign, and so it is no surprise that the art historians in the service of the ERR had only to give the painting a brief glance to decide that it should be sold off or exchanged for a work more suitable to the Nazis' aesthetic sensibilities.

Working shoulder to shoulder with the ERR was the curator Rose Valland, who, since 1939, had worked at the Jeu de Paume (Figure 3.16). What her German colleagues did not know was that she kept a secret record of the works of art and their owners, which she passed on to the French Resistance. Through her inside knowledge, Valland became a crucial figure in the post-war restitution effort, which ultimately restored the Picasso painting to Paul Rosenberg.[86] It subsequently entered the collection of Heinz Berggruen, who, like Rosenberg, was a Jew forced to flee Nazi persecution. Interestingly, Berggruen never mentioned the provenance of the painting.[87] As a result, it is only thanks to Sven Haase's dogged research that this work by Picasso, whose masterpiece Guernica so brilliantly captured a community's torment in the face of war, can now also bring us face to

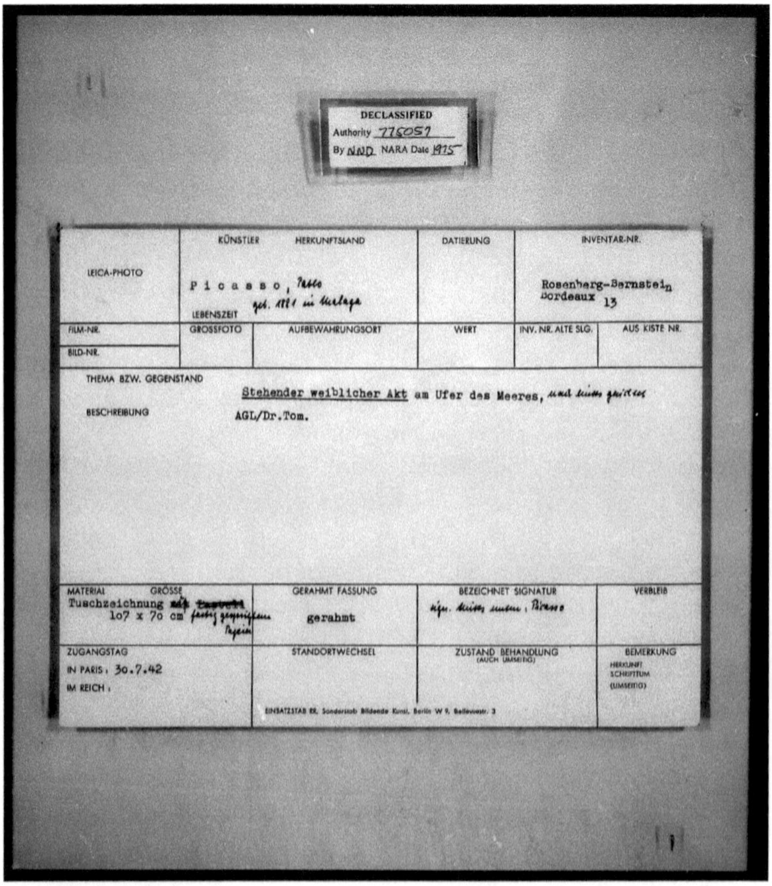

Fig. 3.15. Index card created by the Nazi looting operation Einsatzstab Reichsleiter Rosenberg for the Picasso painting confiscated from Paul Rosenberg. Public domain (Source: National Archives and Records Administration, Washington, DC).

face with both the material and personal suffering unleashed during the Nazi occupation, and indeed with the consequences of the post-war restitution effort.

Allied records

In the immediate post-war period, the victorious Allies attempted to reverse the Nazi campaign of dispossession. The curators and art historians seconded to serve this mission approached their work as

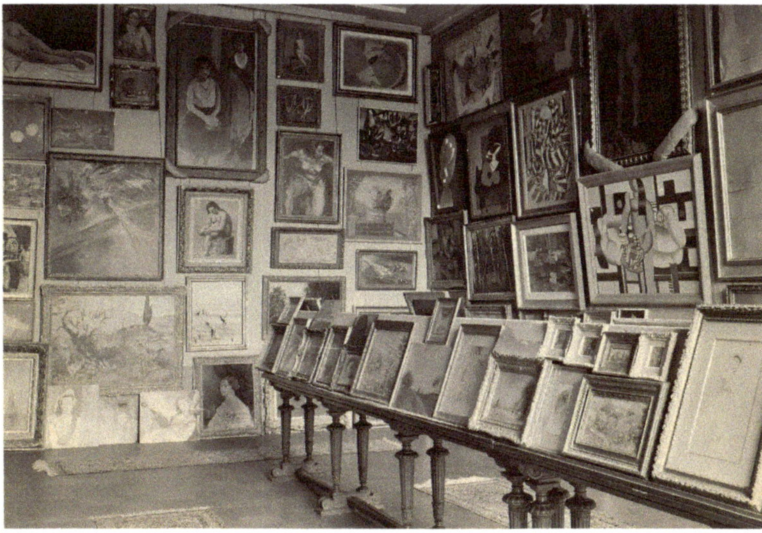

Fig. 3.16. The confiscated Picasso painting hanging on the wall at the Jeu de Paume, which served as the ERR's processing centre for looted art. Public domain (Source: Wikimedia Commons, https://bit.ly/45UGQQU).

if they were cataloguing a museum collection: they created index cards containing information about the objects and their known provenance, with the aim of restoring them to their rightful owners (see Chapter 2). The index cards compiled by the Munich Central Collecting Point are searchable at: www.dhm.de/datenbank/ccp/.[88] For provenance researchers, this is an incredibly rich resource which allows us to quickly and easily ascertain whether an object had passed through the Nazi machinery of confiscations, and whether it was subsequently recovered and restituted. If this digital database were not accessible to us, the same work could only be achieved by a trip to the German national archives, where one would have to search through every single record.

As efficient as they are, we must always bear in mind that archives in Germany and in the formerly Nazi-occupied countries, as well as in the Allied states, contain a wealth of information that has never been digitised. Indeed, none of the cases we have explored in this book could have been resolved using digitised resources alone. Moreover, even very detailed descriptions of these archival holdings do not allow us to determine whether a given object will be mentioned in the files. The finding aids may simply inform us that some 10,000 items looted by the Nazis are mentioned on a given roll of microfilm. Thankfully, large segments of relevant holdings at the National Archives in Washington, DC, are already available in an online database called Fold3.com. This contains a wealth of historical documentation that extends well beyond object records.

To see how important this resource can be, we need only turn to an example from the Kunsthalle Kiel. Their provenance researcher, Kai Hohenfeld, was investigating an oil painting by Vasily Dmitrievich Polenov which the museum had acquired in 1986 from the estate of Georg Schäfer, a Bavarian industrialist and collector of Russian and Polish paintings, who, in turn, had acquired it from the art dealership Galerie Hagman & Gräf in Munich almost 30 years previously (Figure 3.17).[89] When the painting came to the museum, its lack of provenance prior to 1959 was not seen as a cause for concern and it was catalogued with the German title 'Waldweiher' (forest pond).[90] Since this title was not original to the painting, a search for 'Waldweiher' would therefore not have produced any results, but when Hohenfeld entered the name of the painter into Fold3's search field, he was immediately presented with a digital copy of a document from the records of the Munich Central Collecting Point: a list of items from the Taganrog Local History Museum, 'which belong to the Soviet Union' (Figure 3.18).

The first item on the list was a Polenov painting with a slightly different but closely related title: 'Teich mit Weiden' (pond with willows).[91] Crucially, the dimensions of the painting on this list were identical with the Waldweiher in the Kunsthalle's collections.[92] Hohenfeld then also consulted the Lostart.ru database, which documents Russian wartime losses, and found an entry for the painting which the Soviet restitution officers had been unable to recover in 1949. Crucially, the Lostart.ru entry contained a historical photograph, taken in the 1910s in the villa of the businessman and collector Zakhar Antonovich Khandrin, whose collection was 'nationalised' in 1920.[93] Eight years later the Soviet authorities gave the painting to the Taganrog Museum. Although the photograph was of poor quality, it is possible to recognise that the painting hanging on the wall of Khandrin's villa looked identical to the one in the Kunsthalle. It was therefore necessary to rule out the possibility that Polenov had produced two or more versions of the same painting, a suspicion that was eliminated through a literature review which confirmed that no additional similar paintings by the artist are known.[94]

With the painting's connection to the Taganrog Museum confirmed, Hohenfeld turned to the historical literature and the

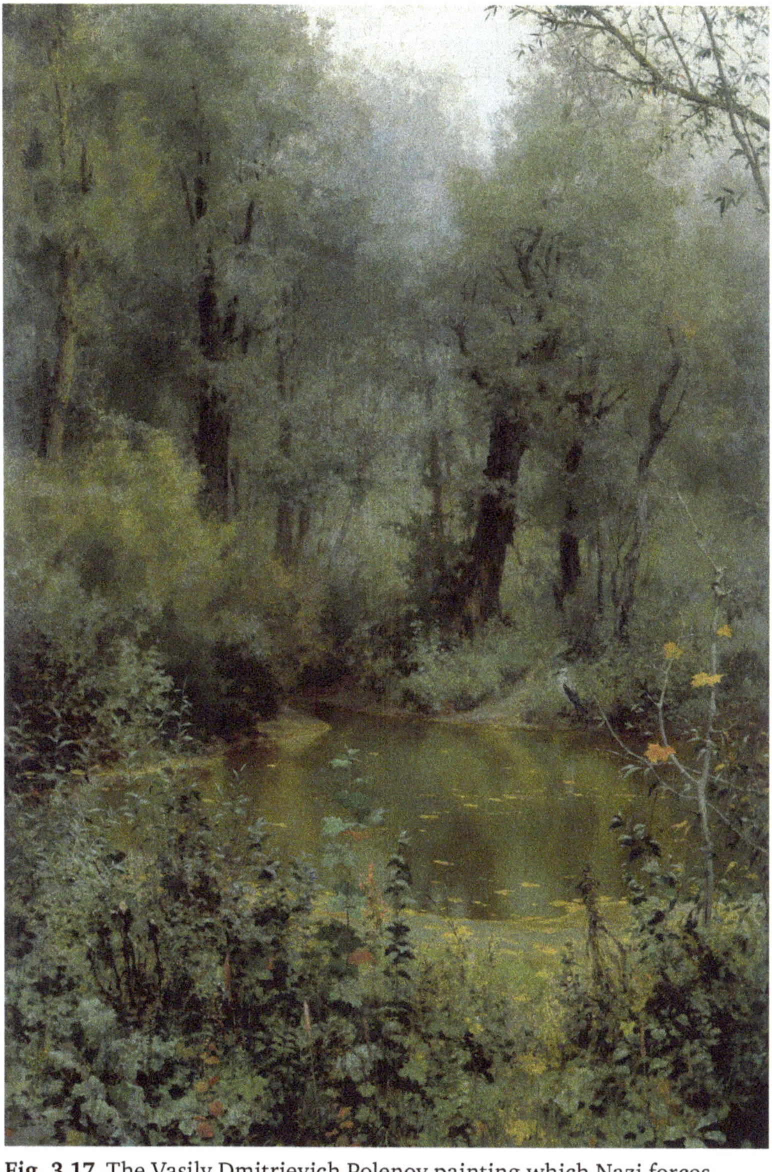

Fig. 3.17. The Vasily Dmitrievich Polenov painting which Nazi forces looted from Taganrog. © Kunsthalle zu Kiel.

archival record to gain an understanding of the German occupation of the city. In October 1941, the Wehrmacht captured Taganrog, a strategic port city in the Rostov region. Sonderkommando 10a followed in the Wehrmacht's footsteps; its members rounded up and executed

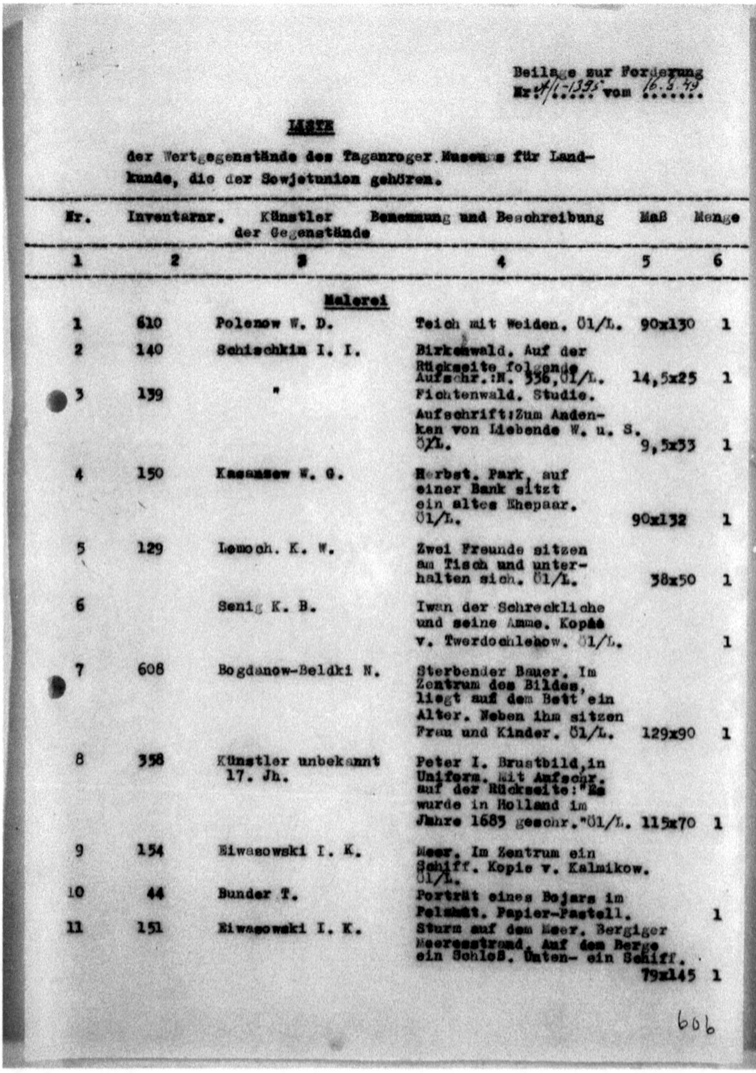

Beilage zur Forderung
Nr. 4/1-1395 vom 16.3.49

LISTE

der Wertgegenstände des Taganroger Museums für Landkunde, die der Sowjetunion gehören.

Nr.	Inventarnr.	Künstler der Gegenstände	Benennung und Beschreibung	Maß	Menge
1	2	3	4	5	6
		Malerei			
1	610	Polenow W. D.	Teich mit Weiden. Öl/L.	90x130	1
2	140	Schischkin I. I.	Birkenwald. Auf der Rückseite folgende Aufschr.: N. 336, Öl/L.	14,5x25	1
3	139	"	Fichtenwald. Studie. Aufschrift: Zum Andenken von Liebende W. u. S. Öl/L.	9,5x33	1
4	150	Kasanzew W. G.	Herbst. Park, auf einer Bank sitzt ein altes Ehepaar. Öl/L.	90x132	1
5	129	Lemoch. K. W.	Zwei Freunde sitzen am Tisch und unterhalten sich. Öl/L.	38x50	1
6		Senig K. B.	Iwan der Schreckliche und seine Amme. Kopie v. Twerdochlebow. Öl/L.		1
7	608	Bogdanow-Beldki N.	Sterbender Bauer. Im Zentrum des Bildes, liegt auf dem Bett ein Alter. Neben ihm sitzen Frau und Kinder. Öl/L.	129x90	1
8	358	Künstler unbekannt 17. Jh.	Peter I. Brustbild, in Uniform. Mit Aufschr. auf der Rückseite: "Es wurde in Holland im Jahre 1683 geschr." Öl/L.	115x70	1
9	154	Eiwasowski I. K.	Meer. Im Zentrum ein Schiff. Kopie v. Kalmikow. Öl/L.		
10	44	Bunder T.	Porträt eines Bojars im Pelzhut. Papier-Pastell.		1
11	151	Eiwasowski I. K.	Sturm auf dem Meer. Bergiger Meeresstrand. Auf dem Berge ein Schloß. Unten- ein Schiff.	79x145	1

606

Fig. 3.18. Soviet list (dated 1949) of items looted from the Taganrog Museum, featuring as the first entry the Polenov painting that eventually re-emerged in the Kunsthalle Kiel. Public domain (Source: National Archives and Records Administration, Washington, DC).

2,500 Jewish men, women and children. As the Wehrmacht and the Einsatzgruppe marched on, a Security Division established its headquarters at the Taganrog Museum. When, in 1942, a member of the ERR paid a visit to the museum, he reported back to his superiors: 'One finds good landscape paintings here, such as, for example, by

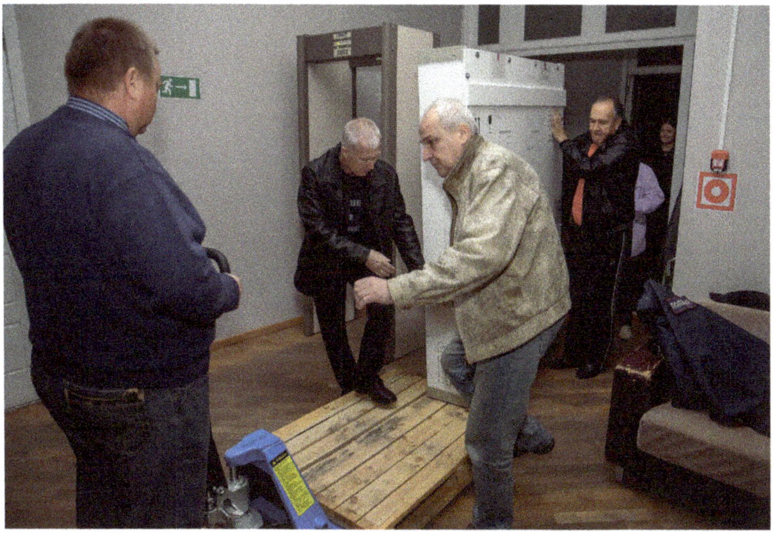

Fig. 3.19. The Polenov painting returns to Taganrog in 2018, more than 75 years after it was looted from the city. © Taganrog Local Government. Photo: Sergey Plishenko.

Polenov.'[95] Despite the fact that the painter was singled out as particularly important, his painting remained in the museum, in contrast to other works which were removed by a German officer and members of the Security Police. In February 1943, a Panzer Propaganda Company shipped 125 paintings, icons and works of decorative art to the Reich for so-called 'security reasons'.[96] In the inventory, the responsible officer had underlined in red those items that were particularly valuable. He did not share the ERR's assessment of the Polenov painting and so it did not enter the ERR depot in Buxheim.

The trail seemed to have gone cold, and Hohenfeld was only able to resolve what happened to the painting when he made contact with his colleagues at the Taganrog Museum. The Taganrog team shared a document which their curators had created after the city's liberation. It detailed that, when the Red Army appeared on the city's outskirts, a 'Sonderführer Lebert', who was said to have belonged to a 'Propaganda Unit', came to the museum on 27 August 1943 and left with the Polenov painting.[97] The document provides a balance sheet of the German occupation of the museum: it recorded a further 4,624 items as missing.[98] Allied restitution officers recovered 73 of these items from the ERR depot in Buxheim, and brought them to the Munich Central Collecting point, where they were catalogued and labelled with 'Russia?' in the records.[99] The path taken by the Polenov painting before it resurfaced in Munich remains a mystery. The records of the art dealership which offered it for sale in the 1950s are inaccessible to researchers.[100] As a result of this remarkable research by Kai Hohenfeld, which started with a simple database search, the Kunsthalle was ultimately able to undo the theft of the German occupiers by restituting the painting to their colleagues in Taganrog (Figure 3.19).[101]

Research strategies

After the initial survey is complete, it is time to devise a clear research strategy to fill in the remaining blanks in the object biographies. At this stage, it is vital that we clearly establish what we know and what we have yet to determine about an object's provenance. There are several possible outcomes here.

In some cases, we will have identified a name, which we can follow up on. In such cases, the research can play out smoothly and face few obstacles, as it was easy to answer the crucial question of who owned the item during this the Nazi period.

A more common scenario is, for example, that we find ourselves with the name of a collector who owned an object in the 1920s, which then entered our museum collections in the 1980s via an art dealer. The important question to ask next is: did the object remain in the collector's hands across the intervening decades, and specifically during the Nazi period? Or did it leave that collection and circulate on the art market before it came to rest in a collection whose name we have yet to discover?

We are now faced with two principal research options. We can attempt to follow the provenance trail backwards in time until we reach the Nazi period. In this case, we would turn to the dealer who sold the object to the museum and ask them if they can tell us anything about its previous owners. If they can provide a name, we simply repeat this process until we are able to connect all the links in the chain of ownership back to the pre-Nazi period. It may turn out that this is simply impossible, for example if the art dealership is unable or unwilling to provide us with further information, or if it has since gone out of business, taking the company records with it. Indeed, it is important to note that, in contrast to government institutions, private companies are generally under no obligation to preserve their archives. Thankfully, the archives of several important and influential art dealers escaped oblivion and are accessible in national, local or special-interest archives that gave them a home (see below).

The unfortunate reality is that, decades after the fact, it is often impossible to simply go back in time. When this is the case, we turn to our second principal strategy, which is to begin with the last pre-Nazi owner whom we can identify. We would then attempt to recreate the chain of ownership, but this time working forwards. This can be more challenging, because the personal records of private individuals are even less likely to be archived than company documents, unless they were highly prominent figures whose papers sparked the interest of local archives, university art history departments or museums and libraries. Nevertheless, it is always worth trying, especially now that many archival holdings are increasingly available online. In some particularly difficult cases, we have to start with the artist or maker who created the object and attempt to discover to whom they sold or gifted it. This can be possible for modern artworks, but is virtually impossible for works created centuries ago. The general rule is that the more highly regarded and valued an object was in the 1930s–40s, the more traces of these works we can expect to find in the archives. For example, an old masterpiece is more likely to have left a paper trail than the work of artists whom we have only come to appreciate in later times.

We can see how this research can play out in practice if we consider the example of the Gilbert Collection at the V&A. As a reminder, Arthur Gilbert was the son of Jewish immigrants who came to London from Eastern Europe. From the 1960s onwards, he began to collect works of decorative art, ultimately creating one of the most important collections of its kind in the world. Although he generously supported charities that looked after Holocaust survivors and commemorated those that rescued them, Arthur never asked in-depth questions about the Nazi-era provenance of the items he added to his collection.[102] His career as a collector came to an end just at the time when the Washington Principles transformed collecting practices (see Chapter 2). In 2008, his collection came to the V&A, where it was the subject of a provenance research project, funded by the Gilbert Trust for the Arts.

The following three case studies illustrate three important provenance research strategies. These case studies will mention archival resources which are explained in more detail later in this chapter. Readers can turn directly to that section to explore further information about the archives, but the case studies illuminate how the research process unfolds and how this determines which archives we would consult.

Starting from a name

This approach can be straightforward if our initial survey of the collection, the review of the museum records or the examination of the objects and literature leads us to a name, which we can use as the direct starting point for deeper archival research. In 1979, Arthur Gilbert acquired a Louis XVI snuffbox made by Joseph-Etienne Blerzy, one of the most prolific and talented makers in eighteenth-century Paris (Figure 3.20).[103] When this box arrived at the V&A, it was accompanied by numerous documents, ranging from correspondence with the London-based art dealer who sold it to Arthur, to copies of scholarly articles about the maker. Crucially, the file also contained a handwritten research note, stating that the box had formerly been in the collection of 'G-R', an acronym that did not appear in the box's provenance when it was sold.

If Charles Truman, the world's expert on snuffboxes (who in the 1980s catalogued the Gilbert Collection) had not determined that 'G-R' stood for 'Maximilian von Goldschmidt-Rothschild', then it would have been much more difficult, if not impossible, to trace the history of the box through the Nazi period.[104] Truman's catalogue also revealed that, before Arthur acquired it, the box had passed through two auctions: just one year prior, in 1978, it was part of the sale of the Henry Ford II Collection at Sotheby's. Prior to that, it was part of the sale of the René Fribourg Collection in 1963, also at Sotheby's.[105] Intriguingly, neither auction catalogue mentioned the Goldschmidt-Rothschild provenance.[106] If we had been unaware of this name, our research would have had to start from the object. This can be extremely challenging, especially for items that lack identifying marks that may clearly and uniquely tie them to the written historical record.

However, this particular box carries the monogram 'LM', which was added many years after its creation, presumably in the nineteenth century. Yet despite this visible 'clue', it is no guarantee that such a feature would be mentioned in the written record – and as we will learn later, not even Maximilian von Goldschmidt-Rothschild recorded this information in his records.[107] We do not know how Truman came to associate Maximilian's name with the box, as he did not provide any reference for the information. Nevertheless, this clue provided an invaluable starting point for further investigation. As Maximilian was not only a major banking and art figure, but also belonged to a renowned family, we are able to quickly establish through an encyclopaedia that Maximilian lived and died in Nazi Germany. We also learn that he lived

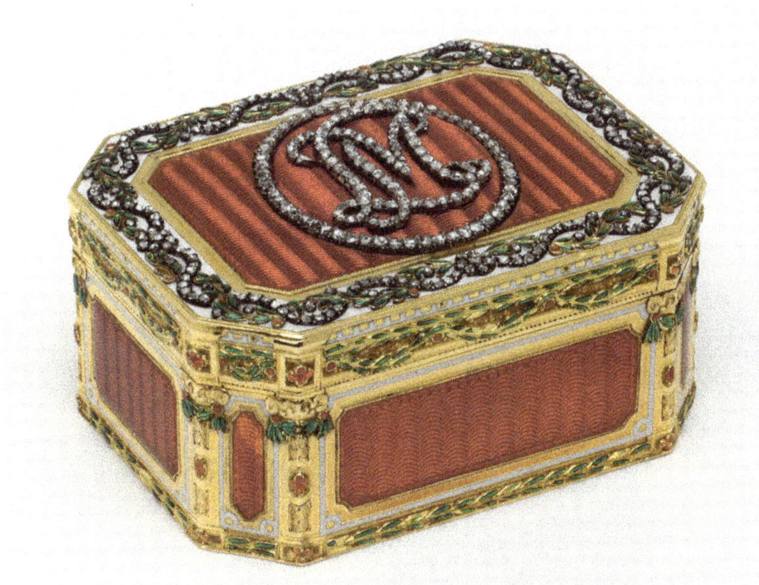

Fig. 3.20. Joseph-Etienne Blerzy gold box, now at the V&A as part of the Gilbert Collection. © The Rosalinde and Arthur Gilbert Collection on loan to the Victoria & Albert Museum, London.

in Frankfurt am Main, which enables us to focus on the local archives, which may hold relevant information.

The city's archives were therefore an obvious starting point. Indeed, an enquiry to the archive revealed that this institution holds several files which tell the story of how Maximilian was forced to sell his collection in the midst of the November 1938 pogrom (Figure 3.21). Like all German Jews, Maximilian had to submit an asset declaration which, as was so often the case, then became the blueprint for his subsequent dispossession.[108] In this context, he produced an inventory of his collection, which comprised more than 1,500 objects, including numerous 'Louis XVI boxes'. But, surprisingly, the inventory did not mention the distinctive monogram 'LM'.[109] On the basis of this limited information, it would have been impossible to confirm that the box now in the Gilbert Collection was part of this inventory. Instead, the files in the city archive and corresponding files from the Hesse Main State Archives at least allow us to reconstruct the way in which the entire collection was taken by the city of Frankfurt and its museums, whose directors approved the asset declaration. In September 1938, the Frankfurt Customs Investigations Office issued

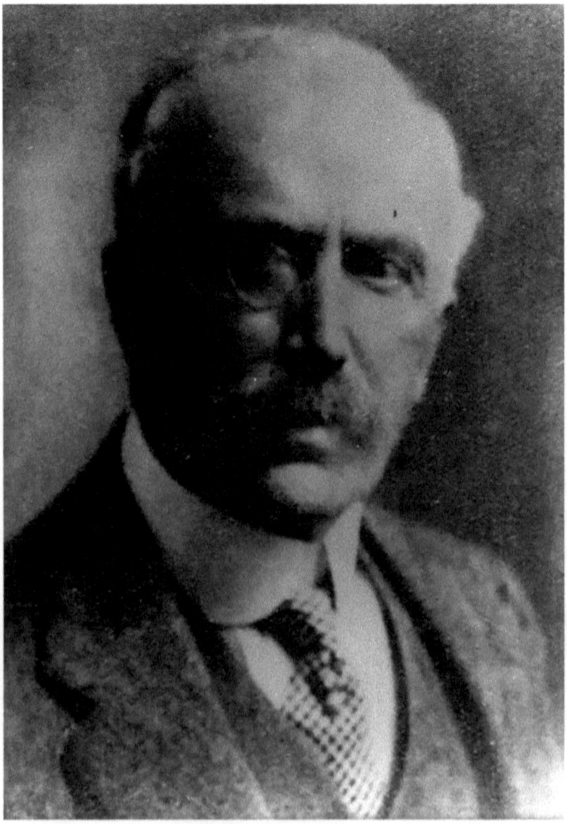

Fig. 3.21. Portrait of the distinguished banker and art collector Maximilian von Goldschmidt-Rothschild, who at the time of the forced sale of his collection was 95 years old. Public domain (Source: Wikimedia Commons, https://bit.ly/3sg8oCF).

a 'Sicherungsanordnung' (freezing order) for Maximilian's assets to prevent him from transferring his wealth abroad. It notes: 'The 96-year-old Max von Goldschmidt-Rothschild is unlikely to emigrate, but most of his fortune consists of liquid assets and it is to be feared that with the imminent emigration of his son Rudolf, parts of his father's fortune will be withdrawn from foreign exchange control.'[110] Crucially, this document also states that the proceeds from any future sale of art would have to be paid into a blocked account.[111] Maximilian would have been under no illusion about the nature of the increasing pressure he was under: his relatives in Vienna had already seen their own collections and personal fortunes plundered by the Nazi authorities.[112]

The mayor of Frankfurt had long desired to seize Maximilian's collection for the city's museums. With the local synagogue in flames, and the Nazi mob brutalising the Jewish population, the mayor decided that now was the time to strike. His negotiators called Maximilian to persuade him to sell his collection, pretending to offer a sympathetic hand in light of 'the events taking place in the city and the imminent danger' Maximilian faced at the hands of the Nazi activists who were making their way towards his residence.[113] Informed that the 'danger was increasing minute by minute', Maximilian agreed to the sale of his collection.[114] Afterwards, the mayor arranged for signs to be erected outside Maximilian's house which stated that it was 'municipal property' so that it would be spared by the brownshirts.[115]

After the eventual sale, the Museum für Kunsthandwerk (Museum of Decorative Arts), whose director was pleased that his galleries would be 'complemented' with items from Maximilian's collections, sent curators to Maximilian's home in order to catalogue the collection. This collection was so vast that the house itself was turned into a branch of the museum (and we should note that Maximilian had already been forced to sell the house to the city for a fraction of its true value).[116]

What the curators lacked in conscience, they more than made up for in diligence – they exhaustively catalogued and recorded all the objects in Maximilian's collection on detailed index cards, which they paired with photographs. These records are kept in the museum, which is now called the Museum Applied Art Frankfurt. Unfortunately, the index cards are not available online, which meant that we could not resolve our research question with a simple database search. Instead, it was only possible to identify the correct box after making a direct request to Katharina Weiler, the provenance researcher at the museum, who shared the relevant index card with the Gilbert Collection.[117] This card featured not only an incredibly meticulous description of the box, but also a number that corresponded to the inventory in the city archives – and a photograph which made it possible to confirm without a shadow of a doubt that the box from Maximilian's collection was identical with the one now in the Gilbert Collection (Figure 3.22).

Now that it was clear that Maximilian had been forced to sell this box to the city of Frankfurt in 1938, the question we had to ask was: what happened to it afterwards? After the war, the bulk of the collection was restituted to Maximilian's family – therefore, it needed to be established whether our box was among the items returned to the rightful owners, or if it had left the museum earlier, whether through an exchange with another institution, or if it had simply been

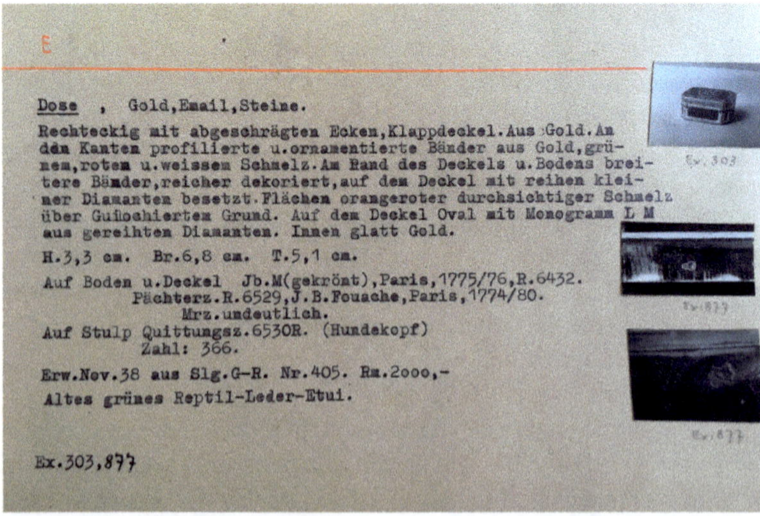
Dose , Gold,Email,Steine.
Rechteckig mit abgeschrägten Ecken,Klappdeckel.Aus Gold.An
den Kanten profilierte u.ornamentierte Bänder aus Gold,grü-
nem,rotem u.weissem Schmelz.Am Rand des Deckels u.Bodens brei-
tere Bänder,reicher dekoriert,auf dem Deckel mit reihen klei-
ner Diamanten besetzt.Flächen orangeroter durchsichtiger Schmelz
über Guillochiertem Grund. Auf dem Deckel Oval mit Monogramm L M
aus gereihten Diamanten. Innen glatt Gold.
H.3,3 cm. Br.6,8 cm. T.5,1 cm.
Auf Boden u.Deckel Jb.M(gekrönt),Paris,1775/76,R.6432.
Pächterz.R.6529,J.B.Fouache,Paris,1774/80.
Mrz.undeutlich.
Auf Stulp Quittungsz.6530R. (Hundekopf)
Zahl: 366.
Erw.Nov.38 aus Slg.G-R. Nr.405. Rm.2000,-
Altes grünes Reptil-Leder-Etui.
Ex.303,877

Fig. 3.22. Index card created by curators in Frankfurt in the wake of the forced sale of the Maximilian von Goldschmidt-Rothschild Collection during the November pogrom. © Museum Angewandte Kunst, Frankfurt am Main.

lost during the chaos of war. The relevant records are again in the City Archives, which confirm that the box was indeed restituted to the family after the conflict.[118]

Working our way backwards

The research will not always be as straightforward as this. Often, we will not discover a reference to a previous owner in the acquisition records, nor on the objects themselves. In this case, our strategy must be to work our way backwards through time.

In 1973, Arthur Gilbert acquired from a London-based art dealer a pair of church gates depicting the annunciation of Christ, which had once adorned an Orthodox church in the Pechersk Lavra monastery in Kyiv (Figure 3.23).[119] When we examine the acquisition records, it rapidly becomes clear that it mattered tremendously to Arthur that these gates came with a powerful stamp of approval from another prolific collector, William Randolph Hearst, one of America's most famous art collectors. The question was now: from whom, when and how did Hearst acquire these gates? The answer lay hidden in the archives of Hearst Castle, where the collection's voluminous index cards are held.

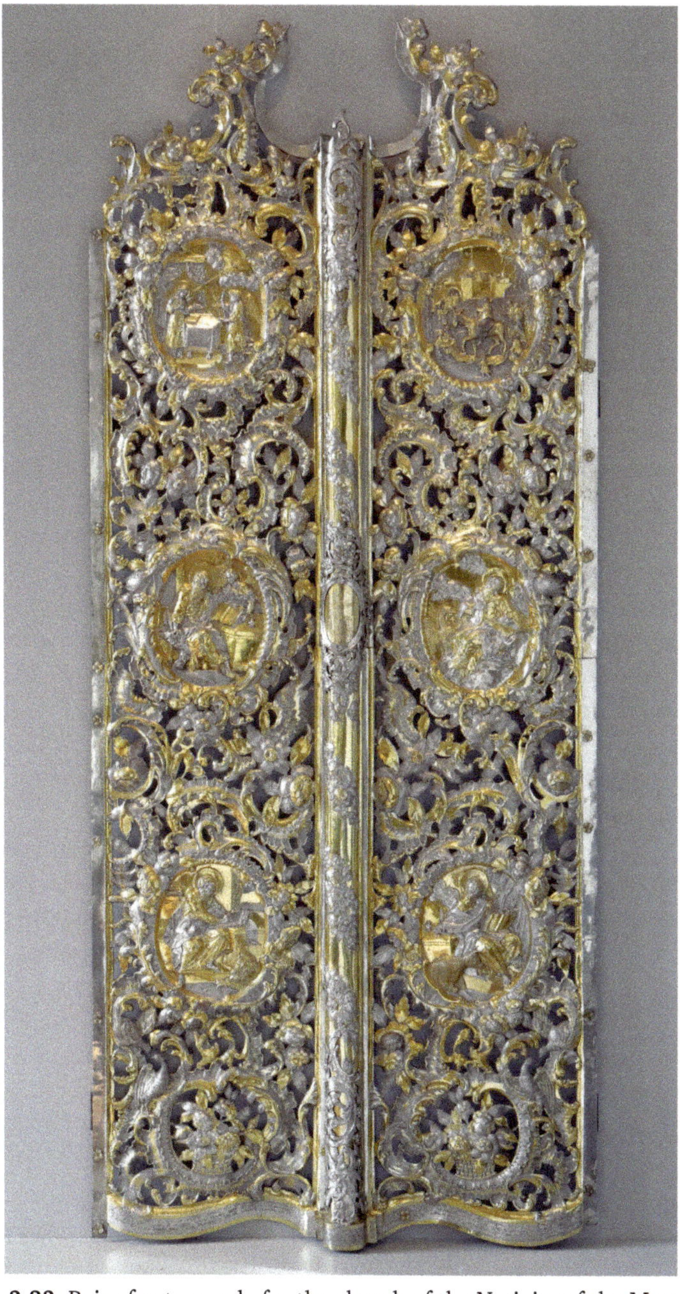

Fig. 3.23. Pair of gates made for the church of the Nativity of the Most Holy Mother of God in the Kyiv-Pechersk Lavra in Kyiv, c. 1784, now at the V&A as part of the Gilbert Collection. © The Rosalinde and Arthur Gilbert Collection on loan to the Victoria & Albert Museum, London.

An enquiry revealed that Hearst bought the gates in 1935 from 'Goldschmidt Galleries'.[120] The curator helpfully pointed out that 'Goldschmidt Galleries' was shorthand for 'J&S Goldschmidt'. With this name, it was now possible to research the history of the gallery in the literature. In the 1850s, Jakob and Selig Meier Goldschmidt established the company in Frankfurt. The gallery enjoyed an outstanding international reputation and had counted the Rothschilds and the Russian imperial family among its clients.[121] The literature, however, did not provide detailed information about the company after the Nazis' seizure of power, nor any specific details about the fateful year of 1935, in which they had sold the gates to Hearst. To find the answers to our questions, we needed to turn to the archival record.

An enquiry to the Federal Office for Central Services and Unresolved Property Issues, which keeps files from the West German compensation offices (see below), unearthed extensive records which made it possible to reconstruct the fate of the company and its owners under the Nazis. At the beginning of 1933, J&S Goldschmidt had two branches in Germany: one in Frankfurt and one in Berlin, which were run by Julius Falk Goldschmidt and Arthur Goldschmidt, respectively.[122] After the Nazis' seizure of power, Arthur Goldschmidt was ordered by the authorities to vacate the Berlin gallery space in order to make room for the Nazi organisation Kameradschaft der deutschen Künstler (Association of German Artists).[123] After he found new premises, the business continued – as it did in Frankfurt.

In 1935, two years after the Nazis had seized power, Julius Goldschmidt decided to close down the gallery in Frankfurt and to emigrate to London. In March that year, he packed up his belongings and placed them in storage with a shipping company, from which they were later confiscated by the Gestapo.[124] The sale of the gates took place seven months later in October 1935, and the index cards from Hearst Castle inform us that they were 'received from London' – where Julius had done business before and where he was now rebuilding his life as an art dealer.[125]

Arthur Goldschmidt held out in Berlin until November 1936, when he too made the decision to flee (Figure 3.24). The belongings and artworks which he left behind were either destroyed by bombs or seized and auctioned off by the Nazi authorities.[126] Like Julius, he chose a major European capital: he went to Paris, where, in November 1937, he received a letter from the Reich Chamber of Culture, informing him that: 'You are no longer allowed to participate in the distribution, reproduction, sale or mediation of the sale of cultural property in

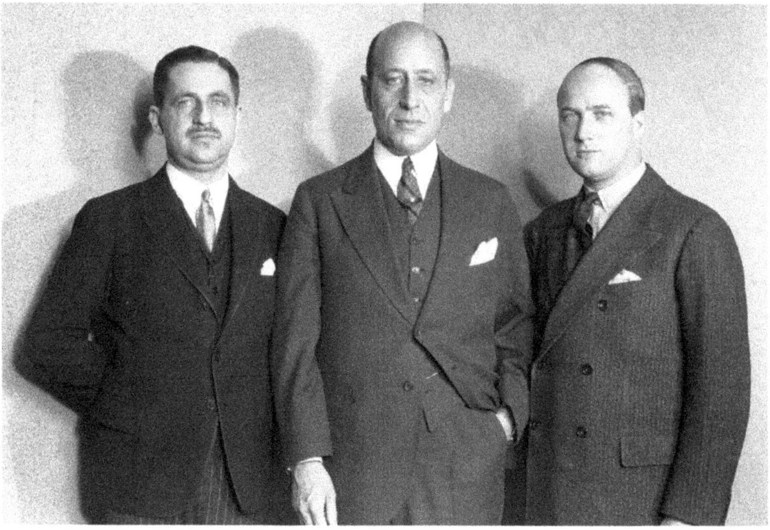

Fig. 3.24. Portrait of Arthur Goldschmidt (middle), co-owner of the J&S Goldschmidt art dealership which was forced into 'liquidation' by the Nazi regime in 1938. © Cleveland Museum for Art.

Germany. I grant you a period of two months for the dissolution of your branches in Berlin and Frankfurt am Main.'[127] In June 1938, the forced 'liquidation' of the company was finalised.[128]

Meanwhile, Arthur had managed to rebuild his life and business in Paris, which was then shattered once again by the outbreak of war. In May 1940, when German troops launched their offensive in the West, Arthur 'was arrested by the French police for his German nationality', as his wife Anna-Marie later recalled.[129] While Arthur was transferred to a French internment camp for foreign nationals, his wife was in hospital, from which she was ruthlessly expelled after the arrival of German soldiers. Arthur and Anna-Marie managed to reunite in Bordeaux: 'When I met my husband again, all our belongings consisted of two dresses for me, which I took from the clinic, and a shirt and trousers for my husband.'[130] Together, they went to Cannes where, upon arrival, they received notification that the Gestapo had seized their Parisian apartment and everything inside.[131] From Cannes, they managed to emigrate to Cuba, from where they went to the United States.[132]

As this complex story shows, working our way backwards from the acquisition file, we were able to reconstruct what happened to the gates and at the same time appreciate the lives of the people whose worlds were torn apart by the Nazis. By tracing this story, we learn that the gates were sold by a Jewish-owned company in 1935, the same year that the Nuremberg Racial Laws came into effect. Nevertheless, many questions remain. We now know that the gates were delivered to Hearst from London, but this could mean that they had been outside Germany for many years prior to the sale. In the post-war restitution and compensation records, the gates do not make an appearance. The company archives did not survive the war, which means that we will not be able to explore the kind of questions that we always have to consider when art dealers are concerned: did the dealer actually own the work, or were they offering it on behalf of someone else? If so, were the owners also the victims of Nazi persecution? Or did the art dealer own the object together with other art dealers – a complicating factor for provenance researchers, but a very common situation where valuable objects are concerned.

Working our way forwards

We can see this process of discovery play out in the opposite direction when we consider a third case, in which the best strategy was to pursue the provenance trail forwards in time from a concrete starting point. In 1987, Arthur Gilbert acquired an table clock from a London-based art dealership, without receiving information about its provenance (Figure 3.25).[133] As it was impossible for us to gain further information from the art dealership, this was the end of the 'backwards' trail.

We therefore had to turn to the object itself. On the clock face, we can see the name 'Kreitt Mayer', which refers to a large family of clock makers who, for generations, were active in Friedberg and in Prague. The ornaments on the base of the clock came from the workshop of Matthias Walbaum, a renowned goldsmith from Augsburg who, despite being a Protestant, created many devotional objects for Catholic patrons. When we begin researching these makers, it does not take very long before we encounter references to this clock. It features a small Jesus figure which, at some point in its history, was reworked to look like an explorer holding a telescope. These unusual features make it relatively easy to identify in the written record. From the 1975 book *Die Augsburger Goldschmiedewerkstatt des Matthias Walbaum*, we learn that the clock had once been part of the collection of Nathan Ruben Fränkel, and we are provided with a reference to the catalogue of his collection, which was published in 1913 in Düsseldorf (Figure 3.26).[134]

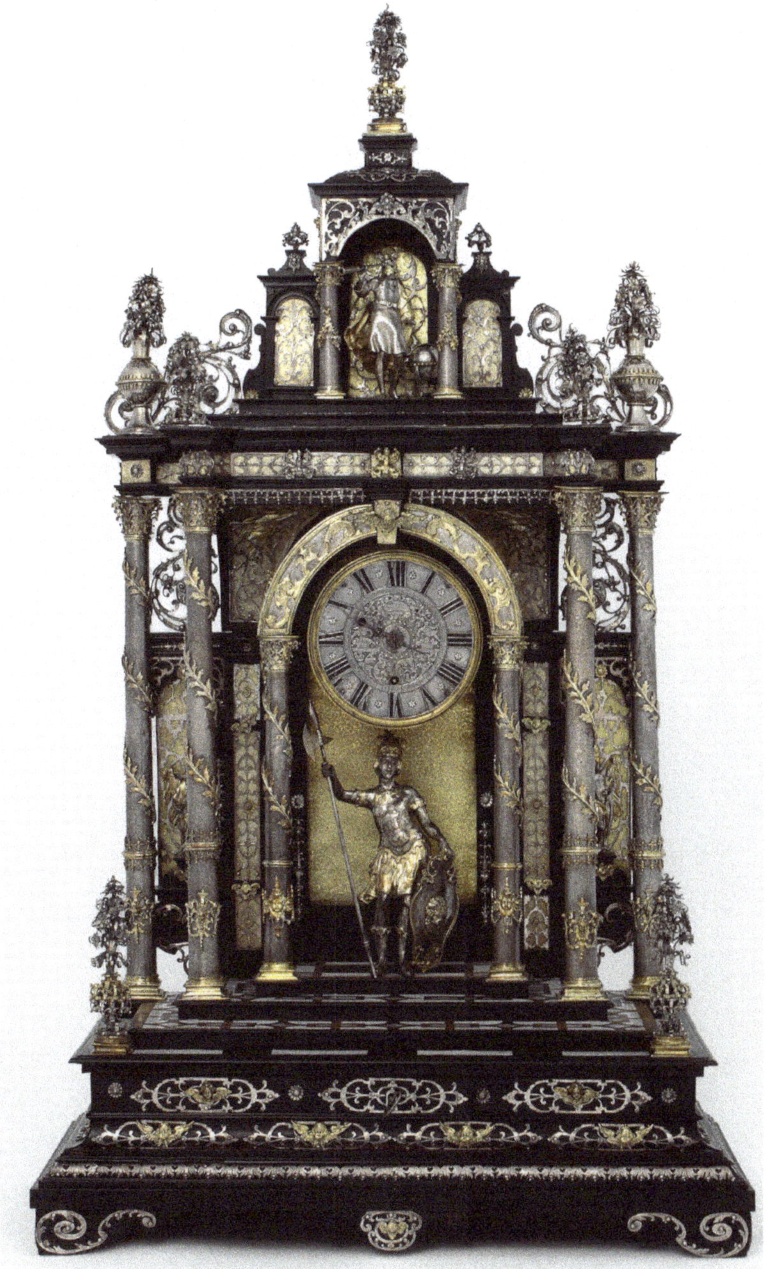

Fig. 3.25. The table clock, now at the V&A as part of the Gilbert Collection. © The Rosalinde and Arthur Gilbert Collection on loan to the Victoria & Albert Museum, London.

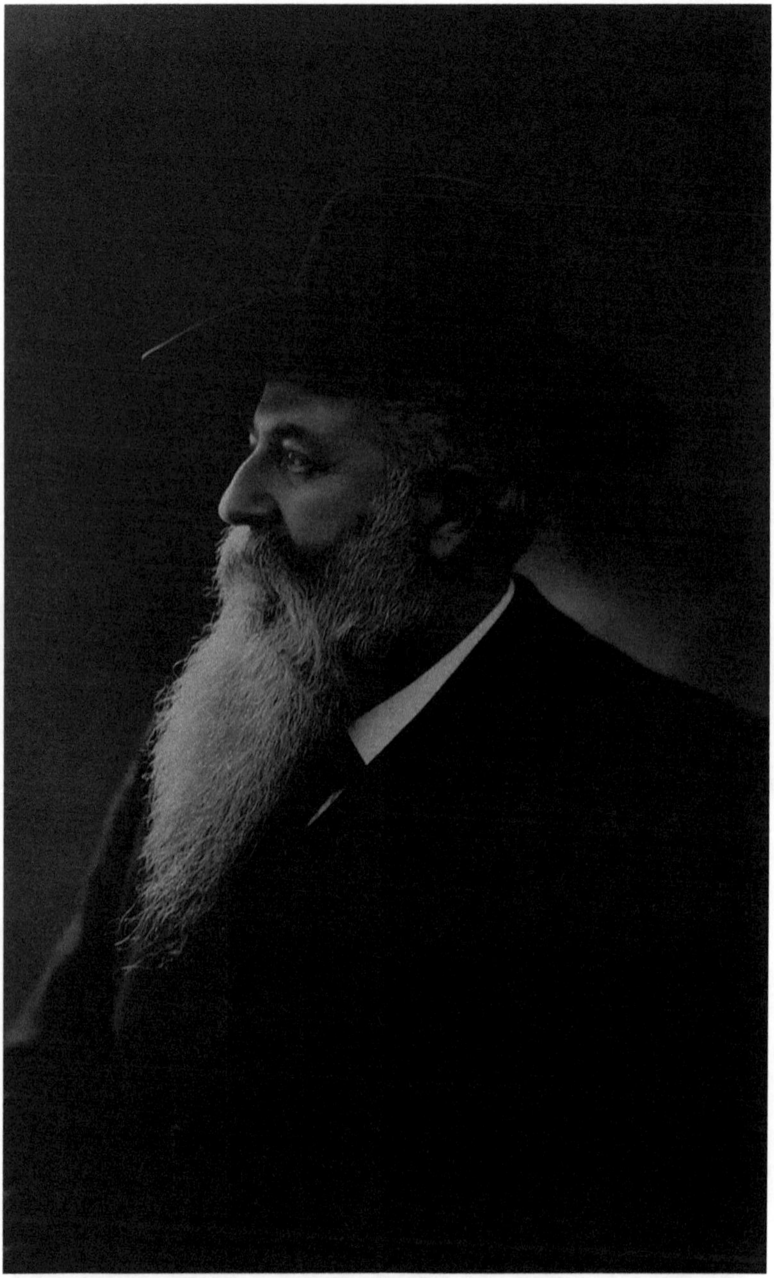

Fig. 3.26. Portrait of Nathan Ruben Fränkel, who, when this photo was taken, could look back on an impressive career as a clock dealer and collector of timepieces. Public domain (Source: Wikimedia Commons, https://bit.ly/3SEaXJN).

This catalogue in turn reveals that Nathan was a successful clock maker from Frankfurt and that, alongside his business, over the decades he built up an encyclopaedic collection of timepieces. The catalogue's foreword was written by his children, who had commissioned the Director of the Kunstgewerbemuseum in Düsseldorf to compile the catalogue in order to celebrate their father's lifetime of collecting.[135] The catalogue contained a list of the 372 clocks that he had collected and 44 photographs of the collection's highlights. Entry number 273 concerns a table clock, and if the detailed description was not enough, on the next page we find a large photograph of the front of the clock, confirming that the one in Arthur Gilbert's collection is the same as that in the Fränkel collection (Figure 3.27).[136] 'Fränkel' is a common Jewish surname. In the foreword, however, the children did not mention that Nathan was born into a large Jewish family, many members of which shared Nathan's passion and business acumen for the world of clocks.[137] After discovering the catalogue, we now know that the clock had been in Nathan's collection until his death in 1909 and that it was still part of the collection when the catalogue was produced in 1913.

The question was now: what happened to the clock after this date in the decades that followed? As we attempt to trace the path taken by the clock, we need to ask ourselves what we can discover about the history of the Fränkel family under the Nazis. Having exhausted the literature, we must turn to the archival record. As with the Goldschmidt-Rothschild case, the city archive was the obvious starting point, but when our enquiries did not produce any useful results, we turned to the Hesse Main State Archive. This holds not only crucial records created by the Nazi authorities, but also the post-war restitution records which detail their dramatic impact. This archive held records pertaining to Friedrich and Klara Fränkel, who ran 'Fränkel & Co', a clock wholesale business, in Frankfurt.

The relevant files and the corresponding records in the Federal Office for Central Services and Unresolved Property Issues contain hundreds of pages which tell the story of how, after the Nazi seizure of power, like so many Jewish-owned business, the Fränkels found themselves in a hostile environment. Important wholesalers refused to supply the company with watches, and many former customers no longer wanted to be seen frequenting a Jewish business.[138] To his employees, Friedrich often expressed his dismay at the torrent of directives that made it more and more difficult for the business to stay afloat. Friedrich became so demoralised that he made the difficult decision to close down the business in 1938 – as it turned out, only a few months

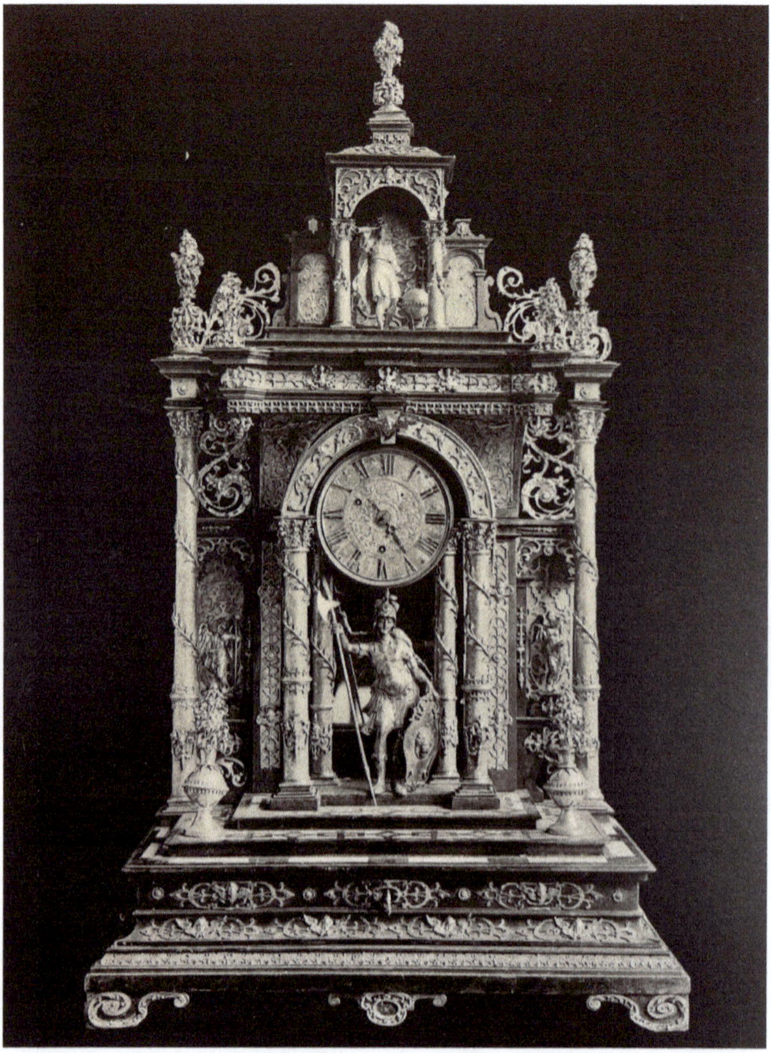

Fig. 3.27. Catalogue of the Nathan Ruben Fränkel Collection, featuring a photograph and a detailed description of the table clock. Public domain (Source: Heinrich Frauenberger, ed., N. R. Fränkels Uhrensammlung, Düsseldorf, 1913).

before the Nazi mob vandalised Jewish businesses across Frankfurt in November.[139]

Afterwards, the remaining stock was sold 'en bloc' to an 'Aryan' watch wholesaler with approval of the Nazi authorities.[140] In the wake of the pogrom night, Friedrich also had to pay the 'Jewish

Capital Levy' for the destruction caused by Nazi thugs.[141] Against this background, it is understandable that the Fränkels saw no future for themselves in Nazi Germany. They made the decision to emigrate and sold their house to an 'Aryan' buyer, who snatched it up at a staggering 80 per cent 'discount'.[142]

The records of the Currency Office, which are also held in the Hesse Main State Archive, tell the story of how the Fränkels were then robbed again before they were allowed to leave the country. Not only did they have to pay the Reich Flight Tax, but in the process of converting their money into francs to start a new life in Paris, they lost 93 per cent of what they had once owned.[143] For the customs officials, who, much like the Finance Officers, had become brutal enforcers and licensed thieves under the Nazis, the Fränkels had to prepare a detailed inventory of everything they owned – all the way down to each pair of socks in their suitcases.[144] Before the Fränkels received their exit permit, they were ordered to surrender their silver to the City Pawn Office and were paid 10 per cent of its true value.[145]

In France, they lived in an apartment in Neuilly. Their friend Denise Paraz testified after the war that: 'In June 1940 when the Germans arrived in the city, they occupied the Fränkels' apartment and set them a tight deadline to leave the apartment without allowing them to take anything with them, apart from some personal items and clothes.'[146] From then on, as Klara recalled, they were 'hounded like animals'.[147] They were saved by a young French woman called Honorine Lathier, who testified after the war that: 'In July 1942, Mr and Mrs Fränkel were wanted by the Gestapo, I took them in and hid them for about 10 days to save them from deportation.'[148] They then lived with the Rouselle family in Clermont de l'Oise, where they had to 'live in primitive conditions'. As a result, Friedrich became 'severely ill' and could no longer leave his bed.[149] Subsequently, a French teacher, Mademoiselle Trouvain, hid Friedrich and Klara for the duration of the war in Clermont.[150]

Living in constant fear of discovery, Friedrich was 'completely exhausted ... hardly spoke and was physically and emotionally changed'.[151] Against all odds, the couple survived the war in hiding, with fake ID papers in the names of 'Pierrefond' and 'Sylla', which they had received from a local priest and the mayor's secretary, but they had to survive without food stamps because the 'danger [of discovery] would have been too large'.[152] In the restitution claims that the Fränkels submitted after the war, they made no mention of the clock. Its fate remains unclear, but at least it has been reconnected with the Fränkel family.

These three examples not only illustrate the two principal research strategies, but also powerfully highlight how, even after a major research effort, questions may still remain. Indeed, Nazi-era provenance research aims not merely to provide concrete answers to specific questions, but also to shine a spotlight on past injustices on the basis of documentary evidence. Sometimes, the sources we seek did not survive in the chaos of emigration and the destruction of war. As a result, it may be that certain provenance gaps will never be filled, but it remains important that we share what we can find with the world. In doing so, we can tell the stories of Nathan and the Goldschmidts, and in the process offer an open invitation to readers and gallery visitors who may be able to pick up the threads and offer unexpected new sources of information. For the V&A, this was the principal motivation for including the items in these case studies so prominently in the special 'Concealed Histories' display (see Chapter 2).

Turning to the literature on the Nazi past

As these examples illustrate, archival research is absolutely essential in most cases. Nevertheless, before we deploy these research strategies, we should ensure that our work has not already been done for us by another researcher, and that we are aware of any useful information that may have been produced. To do so, we must in the first instance go beyond the art-historical literature and into the potentially unfamiliar realm of historical scholarship about the Nazi period. These publications may be highly relevant for grounding and elaborating our understanding of the circumstances in which dispossession unfolded, even if these works rarely directly focus on art. It can be easy to become overwhelmed by the sheer quantity of material, so it is important not to get bogged down in scholarly debates which frequently focus on the macro level.

Our interest remains on the specific facts relating to the objects we are investigating, and the individual (and thus always unique) stories of their former owners. As we piece together information about the pressures these people faced, we will often find that the books that become most useful are those that provide an overview or summary of the policies deployed against particular professions, business sectors and communities in the area where they lived. The key information we need to form an accurate picture of a person's life under the Nazis can often be found in local studies that explore exactly how German society transformed into a violent racial state in a particular region or city. For example, articles in obscure local history journals can help us to illuminate the persecution of Rosa Israels in the small town of Weener, or the effects of the November pogrom in Frankfurt. These local histories allow us to develop a fine-grained understanding of the pressures faced by the victims and how these played out on the ground, rather than in the imaginations of high-level functionaries.

Even the history of Nazi Germany is never black and white; as conscientious researchers, we must remain interested in grey areas, especially as we dedicate ourselves to recovering victims' agency rather than treating them as the passive subjects of Nazi bureaucracy and violence. When we carried out the initial survey, we turned to online catalogues that enabled us to locate publications relevant to specific objects. We can now do the same for the historical context by utilising online historical bibliographies such as the German *Deutsche Historische Bibliografie* (www.historicum.net/metaopac), and specialised resources that catalogue publications relevant to the history of Nazi Germany, and of the occupied territories, such as the catalogues of the United States Holocaust Memorial Museum, Yad Vashem (www.yadvashem.org/collections/bibliography.html) and the Wiener Library (wienerholocaustlibrary.org/what-we-have/search-the-catalogue/).

Provenance research sometimes leads to restitution, which in turn attracts legal scholars, who have produced fascinating insights into these topics. But we must be cautious when we read publications that approach this topic exclusively from a legal perspective, as these inevitably obsess over strict legal definitions or seek to apply a legalistic framework to make sense of past lives. While a knowledge of Nazi laws is of course essential, we must always remember that the Nazis' victims did not live within the pages of a legal text, but in a society that turned increasingly hostile towards them, a society whose cruelty was characterised by everyday acts of humiliation and theft, and in which violent action was often only formalised and codified afterwards.

In addition to developing a nuanced understanding of the circumstances in which the individuals we are investigating lived, we also need to be aware of the fact that the Washington Conference sparked an unprecedented push to investigate the provenance of museum collections, resulting in a vast range of research outputs that often contain a wealth of information for our research. This is particularly important because the nature of the dispossession meant that objects from the same collection often ended up in different institutions.

The *Central Registry of Information on Looted Cultural Property 1933–1945* (www.lootedart.com) is the best entry point, providing a comprehensive overview of research outputs from all over the world. Another important resource is the *Proveana* database (www.proveana.de), which integrates the huge quantities of information created in the context of 25 years of provenance research in German museums, ranging from detailed internal research reports into collections (which are only available for download after registration) to publications, provenance marks and more. What makes the Proveana database so valuable is that it connects many disparate dots in the background: this silent, automatic work makes it possible to discover that the name of a collector, for example, appears in a provenance report that does not carry their name in the title or description, or that a provenance mark has been connected to them.

As one of the principal aims of provenance research has been to achieve restitution, it is no surprise that the various European restitution committees have produced much rich information which will be relevant if our research leads us to the name of an individual whose fate has already been ascertained. The reports produced by the UK Spoliation Advisory Panel are invaluable for researchers due to the level of forensic detail these contain (www.gov.uk/government/collections/reports-of-the-spoliation-advisory-panel). Researching the existing work in these areas allows us not only to identify relevant publications that might otherwise be difficult to find, but also to identify and contact researchers who have worked on similar cases.

Archives

To truly be able to reconstruct a past life for the first time, or to follow up on what we have read elsewhere, it is essential that we carry out archival research. There are two kinds of archives that are particularly relevant here: 1) archives containing documents that were created during the Nazi period, such as those created by Finance Offices, and 2) archives that document the efforts of survivors and the families of the victims to gain recognition and thus compensation for the suffering that they endured during the Nazi period, and their often unsuccessful attempts to reverse the material legacies of persecution (if this venue was open to them in the countries where they lived).

In order to be able to use any such archive effectively, it is essential that we have a name, because this is how the records are organised. It is generally not possible to reliably search archival holdings for a specific work of art because the files are catalogued by personal names, and because the archival finding aids only contain a high-level description of the contents. In order to identify relevant records, it can often be crucial to search not just for files in the name of the collector, but also those of their family members who may have shared important information about their relatives. To reconstruct these family networks and discover the relevant names, we can turn to genealogical tools such as Ancestry.org or Geni.com.

While the way in which this crucial historical record has been scattered across different archives varies from country to country, what remains the same is that we must always think about where these people's lives may have left a trace in the archives and let this guide our enquiries. The Nazi regime brought vast territories under its control and while the various dispossession campaigns were informed by the same murderous logic, they played out slightly differently on the ground, involved different institutions and thus left a different archival footprint. The *EHRI Holocaust Research Infrastructure Project* (www.ehri-project.eu) provides the best possible entry point for anyone interested in pursuing archival research in this area. It features 63 country reports that provide vital orientation and instructions on how to navigate the archival landscape in the respective country. It provides descriptions of 2,235 archival institutions and a staggering 412,536 descriptions of archival holdings and finding guides. In sum, this makes it a truly indispensable resource, especially if used in conjunction with the country-specific information on the Central Registry. These tools allow us to open up the archival landscape relevant to our specific case.[153]

Federal Office for Central Services and Unresolved Property Issues

To illustrate the archival research process at a high level, we can turn to the German example. If the name of the person whose life story we want to reconstruct can in any way be tied to Germany, the first archive we need to contact is the Federal Office for Central Services and Unresolved Property Issues (BADV). To use this archive effectively, it is helpful to be aware of the complicated history which, by chance, transformed an unassuming administrative body into perhaps the most important resource for provenance researchers today.[154]

Tucked away within an unremarkable office building in north-east Berlin, in this institution we gain access to a wealth of post-war restitution records. These are the claims that were made on the basis of the post-war restitution law that applied to West Germany and Berlin, and which found no equivalent in the Soviet-controlled GDR (see Chapter 2). If, during the Nazi period, Jewish people were forced to complete endless forms for Nazi bureaucrats hellbent on their systematic dispossession, after the war the survivors and their families essentially had to recreate this record and submit it in the hope that they might either be reunited with their possessions, or be granted a compensation payment. In order to substantiate their claims, they had to revisit the painful reality of how their lives had been incrementally destroyed by the Nazis. Worse still, during the restitution proceedings, they sometimes came face to face with the same finance officials who had calculated their Reich Flight Tax and who now, in a perverse twist of fate, were deeply involved with the restitution proceedings.[155]

Claims had to be filed at the local level, in the *Land* (German federal state) where the act of dispossession had occurred, leaving the documentary traces of this process scattered across Germany. The ultimate deadline for claims was 1 April 1959, but the proceedings stretched on well into the 1980s, highlighting how difficult and protracted this work could be. By the mid-1980s, it seemed to many that a line had been drawn under the Nazi past, but the sudden fall of the Iron Curtain changed the face of Europe once again. Because there had been no restitution effort in the GDR, a new law was passed to give those who had been dispossessed in East Germany the same opportunity for justice.

A new centralised office was created for this purpose: the BADV. Because its work would inevitably cross multiple jurisdictions and touch upon previous claims that had concerned property thought lost behind the Iron Curtain, the local Finance Offices sent their case files to support the new restitution effort. It is important to note that the files they sent were not the complete records. Each restitution claim essentially played out like a court trial, pitting a claimant against a defendant. In this case, the defendant was the German Reich, whose successor, the Federal Republic of Germany, now appointed finance officers to represent state interests and to ensure that the claims were appropriately tested before a decision was made.

The documentary records of this process were split in two: one part was the state defendant's records, while the other was a more comprehensive file that consolidated information provided by both sides. Frustratingly, only the state's defendant files were sent to support the work of the BADV. Nevertheless, these files can be extremely extensive, often containing carbon copies of the claimants' submissions, and copies of other relevant documents. Although these files often consist only of highly bureaucratic documents, and focus on the exploration of narrow legal issues, the fragmentary pieces of the claimants' voices can still be heard.

In 1998, in the wake of the Washington Conference, the BADV became increasingly concerned with art collections lost under Nazi persecution. They now receive dozens of enquiries each week, which are handled by a single individual, Yvonne Mundt, whose tireless dedication is essential to so much of today's provenance research efforts. In an age where we have become used to information being just a click away, it is important to appreciate just how much personal effort goes into this aspect of provenance research.

In the 1990s, the regional Finance Offices not only sent boxes bulging with thousands of files to the BADV, but also the index cards they had created to navigate this ocean of historical material. When she receives an enquiry, Yvonne Mundt has to search through every filing cabinet of index cards in order to locate the relevant file number. With this in mind, to make effective use of this archive, it is essential to provide Mundt with the name of the person we are interested in, as much information as possible about them, and particularly their date of birth and known places of residence. As we have seen, the spelling of names could vary considerably during this time period, so it is important to consider alternative versions of the same name.

Although the BADV's records can often be incredibly valuable, we must always remain aware that they may not tell us the full story. The BADV was not designed to support provenance research, but if it did not exist, our work would be infinitely more difficult.

State (Landes) archives

As we noted above, the BADV only holds the files produced by the state's defendants' side. The corresponding files that complete this picture will always be located in the *Land* where the act of dispossession occurred, usually in the central *Landesarchiv* (to which they were transferred after it was thought that the last restitution case had been processed and completed). For the case studies that we explored in the Research Strategies sections above, to get the full picture it was necessary to review both the files at the BADV and then at the *Landesarchiv* in the *Land* where the victims were dispossessed. For example, although we could establish much of the Fränkels' story at the BADV in Berlin, it was only possible to read certain crucial witness statements by visiting the *Landesarchiv* in Hesse. It is also advisable to write to the relevant local city archives because in some cases these too may contain important records unavailable elsewhere.

If we were researching a case of an individual dispossessed in Berlin, the files of the West Berlin Restitution Offices (Wiedergutmachungsämter) are kept in the *Berlin Landesarchiv*, an institution housed within a former armaments factory that somehow survived the Allied bombing, and in which countless prisoners of war were worked to death. When the files of the West Berlin Restitution Offices were transferred to the *Landesarchiv* for processing, archivist Martin Luchterhandt could scarcely have imagined that this collection would become an indispensable resource for provenance researchers, and the most-used part of the archive's holdings. Luchterhandt had worked on the history of Nazi persecution and quickly realised that these documents carried an important story that needed to be told. Under his leadership, volunteers transcribed the 400,000 index cards which unlock the vast body of files that together span some four kilometres inside the archival vaults.[156] This invaluable information was then made available in an online database accessible to the public at www.wga-datenbank.de. This is a remarkable resource because the relevant holdings of many other *Landesarchive* are not yet searchable in this fashion; for these, we will have to send a written enquiry to the relevant archive.

Provenance researchers are interested in the objects, but these files were principally focused on the legal questions concerning restitution. In order to find additional context and restore the human story to these events, we must turn from the restitution to the compensation files, which directly addressed the personal suffering of the victims. These are the files in which people could speak about the damage they had suffered to their families, their careers and their livelihoods. These records provide an often shocking picture of persecution, not only through traumatic recollections, but also through the medical records which demonstrated the sometimes decades-long consequences of Nazi brutality. These records are generally kept in the *Landesarchive* of the areas in which the victims resided at the time of their persecution.

In the *Landesarchive*, we are often able to find additional records that help us cast light on the fate of the individuals and the actions of those who mistreated, dispossessed and expelled them. These resources range from Finance Office files to Gestapo records and the records of Nazi culture associations, which had art-historical experts in their ranks to assess collections (provided that these records were not destroyed by the war or set ablaze by the Nazis in the attempt to stop them falling into enemy hands). In some cases, copies of crucial records will be contained in the post-war restitution and compensation files as pieces of evidence, but this is not always the case.

If our aim is to reconstruct as much as possible, it is therefore advisable that we write to the *Landesarchive* asking for information about *all* of the records that they hold with respect to the individuals our research has identified, as well as regarding other persons of interest, such as the art dealers and curators with whom the victims dealt (these individuals' 'de-Nazification' files can often provide revealing insights if read critically). An archive that is particularly important here is the Brandenburg Main State Archives, which holds the records of the Chief Finance President Berlin-Brandenburg, the destructive influence of which spanned far beyond this region. This institution played a central role in the dispossession of refugees and the seizure of the assets belonging to those who were deported and murdered. Within this institution we find the archival holdings of the Asset Liquidation Office (Vermögensverwertungsstelle), which contain more than 40,000 files pertaining to specific individuals. These are currently being digitised, which means that we will soon be able to use this resource to discover artworks without first having to know the name of the dispossessed person.

Summary

As we have seen, the research process will involve numerous different institutions and can at first seem daunting. However, armed with an understanding of how the archival landscape in Germany is organised, we are able to approach this task in a systematic manner using the following steps.

Once we have found a name, we would first send an enquiry to the BADV in Berlin. If restitution proceedings are found related to this name, then we would be able to access these documents at the BADV office. A review of these files would at the very least inform us where the restitution process was initiated and processed, and thus lead us to the corresponding files in the relevant *Landesarchiv.*

We would then contact the *Landesarchiv* to request these documents and any additional materials they may hold related to the individual. This may include compensation files or records pertaining to the individuals and organisations that were mentioned in the BADV records. In most cases, we would need to visit the *Landesarchiv* in person as this documentation can be vast.

When brought together, the materials from across these archives allow us to reconstruct a rich picture of individual lives and restore the victims' voices to the historical record.

Conclusion

If we examine a museum collection with the Nazi period in mind, we open the door to seeing and appreciating the objects in the galleries and storerooms in an entirely new light. All that is required is the readiness to ask a simple question: 'Who owned these objects between 1933 and 1945?' To answer this question requires a willingness to examine the museum records, the objects and the literature, and the tenacity to explore with an open mind where this information leads.

Online databases enable us to discover that additional objects which, at first glance, have nothing to do with the Nazi past, and whose records and labels do not connect them to this past in any obvious way, do in fact carry traces of this history. The aim of this initial survey is always to find a name through which we can illuminate the history behind the object. In some cases, if we find a name in the object's documentation, or if we discover the object in a database, we can immediately embark on archival research, which is almost always essential. In other cases, we will have to work our way forwards or backwards in time until we arrive at the 1933–45 period.

We will always learn much about the objects and the places and times through which they passed, but this does not mean that we will always gain clear answers. In some cases, the link to the past may indeed be broken and we will hit a brick wall that we cannot overcome, no matter from which direction we approach it. The important thing is that we have embarked on the research journey, which, even if we cannot complete the full process, will always generate new knowledge and new ways of understanding the objects in a collection. If we discover that these items once belonged to people whose lives were destroyed in the name of Nazi ideology, or if we find that the artworks themselves had drawn the racist wrath of the regime, then it is no longer possible to interpret the objects based on their artistic merit alone – unlike the generations of curators, art historians and visitors who did not know how to ask these questions, and indeed sometimes deliberately chose not to.

These are no longer objects that merely carry an unresolved 'question mark' hovering over their provenance; they become a tangible link to the Nazi past and we can now, through our archival research, picture them not only in artists' studios, but in the personal homes of former owners whose lives were uprooted or cut short. Beyond the personal level, we can also see the objects as vehicles that can open up a wider conversation not only about the history of persecution, occupation and extermination, but also about the decades that followed – the effort to reverse the material consequences of the Nazi campaign of dispossession, and indeed the role of museums, which owe it to themselves and to their visitors to tell this story.

Further reading and resources

At the 1998 Washington Conference, American and British museums made a clear commitment to researching the Nazi-era provenance of their collections. The curators tasked with carrying out this important work were faced with an enormous challenge, as they had never before thought about their collections in this light and initially struggled to understand how to best approach it. To address this serious problem, the American Alliance of Museums commissioned the *AAM Guide to Provenance Research*, which was produced in just six months by Nancy H. Yeide, Konstantin Akinsha and Amy L. Walsh, and was published in 2001. It provided an incredibly rich overview of research strategies and resources for Nazi-era provenance research and quickly became the standard work in the field, and the 'go-to' guide for provenance researchers in English-speaking countries. Despite the fact that our understanding of this topic has evolved dramatically since its publication, and many new resources have become available, this book remains required reading for anyone interested in researching the Nazi-era provenance of a museum collection.

The need to carry out provenance research was felt with particular urgency in Germany, where the government has made considerable financial resources available to support it. In 2020, the German Lost Art Foundation in conjunction with the Arbeitskreis Provenienzforschung (which represents the research community) published a remarkable provenance research manual with the precise if ungainly title *Provenance Research Manual to Identify Cultural Property Seized due to Persecution during the National-Socialist Era*. This book, although concise, embodies decades' worth of the knowledge and experience gained within German museums working to explore the provenance of their collections. It provides an overview of research strategies and offers principles that can be applied to any collection. Crucially, it contains an appendix of resources that have become available since the publication of the *AAM Guide for Provenance Research*. Taken together, these two manuals will be read with great benefit by anyone interested in embarking on this important work.

As we have seen, the core research strategy remains the same, but the resources we will use along the way depend greatly upon the circumstances of the specific case and the objects involved. The key resources for each research step are mentioned in the relevant sections of the current chapter, but due to the increasing interest in provenance research, new resources are always becoming available. The best way to keep abreast of this changing landscape (and to identify extremely specialised resources) is to regularly consult the websites of the Getty Research Institute (www.getty.edu/research) and arthistoricum.net, as well as Proveana.de and the Central Registry of Information on Looted Cultural Property 1933–45 (lootedart.com), which also keeps a record of newly accessible archives.

Notes

1 Victoria & Albert Museum 2023, 2R-3.
2 On provenance research into Judaica, see Cohen et al. 2019.
3 See, for example, Weitz 2020.
4 On this approach: Yeide et al. 2001, 15–17; Kocourek et al. 2019, 51–2.
5 Kenzler 2014, 138–40.
6 Kenzler 2014, 142–3.
7 Kenzler 2014, 135.
8 Kenzler 2014, 138–9.
9 Wessels 1991, 293–5.
10 Kenzler 2014, 140.
11 Wessels 1991, 298.
12 Kenzler 2014, 141.
13 Kenzler 2014, 141.
14 Kenzler 2014, 143.
15 Kenzler 2014, 143.
16 Kenzler 2014, 138–9.
17 Kenzler 2014, 145.
18 Stolberg and Lehmann 2020, 55–6. On books, see Pearson 2019; Alker-Windbichler et al. 2017, 16–24.
19 Kocourek et al. 2019, 41–7.
20 Eßl 2020, 155.
21 Eßl 2020, 154–5.
22 Eßl 2020, 155.
23 Other important databases of provenance marks, which are continuously being updated by provenance researchers, include: lootedculturalassets.de, ProvenienzWiki (provenienz.gbv.de) and the Austrian Database of Provenance Mark (provenienz.collectiveaccess.de) (all accessed 22 November 2023).
24 Eßl 2020, 155–6.

25 Eßl 2020, 156–9.
26 Eßl 2020, 159–60.
27 Eßl 2020, 159–60.
28 Eßl 2020, 160.
29 On this process, see: Yeide et al. 2001, 21–7; Kocourek et al. 2019, 60–6.
30 Garrad & Co., invoice of 9 November 1987. GC/9/3/127. Victoria and Albert Museum Archive, London.
31 Truman 1991, 233.
32 Holzhausen 1935, 18.
33 von Falke 1912.
34 Kugel 2012, 354.
35 Goodman 2015, 208.
36 Goodman 2015, 117–18.
37 Goodman 2015, 125–7.
38 Inventory of the Eugen Gutmann Collection. 91221736. National Records and Archives Administration, Washington, DC.
39 Hans Sauermann, letter of 4 April 1943 to Robert Schmidt. F 43, Nr. 351. Bayerisches Wirtschaftsarchiv, München; Winkler 2005, 226–31.
40 Goodman 2015, 155–6.
41 Christie's 1983, lot 83.
42 See also Yeide et al. 2001, 259–96.
43 Lauterbach 2018, 79–80.
44 Baresel-Brand 2005, 60.
45 Hartmann 2005.
46 Merz 2023, 100–1.
47 https://www.lostart.de/de/Verlust/309711 (accessed 6 December 2023).
48 Edith Eberstadt, restitution claim of 11 July 1957. Abt. 518, Nr. 11266. Hessisches Hauptstaatsarchiv, Wiesbaden.
49 See the various reports in Hesse Main State Archive, Wiesbaden, Abt. 519/3 Nr. 16.657.
50 G. Eberstadt, affidavit of 23 March 1960. Abt. 518, Nr. 11266. Hessisches Hauptstaatsarchiv, Wiesbaden.
51 G. Eberstadt, affidavit.
52 Gestapo Wiesbaden, letter of 25 October 1937 to the Frankfurt Currency Office. Abt. 5193 Nr. 34817. Hessisches Haupstaatsarchiv, Wiesbaden.
53 Cited in Fritz Mertens, letter of 12 July 1938 to the Kassel Currency Office, 4. Abt. 519/3 Nr. 10150. Hessisches Hauptstaatsarchiv, Wiesbaden.
54 G. Eberstadt, affidavit.
55 Fritz Mertens, letter of 12 July 1938.
56 Ernst Flersheim, letter of 30 August 1943 to Willy Dreyfus. Abt. 518, Nr. 11266. Hessisches Hauptstaatsarchiv, Wiesbaden.
57 Dutch Red Cross, certificate of 18 August 1960 with respect to Gertrud Flersheim and certificate of 12 July 1960 with respect to Ernst Flersheim. Abt. 518, Nr. 11266. Hessisches Hauptstaatsarchiv, Wiesbaden.
58 Hugo Helbing 1937, lot 32.
59 Hugo Helbing 1937, 2.
60 Merz 2023, 104.
61 Merz 2023, 105.
62 Merz 2023, 105.
63 https://www.culture.gouv.fr/Nous-connaitre/Organisation-du-ministere/Le-secretariat-general/Mission-de-recherche-et-de-restitution-des-biens-culturels-spolies-entre-1933-et-1945/Recherche-de-provenance-outils-et-methode/Repertoire-des-biens-spolies-RBS#conseils (accessed 22 November 2023).
64 Hüneke 1997.
65 Harald Horst Halvorsen, letter of 14 December 1938 to Tate Gallery. TG 4/2/757/1. Tate Archive, London.
66 Huemer 2014.
67 The project did not include sales catalogues that happened not to be in the libraries visited by the research project.
68 Bähr 2014.

69 S. J. Phillips, invoice of 23 October 1970. GC/9/3/262. Victoria & Albert Museum Archive, London.
70 Hans W. Lange 1939, lot 511.
71 Pabstmann 2019, 282–3.
72 Postcard of 17 April 1937 to the Fahlberg-List AG. I 53, Nr. 2367. Landesarchiv Sachsen-Anhalt, Magdeburg.
73 Executive Board of the Fahlberg-List AG, letter of 26 April 1937 to the Supervisory Board. I 53, Nr. 2367. Landesarchiv Sachsen-Anhalt, Magdeburg.
74 Executive Board of the Fahlberg-List AG, letter of 29 April 1937 to the Magdeburg Nazi Party Head Office. I 53, Nr. 2367. Landesarchiv Sachsen-Anhalt, Magdeburg.
75 F. E. List, letter of 22 June 1937 to the Fahlberg-List AG. I 53, Nr. 2367. Landesarchiv Sachsen-Anhalt, Magdeburg.
76 Fahlberg-List AG, letter of 25 November 1938 to Helene List. I 53, Nr. 2367. Landesarchiv Sachsen-Anhalt, Magdeburg.
77 Reich Office for Genealogical Research, certificate of 4 July 1938 with respect to Helene List. I 53, Nr. 2367. Landesarchiv Sachsen-Anhalt, Madgeburg.
78 Fritz Artl, letter of 1 December 1938 to the Fahlberg-List AG. I 53, Nr. 2367. Landesarchiv Sachsen-Anhalt, Magdeburg.
79 Pabstmann 2019, 285–6.
80 Haase 2018, 40.
81 It seems likely that the double-barrelled name 'Rosenberg-Bernstein' on the back of the painting and which appears in the ERR records was a result of artworks belonging to Rosenberg and to Bernstein being processed at the same time (see https://www.fold3.com/image/306275445, accessed 22 November 2023).
82 Haase 2018, 39.
83 Haase 2018, 40.
84 Haase 2018, 81.
85 https://www.errproject.org/jeudepaume/card_view.php?CardId=14595 (accessed 6 December 2023).
86 Haase 2018, 44–5.
87 Haase 2018, 41.
88 Enderlein 2009.
89 Kunsthalle zu Kiel 2017, 12.
90 Kunsthalle zu Kiel 2017, 13.
91 'Liste der Wertgegenstände des Taganroger Museums für Landeskunde, die der Sowjetunion gehören' (16 August 1949). https://www.fold3.com/image/269932310 (accessed 6 December 2023).
92 Kunsthalle zu Kiel 2017, 13.
93 http://www.lostart.ru/catalog/ru/tom13/2695/3120/72314 (accessed 5 December 2023).
94 Kunsthalle zu Kiel 2017, 14.
95 Kunsthalle zu Kiel 2017, 9.
96 Kunsthalle zu Kiel 2017, 9.
97 Kunsthalle zu Kiel 2017, 10.
98 Kunsthalle zu Kiel 2017, 10.
99 Kunsthalle zu Kiel 2017, 10.
100 Kunsthalle zu Kiel 2017, 11.
101 Kunsthalle zu Kiel 2017, 14.
102 Schuhmacher 2021b.
103 S. J. Phillips, invoice of 5 October 1979. GC/9/3/261. Victoria & Albert Museum Archive, London.
104 Truman 1991, 100.
105 Truman 1991, 100.
106 Sotheby's 1963, lot 296; Sotheby's 1978, lot 23.
107 Inventory of the Maximilian von Goldschmidt-Rothschild Collection (1938). III/5, 47. Institut für Stadtgeschichte, Frankfurt am Main.
108 Bruno Müller, report of 29 March 1946 on the acquisition of the Maximilian von Goldschmidt-Rothschild Collection. Rechneiamt IV/2. Institut für Stadtgeschichte, Frankfurt am Main, 2R-3.

109 Inventory of the Maximilian von Goldschmidt-Rothschild Collection (1938), 14.
110 Frankfurt Customs Investigations Office, freezing order of 24 September 1938 against Maximilian von Goldschmidt-Rothschild. Nr. 519/3. Hessisches Hauptstaatsarchiv, Wiesbaden, 1.
111 Frankfurt Customs Investigations Office, freezing order, 2.
112 Alexander Berg, statement of 8 March 1946 with respect to the acquisition of the Maximilian von Goldschmidt-Rothschild Collection. Rechneiamt, IV/2. Institut für Stadtgeschichte, Frankfurt am Main, 57.
113 Berg, statement of 8 March 1946, 58.
114 Berg, statement of 8 March 1946, 58.
115 Müller, report of 29 March 1946, 4.
116 Müller, report of 29 March 1946, 4R.
117 Index card with respect to the Maximilian von Goldschmidt-Rothschild Collection (no. 405), received from Katharina Weiler on 26 July 2018. Museum Angewandte Kunst, Frankfurt am Main. On the sale of the Maximilian von Goldschmidt-Rothschild Collection, see Weiler 2019.
118 Hans Bräutigam, receipt of 3 February with respect to items from the Maximilian von Goldschmidt-Rothschild Collection. Kulturamt 777. Institut für Stadtgeschichte, Frankfurt am Main, 177.
119 S. J. Phillips, invoice of 6 November 1973. GC/9/3/261. Victoria and Albert Museum Archives, London.
120 Inventory cards nos. 10199 and 10200, received from Mary Levkoff on 24 July 2018. Hearst Castle, San Simeon, California.
121 Arnsberg 1983, 160–1.
122 Memo of 25 September 1964 with respect to J&S Goldschmidt, 2. VV 6240-93/18. Bundesamt für zentrale Dienste und offene Vermögensfragen, Berlin.
123 Arthur Goldschmidt, affidavit of 19 February 1957, 1. VV 6240-93/18. Bundesamt für zentrale Dienste und offene Vermögensfragen, Berlin.
124 H. Delliehausen, receipt of 7 March 1935. VV 6240-93/18. Bundesamt für zentrale Dienste und offene Vermögensfragen, Berlin; Helene Goldschmidt, letter of 23 November 1948 to the Bad Nauheim Central Registration Office. Bundesamt für zentrale Dienste und offene Vermögensfragen, Berlin.
125 Inventory cards nos. 10199 and 10200, Hearst Castle.
126 Memo of 25 September 1964 with respect to J&S Goldschmidt, 1.
127 Reich Chamber of Fine Arts, letter of 18 November 1937 to Arthur Goldschmidt. VV 6240-93/18. Bundesamt für zentrale Dienste und Offene Vermögensfragen.
128 Memo of 25 September 1964 with respect to J&S Goldschmidt, 2.
129 Anne-Marie Goldschmidt, affidavit of 21 January 1967, 2. VV 6240-93. Bundesamt für zentrale Dienste und offene Vermögensfragen, Berlin.
130 Anne-Marie Goldschmidt, affidavit, 2.
131 Anne-Marie Goldschmidt, affidavit, 3.
132 Arthur Goldschmidt, affidavit, 2.
133 S. J. Phillips, invoice of 14 April 1987. GC/9/3/263. Victoria and Albert Museum Archives, London.
134 Löwe 1975, 102.
135 Frauberger 1913, vii–viii.
136 Frauberger 1913, 41.
137 Abeler 1977, 188.
138 Wiesbaden Compensation Office, decision with respect to the claim submitted by Claire Fraenkel, 1960, pp. 297–8. Abt. 518, Nr. 29644. Hessisches Hauptstaatsarchiv, Wiesbaden.
139 Claire Fraenkel, Appendix I, 1958, pp. 203–4. Abt. 518, Nr. 29644. Hessisches Hauptstaatsarchiv, Wiesbaden.
140 Wiesbaden Compensation Office, decision, 297.
141 Frankfurt (Main)-Ost Finance Office, demand for payment of 21 December 1938 with respect to the Jewish Capital Levy. Abt. 518, Nr. 29644. Hessisches Hauptstaatsarchiv, Wiesbaden.
142 Friedrich Fraenkel, restitution claim of 1 November 1948 submitted to the Central Filing Agency Bad Nauheim. 095019. Bundesamt für zentrale Dienste und offene Vermögensfragen, Berlin.

143 Frankfurt (Main)-Ost Finance Office, demand for payment of the Reich Flight Tax of 18 January 1939 addressed to Friedrich Fraenkel. Abt. 518, Nr. 29644. Hessisches Hauptstaatsarchiv, Wiesbaden.

144 Friedrich Fraenkel, inventory of 2 January 1939. Abt. 518, Nr. 1452. Hessisches Hauptstaatsarchiv, Wiesbaden.

145 Frankfurt am Main Office for Property Control and Compensation, decision of 19 May 1953 with respect to Friedrich and Klara Fraenkel. VV 6240-118-18. Bundesamt für zentrale Dienste und offene Vermögensfragen, Berlin.

146 Denise Paraz, affidavit of 16 November 1961. VV 66240-11818. Bundesamt für zentrale Dienste und offene Vermögensfragen, Berlin.

147 Claire Fraenkel, affidavit of 2 September 1957. Abt. 518, Nr. 29644. Hessisches Hauptstaatsarchiv, Wiesbaden.

148 Honorine Lathier, affidavit of 22 August 1953. Abt. 518, Nr. 29644. Hessisches Hauptstaatsarchiv, Wiesbaden.

149 Claire Fraenkel, affidavit.

150 Georges Fleury, affidavit of 1 September 1957. Abt. 518, Nr. 29644. Hessisches Hauptstaatsarchiv, Wiesbaden.

151 Claire Fraenkel, affidavit.

152 Claire Fraenkel, affidavit.

153 The archival research guides on the website of the ERR Project also provide vital orientation: https://www.errproject.org/guide.php (accessed 23 November 2023).

154 Yvonne Mundt, interview on the Federal Office for Central Services and Unresolved Property Issues conducted by Jacques Schuhmacher, 5 April 2022.

155 Mundt, interview, 2022.

156 Martin Luchterhandt, interview on the Landesarchiv Berlin conducted by Jacques Schuhmacher, 29 March 2022.

Published sources and bibliography

Abeler, Jürgen. 1977. *Meister der Uhrmacherkunst*. Wuppertal: Uhrenmuseum.

Adam, Uwe Dietrich. 2003. *Judenpolitik im Dritten Reich*. Düsseldorf: Droste.

Aktives Museum Faschismus und Widerstand in Berlin. 2011. *Gute Geschäfte: Kunsthandel in Berlin 1933–1945. Ausstellung des Aktiven Museums im Centrum Judaicum (10. April–31. Juli 2011) und im Landesarchiv Berlin (20. Oktober 2011–27. Januar 2012)*. Berlin: Aktives Museum Faschismus und Widerstand in Berlin.

Albright, Madeleine. 1999. 'Keynote address'. In *Proceedings of the Washington Conference on Holocaust-Era Assets (November 30–December 3, 1998)*, edited by US Department of State, 29–33. Washington, DC: Government Printing Office.

Alexander, Edward P., and Mary Alexander. 2008. *Museums in Motion: An introduction to the history and functions of museums*. 2nd ed. Plymouth: AlaMira.

Alexander, M. Darsie, and Sam Sackeroff, eds. 2021. *Afterlives: Recovering the lost stories of looted art*. New Haven, CT: Yale University Press.

Alker-Windbichler, Stefan, Bruno Bauer and Markus Stumpf. 2017. *NS-Provenienzforschung und Restitution an Bibliotheken*. Berlin: De Gruyter Sauer.

American Commission for the Protection and Salvage of Artistic and Historic Monuments in War Areas. 1946. *Report of the American Commission for the Protection and Salvage of Artistic and Historic Monuments in War Areas*. Washington, DC: Government Printing Office.

Andratschke, Claudia, and Maik Jachens, eds. 2020. *Nach dem Erstcheck: Provenienzforschung nachhaltig vermitteln. Eine Dokumentation der Tagung 'Nach dem Erstcheck – Provenienzforschung nachhaltig vermitteln' am 4.11.2019 im StadtMuseum Einbeck*. Hannover: Netzwerk Provenienzforschung in Niedersachsen.

Arbeitskreis Provenienzforschung. 2018. *Leitfaden zur Standardisierung von Provenienzangaben*. Hamburg: Arbeitskreis Provenienzforschung. https://www.arbeitskreis-provenienzforschung.org/wp-content/uploads/2022/10/Leitfaden_APFeV_online.pdf (accessed 6 December 23).

Arendt, Hannah. 1964. *Eichmann in Jerusalem: Ein Bericht von der Banalität des Bösen*. Munich: Piper.

Arnsberg, Paul. 1983. *Die Geschichte der Frankfurter Juden seit der Französischen Revolution*, vol. 3. Darmstadt: Eduard Roether.

Artinger, Kai. 2020. *Das Kunstmuseum Stuttgart im Nationalsozialismus: Der Traum vom Museum 'Schwäbischer' Kunst*. Cologne: Wienand.

Arts Council England. 2022. *Restitution and Repatriation: A practical guide for museums in England*. London: Arts Council England. https://www.artscouncil.org.uk/supporting-arts-museums-and-libraries/supporting-collections-and-cultural-property/restitution-and (accessed 6 December 2023).

Association of Art Museum Directors. 1998. 'Report of the Association of Art Museum Directors (AAMD) Task Force on the Spoliation of Art during the Nazi/World War II Era (1933–1945), June 4, 1998'. https://aamd.org/sites/default/files/document/Report%20on%20the%20Spoliation%20of%20Nazi%20Era%20Art.pdf (accessed 6 December 2023).

Bach, Christine, and Caroline Lange. 2018. '"Sieben Kisten mit jüdischem Material": Der Raub der Judaica in Unterfranken 1938'. In *'Sieben Kisten mit jüdischem Material': Von Raub und Wiederentdeckung 1938 bis heute*, edited by Jüdisches Museum München and Museum für Franken in Würzburg, 91–104. Berlin/Leipzig: Hentrich & Hentrich.

Baensch, Tanja. 2016. 'Einführung'. In *Museen im Nationalsozialismus: Akteure – Orte – Politik*, edited by Tanja Baensch, Kristina Kratz-Kessemeier and Dorothee Wimmer, 11–19. Cologne/Weimar/Vienna: Böhlau.

Bähr, Astrid. 2014. *German Sales 1930–1945: Bibliographie der Auktionskataloge aus Deutschland, Österreich und der Schweiz*. Berlin: Kunstbibliothek/Staatliche Museen zu Berlin. http://archiv.ub.uni-heidelberg.de/artdok/volltexte/2013/2251 (accessed 6 December 23).

Bajohr, Frank. 2000. '"Arisierung" als gesellschaftlicher Prozeß: Verhalten, Strategien und Handlungsspielräume jüdischer Eigentümer und "arischer" Erwerber'. In *'Arisierung' im Nationalsozialismus: Volksgemeinschaft, Raub und Gedächtnis*, edited by Irmtrud Wojak and Peter Hayes, 15–30. Frankfurt am Main/New York: Campus.

Bajohr, Frank. 2002. *'Aryanisation' in Hamburg: The economic exclusion of Jews and the confiscation of their property in Nazi Germany*. New York/Oxford: Berghahn.

Baresel-Brand, Andrea. 2005. 'Verantwortung wahrgenommen: Die Koordinierungsstelle für Kulturgutverluste'. In *Verluste: Kulturgutverluste, Provenienzforschung, Restitution. Sammlungsgut mit belasteter Herkuft in Museen, Bibliotheken und Archiven*, edited by Landesstelle für die nichtstaatlichen Museen in Bayern, 59–66. Munich/Berlin: Deutscher Kunstverlag.

Barkai, Avraham. 1988. *Vom Boykott zur 'Entjudung': Der wirtschaftliche Existenzkampf der Juden im Dritten Reich 1933–1945*. Frankfurt am Main: Fischer.

Benz, Wolfgang. 2010. *'Der ewige Jude': Metaphern und Methoden nationalsozialistischer Propaganda*. Berlin: Metropol.

Bernsau, Tanja. 2013. *Die Besatzer als Kuratoren? Der Central Collecting Point Wiesbaden als Drehscheibe für den Wiederaufbau der Museumslandschaft nach 1945*. Berlin/Münster: Lit.

Bernsau, Tanja. 2016. *Spione für den Kulturgüterschutz: Die Art Looting Investigation Unit*. Saarbrücken: Akademikerverlag.

Bertz, Inka, and Michael Dorrmann. 2008. *Raub und Restitution: Kulturgut aus jüdischem Besitz von 1933 bis heute*. Göttingen: Wallstein.

Bevins, Richard. 1999. 'Britain and the restitution of art looted from occupied countries during the Second World War'. In *Proceedings of the Washington Conference on Holocaust-Era Assets (November 30–December 3, 1998)*, edited by US Department of State, 503–11. Washington, DC: Government Printing Office.

Botsch, Gideon. 2008. 'Raub zum Zweck der Gegnerforschung'. In *Raub und Restitution: Kulturgut aus jüdischem Besitz von 1933 bis heute*, edited by Inka Bertz and Michael Dorrmann, 91–8. Göttingen: Wallstein.

Brenner, Hildegard. 1963. *Die Kunstpolitik im Nationalsozialismus*. Reinbek: Rowohlt.

Briel, Cornelia. 2013. *Beschlagnahmt, erpresst, erbeutet: NS-Raubgut, Reichstauschstelle und Preußische Staatsbibliothek zwischen 1933 und 1945*. Munich: Akademie.

Bureau Central des Restitutions, ed. 1947–9. *Répertoire des biens spoliés en France durant la guerre, 1939–1945*. Berlin.

Burleigh, Michael. 1995. *Death and Deliverance: 'Euthanasia' in Germany 1900–1945*. Cambridge: Cambridge University Press.

Burleigh, Michael, and Wolfgang Wippermann. 1991. *The Racial State: Germany 1933–45*. Cambridge: Cambridge University Press.

Cesarani, David. 2016. *Final Solution: The fate of the Jews 1933–49*. London: Macmillan.

Christie's, ed. 1983. *Important Gold Boxes: Auction in Geneva, 10 May 1983*. Geneva: Christie's.

Cohen, Julie-Marthe, Felicitas Heimann-Jelinek and Ruth Jolanda Weinberger. 2019. *Handbook on Judaica Provenance Research: Ceremonial objects*. New York: Conference on Jewish Material Claims Against Germany. https://art.claimscon.org/wp-content/uploads//2019/09/Judaica-Handbook_17-Sep-2019.pdf (accessed 6 December 2023).

Commission for Looted Art in Europe. 2011. 'Introduction to the National Archives' records on Nazi-era looted cultural property, 1939–1961'. London: National Archives. https://cdn.nationalarchives.gov.uk/documents/records/looted-art-in-depth-intro.pdf (accessed 6 December 2023).

Conze, Eckart, and Bernd Reifenberg, eds. 2006. *Displaced Books: NS-Raubgut in der Universitätsbibliothek Marburg*. Marburg: Universitätsbibliothek Marburg.

Daub, Ute. 1999. 'Die Stadt Frankfurt am Main macht sich "judenfrei": Zur Konzentrierung, Verbannung und Ghettoisierung der jüdischen Bevölkerung zwischen 1938 und 1943'. In *'Nach der Kristallnacht': Jüdisches Leben und antijüdische Politik in Frankfurt am Main 1938–1945*, edited by Monica Kingreen, 319–56. Frankfurt am Main/New York: Campus.

Davidson, Douglas. 2015. 'Just and fair solutions: A view from the United States'. In *Fair and Just Solutions? Alternatives to litigation in Nazi-looted art disputes. Status quo and new developments*, edited by Evelien Campfens, 91–101. The Hague: Eleven.

Dean, Martin. 2008. *Robbing the Jews: The confiscation of Jewish property in the Holocaust 1933–1945*. Cambridge: Cambridge University Press.

Deinert, Juliane. 2011. 'Bücher von politisch und rassisch verfolgten: Walter Heise'. In *NS-Raub- und Beutegut an der SUB Göttingen*, edited by Nicole Bartels, Juliane Deinert, Wilfried Enderle, Helmut Rohlfing and Frank Möbus, 50–5. Göttingen: Universitätsverlag Göttingen.

Deutsches Zentrum Kulturgutverluste, ed. 2019. *Provenienzforschung in deutschen Sammlungen: Einblicke in zehn Jahre Projektförderung*. Berlin: De Gruyter.

Edsel, Robert M. 2009. *Monuments Men: Allied heroes, Nazi thieves, and the greatest treasure hunt in history*. New York: Center Street.

Eizenstat, Stuart E. 1997. 'Introduction'. In *US and Allied Efforts to Recover and Restore Gold and other Assets Stolen or Hidden by Germans during World War II*, edited by US Department of State, i–xii. Washington, DC: Government Printing Office.

Eizenstat, Stuart E. 1999. 'Concluding statement: United States'. In *Proceedings of the Washington Conference on Holocaust-Era Assets (November 30–December 3, 1998)*, edited by US Department of State, 125–32. Washington, DC: Government Printing Office.

Eizenstat, Stuart E. 2003. *Imperfect Justice: Looted assets, slave labour, and the unfinished business of World War II*. New York: Public Affairs.

Enderlein, Angelika. 2006. *Der Berliner Kunsthandel in der Weimarer Republik und im NS-Staat: Zum Schicksal der Sammlung Graetz*. Berlin: Akademie.

Enderlein, Angelika. 2009. 'Introduction of the new database of the "Central Collecting Point Munich" (MCCP)'. In *Holocaust Era Assets: Conference Proceedings, Prague, 26–30 June 2009*, edited by Jiří Schneider, Jakub Klepal and Irena Kalhousová, 908–28. Prague: Forum 2000 Foundation.

Eßl, Julia. 2015. 'Die Sammlung Feldmann: Spuren – Fragmente – Dokumente. Wege einer Rekonstruktion'. In *Spurensuche: Die Sammlung Arthur Feldmann und die Albertina*, edited by Achim Gnann and Heinz Schödl, 9–23. Vienna/Cologne/Weimar: Böhlau.

Eßl, Julia. 2020. '"[…] wie sich das Schicksal unserer Sammlung endgültig gestaltet". Die Sammlung Heumann, Chemnitz'. In *Eigentum verpflichtet: Eine Kunstsammlung auf dem Prüfstand*, edited by Claudia Emmert, Ina Neddermeyer and Mark Niehoff, 150–61. Berlin: Neofelis.

Estreicher, Karol. 1944. *Cultural Losses of Poland: Index of Polish cultural losses during the German occupation, 1939–1944*. London: n.p.

Evans, Richard J. 2003. *The Coming of the Third Reich*. London: Allen Lane.

Evans, Richard J. 2005. *The Third Reich in Power*. London: Allen Lane.

Evans, Richard J. 2008. *The Third Reich at War*. London: Allen Lane.

Farmer, Walter I. 2000. *The Safekeepers: A memoir of the arts at the end of World War II*. Berlin: Walter de Gruyter.

Feigenbaum, Gail, and Inge Reist, eds. 2012. *Provenance: An alternate history of art*. Los Angeles: Getty Research Institute.

Fiedler, Wilfried. 2000. 'Die Alliierte (Londoner) Erklärung vom 5.1.1943: Inhalt, Auslegung und Rechtsnatur in der Diskussion der Nachkriegsjahre'. In *Private Law in the International Arena: From national conflict rules towards harmonization and unification*, edited by Jürgen Badedow, Isaak Meier, Anton K. Schnyder, Talia Einhorn and Daniel Girsberger, 197–216. The Hague: T.M.C. Asser Press.

Finkenberger, Martin. 2008. '"Während meines ganzen Lebens habe ich die Juden erforscht, wie ein Bakteriologe einen gefährlichen Bazillus studiert": Johann von Leers (1902–1965) als antisemitischer Propagandaexperte bis 1945'. *Bulletin des Deutschen Historischen Instituts Moskau* 2: 88–99.

Fischer, Torben, and Matthias N. Lorenz, eds. 2015. *Lexion der 'Vergangenheitsbewältigung' in Deutschland: Debatten- und Diskursgeschichte des Nationalsozialismus nach 1945*. 3rd ed. Bielefeld: Transcript.

Fisher, Wesley A., and Ruth Weinberger. 2014. 'Holocaust-era looted art: A current world-wide overview'. https://art.claimscon.org/wp-content/uploads/2014/11/Worldwide-Overview.pdf (accessed 6 December 2023).

Frauberger, Heinrich. 1913. *N.R. Fränkel's Uhrensammlung*. Düsseldorf: Schmitz & Olbertz.

Friedenberger, Martin. 2008. *Fiskalische Ausplünderung: Die Berliner Steuer- und Finanzverwaltung und die jüdische Bevölkerung 1933–1945*. Berlin: Metropol.

Friedländer, Saul. 1998. *Nazi Germany and the Jews: The years of persecution 1933–1939*. New York: Harper Perennial.

Fuhrmeister, Christian, and Meike Hopp. 2019. 'Rethinking provenance research'. *Getty Research Journal* 11 (1): 213–31.

Genschel, Helmut. 1980. *Die Verdrängung der Juden aus der Wirtschaft im Dritten Reich*. Berlin/Frankfurt am Main: Haag und Herchen.

Geschichtswerkstatt Offenbach. 2011. *Fast vergessen: Das amerikanische Bücherdepot in Offenbach am Main von 1945 bis 1949*. Offenbach am Main: Offenbacher Edition.

Golenia, Patrick, Kristina Kratz-Kessemeier and Isabelle Le Masne de Chermont. 2016. *Paul Graupe (1881–1953): Ein Berliner Kunsthändler zwischen Republik, Nationalsozialismus und Exil*. Cologne/Weimar/Vienna: Böhlau.

Goodman, Simon. 2015. *The Orpheus Clock: The search for my family's art treasures stolen by the Nazis*. Melbourne: Scribe.

Goschler, Constantin. 2007. 'Jewish property and the politics of restitution in Germany after 1945'. In *Robbery and Restitution: The conflict over Jewish property in Europe*, edited by Martin Dean, Constantin Goschler and Philipp Ther, 113–33. New York/Oxford: Berghahn.

Gritzbach, Erich, ed. 1939. *Hermann Göring: Reden und Aufsätze*. 3rd ed. Munich: Zentralverlag der NSDAP.

Gruner, Wolf, ed. 2019. *The Persecution and Murder of the European Jews by Nazi Germany 1933–45*, vol. 1. Oldenbourg: De Gruyter.

Haase, Sven. 2018. 'Der Kunstraub der Nationalsozialisten in Frankreich: Werke im Museum Berggruen'. In *Biografien der Bilder: Provenienzen im Museum Berggruen*, edited by Petra Winter, Doris Kachel and Sven Haase, 36–49. Berlin: Deutscher Kunstverlag.

Haidemann, Anita, and Judith Rauser, eds. 2022. *The Collector Curt Glaser: From champion of modernism to refugee*. Berlin/Munich: Deutscher Kunstverlag.

Hartmann, Uwe. 2005. 'Das Internetportal www.lostart.de: Ziele und Möglichkeiten'. In *Verluste: Kulturgutverluste, Provenienzforschung, Restitution. Sammlungsgut mit belasteter Herkuft in Museen, Bibliotheken und Archiven*, edited by Landesstelle für die nichtstaatlichen Museen in Bayern, 67–77. Munich/Berlin: Deutscher Kunstverlag.

Haupt, Herbert. 'Die Rolle des Kunsthistorischen Museums bei der Beschlagnahme, Bergung und Rückführung von Kunstgut in den Jahren 1938–1945'. In *Kunstraub, Kunstbergung und Restitution in Österreich 1938 bis heute*, edited by Theodor Brückler, 53–75. Vienna/Cologne/Weimar: Böhlau.

Heidt, Sheila. 2017. *Restitutionsbegehren bei NS-Raubkunst: Praxisleitfaden zur Handreichung zur Umsetzung der 'Erklärung der Bundesregierung, der Länder und der kommunalen Spitzenverbände zur Auffindung und zur Rückgabe NS-verfolgungsbedingt entzogenen Kulturgutes, insbesondere aus jüdischem Besitz'*. Berlin: Duncker & Humblot.

Heim, Susanne, ed. 2019. *The Persecution and Murder of the European Jews by Nazi Germany 1933–45*, vol. 2. Oldenbourg: De Gruyter.

Helbing, Hugo, ed. 1937. *Sammlungen und Kunstwerke aus rheinischem und süddeutschen Besitz: Versteigerung am 11., 12. und 13. Mai 1937*. Frankfurt am Main: Hugo Helbing.

Hemke, Christina. 2018. 'Der Einsatzstab Reichsleiter Rosenberg und die "M-Aktion"'. In *Im Schatten des totalen Krieges: Raubgut, Kriegsgefangschaft und Zwangsarbeit*, edited by Christina Hemke and Karl-Heinz Ziessow, 185–96. Cloppenburg: Stiftung Museumsdorf Cloppenburg.

Herf, Jeffrey. 2009. *The Jewish Enemy: Nazi propaganda during World War II and the Holocaust.* Cambridge, MA: Harvard University Press.

Herman, Alexander. 2021. *Restitution: The return of cultural artefacts.* London: Lund Humphries.

Heuss, Anja. 2000. *Kunst- und Kulturgutraub: Eine vergleichende Studie zur Besatzungspolitik der Nationalsozialisten in Frankreich und der Sowjetunion.* Heidelberg: Universitätsverlag C. Winter.

Heuss, Anja. 2008a. 'Das Testament von Emma Budge'. In *Raub und Restitution: Kulturgut aus jüdischem Besitz von 1933 bis heute*, edited by Inka Bertz and Michael Dorrmann, 83–90. Göttingen: Wallstein.

Heuss, Anja. 2008b. 'Die Sammlung Littmann und die Aktion "Entartete Kunst"'. In *Raub und Restitution: Kulturgut aus jüdischem Besitz von 1933 bis heute*, edited by Inka Bertz and Michael Dorrmann, 69–74. Göttingen: Wallstein.

Holzhausen, Walter. 1935. *Johann Christian Neuber: Ein sächsischer Meister des 18. Jahrhunderts.* Dresden: C. Heinrich.

Hoogewoud, F. J. 1992. 'The Nazi looting of books and its American "antithesis": Selected pictures from the Offenbach Archival Depot's photographic history and its supplement'. *Studia Rosenthaliana* 26 (1/2): 158–92.

Hopp, Meike. 2012. *Kunsthandel im Nationalsozialismus: Adolf Weinmüller in München und Wien.* Cologne/Weimar/Vienna: Böhlau.

Hoppe, Jens. 2002. *Jüdische Geschichte und Kultur in Museen: Zur nichtjüdischen Museologie des Jüdischen in Deutschland.* Münster: Waxmann.

Hördler, Stefan. 2020. 'Administered plundering. dispossession and corruption in the concentration camp system'. In *Dispossession: Plundering German Jewry, 1933–1953*, edited by Christoph Kreutzmüller and Jonathan R. Zatlin, 236–59. Ann Arbor: University of Michigan Press.

Howe, Thomas C. 1946. *Salt Mines and Castles: The discovery and restitution of looted European art.* New York: Bobbs-Merrill.

Huemer, Christian. 2014. 'The "German Sales 1930–1945" database project'. *Collections: A journal for museum and archives professionals* 10 (3): 273–8.

Hüneke, Andreas. 1997. 'Fischers Liste: Die kunsthistorische Forschung und die "Entartete Kunst". Zu dem Fund in London'. *Frankfurter Allgemeine Zeitung*, 9 May 1997, 33.

Hüneke, Andreas. 2007. 'Die "Verwertung" der "entarteten" Kunst zwischen Ideologie und Kommerz'. In *Museen im Zwielicht: Ankaufspolitik 1933–1945. Die eigene Geschichte*, edited by Koordinierungsstelle für Kulturgutverluste Magdeburg, 81–8. Magdeburg: Koordinierungsstelle für Kulturgutverluste.

Hüneke, Andreas, and Mario-Andreas von Lüttichau. 1998. 'Rekonstruktion der Ausstellung "Entartete Kunst" (München, 19. Juli–30. November 1937)'. In *Die 'Kunststadt' München 1937: Nationalsozialismus und 'Entartete Kunst'*, edited by Peter-Klaus Schuster, 120–82. Munich: Prestel.

Jenkins, Paul. 2015. 'Independent review of the Spoliation Advisory Panel'. London: Department for Culture, Media and Sport. https://assets.publishing.service.gov.uk/government/uploads/system/uploads/attachment_data/file/415966/SAP_-_Final_Report.pdf (accessed 6 December 2023).

Jeuthe, Gesa. 2007. 'Die Moderne unter dem Hammer: Zur "Verwertung" der "entarteten" Kunst durch die Luzerner Galerie Fischer 1939'. In *Angriff auf die Avantgarde: Kunst und Kunstpolitik im Nationalsozialismus*, edited by Uwe Fleckner, 189–305. Berlin: De Gruyter.

Kaplan, Marion A. 1998. *Between Dignity and Despair: Jewish life in Nazi Germany.* Oxford: Oxford University Press.

Karrels, Nancy. 2019. 'Exhibiting provenance in the university museum: A case study'. In *Collecting and Provenance: A multidisciplinary approach*, edited by Jane Milosch and Nick Pearce, 87–99. Lanham, MD: Rowman & Littlefield.

Kenzler, Marcus. 2014. 'Die "Arisierung" jüdischen Eigentums in Oldenburg: Der Fall Rosalie Israels'. In *Oldenburger Jahrbuch*, edited by Natur- und Heimatkunde e.V. Oldenburger Landesverein für Geschichte, 133–46. Oldenburg: Isensee Verlag.

Kocourek, Jana, Katja Lindenau, Ilse von zur Mühlen and Johanna Poltermann. 2019. 'Methods of provenance research'. In *Provenance Research Manual to Identify Cultural Property Seized due to Persecution during the National Socialist Era*, edited by Deutsches Zentrum Kulturgutverluste, 39–51. Magdeburg: Deutsches Zentrum Kulturgutverluste. https://kulturgutverluste.de/sites/default/files/2023-06/Manual.pdf (accessed 6 December 2023).

Krejčová, Helena. 2019. *Navracení Identity – Returning Identity*. Prague: Centrum pro dokumentaci majetkových převodů kulturních statků obětí II.

Kugel, Alexis. 2012. *Gold, Jasper and Carnelian: Johann Christian Neuber at the Saxon court*. London: Paul Holberton.

Kugelmann, Cilly, ed. 2006. *Heimat und Exil: Emigration der deutschen Juden nach 1933*. Frankfurt am Main: Jüdischer Verlag im Suhrkamp Verlag.

Kuller, Christiane. 2013. *Bürokratie und Verbrechen*. Munich: Oldenbourg Wissenschaftsverlag.

Kunsthalle Mannheim, ed. 2020. *(Wieder)-Entdecken: Die Kunsthalle 1933 bis 1945 und die Folgen*. Berlin: Deutscher Kunstverlag.

Kunsthalle zu Kiel. 2017. *Provenienzforschung an der Kunsthalle zu Kiel: Gemälde und Skulpturen*. Kiel: Kunsthalle zu Kiel. https://www.kunsthalle-kiel.de/file/dossier_provenienzforschung_gemaelde_skulpturen.pdf (accessed 6 December 2023).

Kurtz, Michael J. 2006. *America and the Return of Nazi Contraband: The recovery of Europe's cultural treasures*. Cambridge: Cambridge University Press.

Lange, Hans W., ed. 1939. *Die Sammlung List, Magdeburg: Europäisches Kunstgewerbe des 13. bis 18. Jahrhunderts. Versteigerung am 28., 29. und 30. März 1939*. Berlin: Hans W. Lange.

Langfeld, Gregor, Margriet Schavemaker and Margreeth Soeting, eds. 2015. *The Stedelijk Museum and the Second World War*. Amsterdam: Bas Lubberhuizen.

Lauterbach, Iris. 2018. *The Central Collecting Point in Munich: A new beginning for the restitution and protection of art*. Los Angeles: Getty Research Institute.

Le Masne de Chermont, Isabelle, and Laurence Sigal-Klagsbald, eds. 2008. *À qui appartenaient ces tableaux? La politique française de recherche de provenance de garde et de restitution des oeuvres d'art pillées durant la Seconde Guerre Mondiale*. Paris: Réunion des Musées Nationaux.

Lejeune, Barbara. 2007. 'The effects of online catalogues in London and other museums: A study of an alternative way of access'. *Papers from the Institute of Archaeology* 18 (1): 79–97.

Lewis, Geoffrey. 2016. 'The ICOM Code of Ethics for Museums'. In *Museums, Ethics, and Cultural Heritage*, edited by Bernice L. Murphy, 45–53. Oxford: Routledge.

Liebighaus Skulpturensammlung, ed. 2017. *Eindeutig bis zweifelhaft: Skulpturen und ihre Geschichten*. Frankfurt am Main: Liebieghaus Skulpturensammlung.

Lillteicher, Jürgen. 2007a. *Raub, Recht und Restitution: Die Rückerstattung jüdischen Eigentums in der frühen Bundesrepublik*. Göttingen: Wallstein.

Lillteicher, Jürgen. 2007b. 'West Germany and the restitution of Jewish property in Europe'. In *Robbery and Restitution: The conflict over Jewish property in Europe*, edited by Martin Dean, Constantin Goschler and Philipp Ther, 99–112. New York/Oxford: Berghahn.

Löhr, Hanns Christian. 2009. *Der eiserne Sammler: Die Kollektion Hermann Göring. Kunst und Korruption im 'Dritten Reich'*. Berlin: Gebr. Mann Verlag.

Löhr, Hanns Christian. 2016. *Das Braune Haus der Kunst: Hitler und der 'Sonderauftrag Linz'. Kunstbeschaffung im Nationalsozialismus*. 2nd ed. Berlin: Gebr. Mann Verlag.

Löhr, Hanns Christian. 2018. *Kunst als Waffe: Der Einsatzstab Reichsleiter Rosenberg. Ideologie und Kunstraub im 'Dritten Reich'*. Berlin: Gebr. Mann Verlag.

Longerich, Peter. 2010. *Holocaust: The Nazi persecution and murder of the Jews*. Oxford: Oxford University Press.

Löwe, Regina. 1975. *Die Augsburger Goldschmiedewerkstatt des Matthias Walbaum*. Munich: Deutscher Kunstverlag.

Mallon, MacKenzie. 2022. 'Discriminating thieves: Exhibiting Nazi-era provenance'. *Curator: The Museum Journal* 65 (1): 43–61.

Marck, Annemarie, and Eelke Muller. 2015. 'National panels advising on Nazi-looted art in Austria, France, the United Kingdom, the Netherlands and Germany: A brief overview'. In *Fair and Just Solutions? Alternatives to litigation in Nazi-looted art disputes: Status quo and new developments*, edited by Evelien Campfens, 41–89. The Hague: Eleven.

Masurovsky, Marc. 2020. 'The current state of Nazi-era provenance research, and access to Nazi-era research resources and archives'. In *Provenance Research Today: Principles, practice, problems*, edited by Arthur Tompkins, 136–49. London: Lund Humphries.

Matthes, Olaf, and Christina Ewald. 2017. 'Verbot von Museumsbesuchen für Juden'. In *Hamburger Schlüsseldokumente zur deutsch-jüdischen Geschichte*. https://dx.doi.org/10.23691/jgo:article-200.de.v1.

Mazower, Mark. 2008. *Hitler's Empire: Nazi rule in occupied Europe*. London: Allen Lane.

Meinl, Susanne. 2007. 'Ganz normale Finanzbeamte? Die Verwalter und Verwerter "jüdischen Besitzes"'. In *Vor der Vernichtung: Die staatliche Enteignung der Juden im Nationalsozialismus*, edited by Katharina Stengel, 140–57. Frankfurt am Main/New York: Campus.

Meinl, Susanne, and Jutta Zwilling. 2005. *Legalisierter Raub: Die Ausplünderung der Juden im Nationalsozialismus durch die Reichsfinanzverwaltung in Hessen*. Frankfurt am Main/New York: Campus.

Merz, Miriam Olivia. 2023. 'Provenienz: Sammlung Ernst und Gertrud Flersheim, Frankfurt am Main'. In *Kulturgüter, Provenienzen und Restitution: Objektgeschichten aus Frankfurter Museen, Sammlungen und Bibliotheken*, edited by Franziska Kiermeier, Maike Brüggen and Evelyn Brockhoff, 100–16. Frankfurt am Main: Henrich Editionen.

Metropolitan Museum of Art. 'Collections management policy, approved by the Board of Trustees on May 9, 2023'. https://www.metmuseum.org/-/media/files/about-the-met/policies-and-documents/collections-management-policy/Collections-Management-Policy-May-2023.pdf (accessed 6 December 2023).

Michels, Karen. 2021. *Emma und Henry Budge oder wie Hamburg einmal ein Porzellan-Palais entging*. Göttingen: Wallstein.

Milosch, Jane, and Andrea Hull. 2019. 'Provenance research in museums: From the back of the house to the front'. In *Collecting and Provenance: A multidisciplinary approach*, edited by Jane Milosch and Nick Pearce, 37–60. Lanham, MD: Rowman & Littlefield.

Milosch, Jane, and Nick Pearce, eds. 2019. *Collecting and Provenance: A multidisciplinary approach*. Lanham, MD: Rowman & Littlefield.

Mixon, Marina. 2005. 'Spoliation research in museums and galleries in the United Kingdom'. In *Vitalizing Memory: International perspectives on provenance research*, edited by American Association of Museums, 16–19. Washington, DC: American Association of Museums.

Mommsen, Hans. 1966. *Beamtentum im Dritten Reich*. Stuttgart: Deutsche Verlagsanstalt.

Müller, Wiebke. 2016. 'Das Silber der Hamburger Juden: Eine bis heute währende "Rettungsgeschichte"?' In *Raubkunst? Provenienzforschung zu den Sammlungen des Museum für Kunst und Gewerbe Hamburg*, edited by Sabine Schulze and Silke Reuther, 74–87. Hamburg: Museum für Kunst und Gewerbe Hamburg.

Müller-Kelwing, Karin. 2020. *Zwischen Kunst, Wissenschaft und Politik: Die Staatlichen Sammlungen für Kunst und Wissenschaft in Dresden und ihre Mitarbeiter im Nationalsozialismus*. Vienna/Cologne/Weimar: Böhlau.

Museum Boijmans van Beuningen, ed. 2018. *A Controversial Past: Museum Boijmans van Beuningen and the Second World War*. Rotterdam: Museum Boijmans van Beuningen.

National Archives. 2016. 'OSS Art Looting Investigation Unit Reports'. https://www.archives.gov/research/holocaust/art/oss-art-looting-investigation-unit-reports.html#contents (accessed 6 December 2023).

Network of European Restitution Committees. 2019. *Guide to the Work of the Restitution Committees*. Paris: Network of European Restitution Committees. https://www.provenienzforschung.gv.at/wp-content/uploads/Guide-to-the-work-of-the-Restitution-Committees.pdf (accessed 6 December 2023).

Nicholas, Lynn H. 1995. *The Rape of Europa: The fate of Europe's treasures in the Third Reich and the Second World War*. New York: Vintage.

Nicholas, Lynn H. 1999. 'Presenter statement'. In *Proceedings of the Washington Conference on Holocaust-Era Assets (November 30–December 3, 1998)*, edited by US Department of State, 449–52. Washington, DC: Government Printing Office.

Nietzel, Benno. 2020. 'Restitution, memory and denial: Assessing the legacy of dispossession in postwar Germany'. In *Dispossession: Plundering German Jewry, 1933–1953*, edited by Christoph Kreutzmüller and Jonathan R. Zatlin, 263–81. Ann Arbor: University of Michigan Press.

O'Donnell, Nicholas M. 2017. *A Tragic Fate: Law and ethics in the battle over Nazi-looted art*. Chicago: Ankerwycke.

O'Donnell, Nicholas M. 2021. 'United States of America'. In *Museums and the Holocaust*, edited by Ruth Redmond-Cooper, 229–53. 2nd ed. Builth Wells: Institute of Art and Law.
Osterloh, Jörg. 2000. *'Ausschaltung der Juden und des jüdischen Geistes': Nationalsozialistische Kulturpolitik 1920–1945*. Frankfurt am Main: Campus.
Paas, Sigrun. 1983. 'Verfolgt und verführt: Kunst unterm Hakenkreuz in Hamburg, 1933–1945'. In *Verfolgt und verführt: Kunst unterm Hakenkreuz in Hamburg, 1933–1945*, edited by Hamburger Kunsthalle, 11–20. Marburg: Jonas.
Pabstmann, Sven. 2019. 'Die Sammlung des Chemiefabrikanten Dr Adolf List in Magdeburg: Provenienzforschung zu Kunstgewerbe im Bremer Focke-Museum'. In *Provenienzforschung in deutschen Sammlungen: Einblicke in zehn Jahre Projektförderung*, edited by Deutsches Zentrum Kulturgutverluste, 281–8. Berlin: De Gruyter.
Palmer, Norman. 2000. *Museums and the Holocaust*. Leicester: Institute of Art and Law.
Paver, Chloe E. M. 2018. *Exhibiting the Nazi Past: Museum objects between the material and the immaterial*. Basingstoke: Palgrave Macmillan.
Pearson, David. 2019. *Provenance Research in Book History: A handbook*. Oxford: Bodleian Library/Oak Knoll Press.
Perschke, Reena. 2016. 'Zwischen Kollaboration und Widerstand: Die Museen von Carnac und Vannes während der Besatzung der Bretagne 1940–1944'. In *Museen im Nationalsozialismus: Akteure – Orte – Politik*, edited by Tanja Baensch, Kristina Kratz-Kessemeier and Dorothee Wimmer, 323–38. Cologne/Weimar/Vienna: Böhlau.
Peters, Olaf, ed. 2014a. *Degenerate Art: The attack on modern art in Nazi Germany, 1937*. Munich/London/New York: Prestel Verlag.
Peters, Olaf. 2014b. 'Genesis, conception, and consequences: The "Entartete Kunst" exhibition in Munich in 1937'. In *Degenerate Art: The attack on modern art in Nazi Germany, 1937*, edited by Olaf Peters, 106–25. Munich/London/New York: Prestel Verlag.
Petropoulos, Jonathan. 1996. *Art as Politics in the Third Reich*. Chapel Hill: University of North Carolina Press.
Petropoulos, Jonathan. 1999. 'Art looting during the Third Reich: An overview with recommendations for further research'. In *Proceedings of the Washington Conference on Holocaust-Era Assets (November 30–December 3, 1998)*, edited by US Department of State, 441–8. Washington, DC: Government Printing Office.
Petropoulos, Jonathan. 2000. *The Faustian Bargain: The art world in Nazi Germany*. London: Allen Lane.
Piper, Ernst. 2005. *Alfred Rosenberg: Hitlers Chefideologe*. Munich: Blessing.
Ploil, Ernst. 2014. 'The "Entartete Kunst" exhibitions in Austria'. In *Degenerate Art: The attack on modern art in Nazi Germany, 1937*, edited by Olaf Peters, 126–35. Munich/London/New York: Prestel Verlag.
Pross, Christian. 2001. *Wiedergutmachung: Der Kleinkrieg gegen die Opfer*. Berlin: Philo.
Rabinbach, Anson, and Sander L. Gilman, eds. 2013. *The Third Reich Sourcebook*. Berkeley: University of California Press.
Redmond-Cooper, Ruth, ed. 2021. *Museums and the Holocaust*. 2nd ed. Builth Wells: Institute of Art and Law.
Reed, Victoria. 2013. 'Due diligence, provenance research, and the acquisition process at the Museum of Fine Arts, Boston'. *DePaul Journal of Art, Technology & Intellectual Property Law* 23 (2): 363–73.
Reinhardt, Georg, ed. 1996. *Im Malstrom des Lebens versunken: Elfriede Lohse-Wächtler, 1899–1940. Leben und Werk*. Cologne: Wienand.
Reininghaus, Alexandra, ed. 2009. *Recollecting: Raub und Restitution*. Vienna: Passagen-Verlag.
Rorimer, James J. 1950. *Survival: The salvage and protection of art in war*. New York: Abelard Press.
Safrian, Hans. 2000. 'Expediting expropriation and expulsion: The impact of the "Vienna model" on anti-Jewish policies in Nazi Germany, 1938'. *Holocaust and Genocide Studies* 14 (3): 390–414.
Safrian, Hans, and Hans Witek. 2008. *Und keiner war dabei: Dokumente des alltäglichen Antisemitismus in Wien 1938*. Vienna: Picus Verlag.
Schilde, Kurt, Rolf Scholz and Sylvia Walleczek. 1996. *SA-Gefängnis Papestraße: Spuren und Zeugnisse*. Berlin: Overall Verlag.

Schoenmakers, Christine. 2020. 'The "legal" theft of Jewish assets: The German Gold Discount Bank (Dego)'. In *Dispossession: Plundering German Jewry, 1933–1953*, edited by Christoph Kreutzmüller and Jonathan R. Zatlin, 71–103. Ann Arbor: University of Michigan Press.

Schuhmacher, Jacques. 2021a. 'British museums and Nazi-era provenance research'. In *Museums and the Holocaust*, edited by Ruth Redmond-Cooper, 34–50. 2nd ed. Builth Wells: Institute of Art and Law.

Schuhmacher, Jacques. 2021b. 'Concealed histories: Researching Nazi looting in the Gilbert Collection'. In *Masterpieces in Miniature: Treasures from the Rosalinde and Arthur Gilbert Collection*, edited by Alice Minter, 100–5. London: V&A Publishing.

Schultze-Naumburg, Paul. 1928. *Kunst und Rasse*. Munich: Lehmann.

Schwarz, Birgit. 2018. *Hitlers Sonderauftrag Ostmark: Kunstraub und Museumspolitik im Nationalsozialismus*. Vienna/Cologne/Weimar: Böhlau Verlag.

Schwärzler, Monika. 2000. 'Objekte wie du und ich: Anmerkungen zu Arno Gisingers fotografischer Präsentation von Objekten'. In *InventArisiert: Enteignung von Möbeln aus jüdischem Besitz*, edited by Ilsebill Barta-Fliedl and Herbert Posch, 54–63. Vienna: Turia+Kant.

Smyth, Craig Hugh. 1988. *Repatriation of Art from the Collecting Point in Munich after World War II: Background and beginnings*. Maarssen: Gary Schwartz.

Sotheby's, ed. 1963. *Gold Snuff Boxes, Miniatures and Objects of Vertu from the Collection of the Late Rene Fribourg: Auction in London, 14 October 1963*. London: Sotheby's.

Sotheby's, ed. 1978. *Highly Important French Furniture, Decorations, Porcelain, Works of Art and Gold Boxes from the Collection of Henry Ford II: Auction in New York, 25 February 1978*. New York: Sotheby's.

Spoliation Advisory Panel. 2006. 'Report of the Spoliation Advisory Panel in respect of four drawings now in the possession of the British Museum'. London: Department for Culture, Media and Sport. https://assets.publishing.service.gov.uk/government/uploads/system/uploads/attachment_data/file/231795/1052.pdf (accessed 6 December 2023).

Spoliation Advisory Panel. 2014. 'Report of the Spoliation Advisory Panel in respect of three Meissen figures in the possession of the Victoria and Albert Museum'. London: Department for Culture, Media and Sport. https://assets.publishing.service.gov.uk/government/uploads/system/uploads/attachment_data/file/318667/40796_HC_208_accessible.pdf (accessed 6 December 2023).

Stadtmuseum Düsseldorf. 1998. *Betrifft: 'Aktion 3'. Deutsche verwerten jüdische Nachbarn. Dokumente zur Arisierung*. Berlin: Aufbau.

Stargardt, Nicholas. 2015. *The German War: A nation under Arms, 1939–45*. London: Bodley Head.

Steber, Martina, and Bernhard Gotto. 2014. 'Volksgemeinschaft: Writing the social history of the Nazi regime'. In *Visions of Community in Nazi Germany: Social engineering and private lives*, edited by Martina Steber and Bernhard Gotto, 1–25. Oxford: Oxford University Press.

Steinbach, Stefanie. 2018. *Erkennen, erfassen, bekämpfen: Gegnerforschung im Sicherheitsdienst der SS*. Berlin: Metropol.

Steinweis, Alan E. 1991. 'German cultural imperialism in Czechoslovakia and Poland, 1938–1945'. *International History Review* 13 (3): 466–80.

Steinweis, Alan E. 1993. *Art, Ideology and Economics in Nazi Germany: The Reich chambers of music, theater, and the visual arts*. Chapel Hill: University of North Carolina Press.

Steinweis, Alan E. 2008. *Studying the Jew: Scholarly antisemitism in Nazi Germany*. Cambridge, MA: Harvard University Press.

Steinweis, Alan E. 2009. *Kristallnacht 1938*. Cambridge, MA: Belknap Press of Harvard University Press.

Stiftung Sächsische Gedenkstätten zur Erinnerung an die Opfer politischer Gewaltherrschaft, ed. 2000. *'... das oft aufsteigende Gefühl des Verlassenseins': Arbeiten der Malerin Elfriede Lohse-Wächtler in den Psychiatrien Hamburg-Friedrichsberg (1929) und Arnsdorf (1932–1940)*. Dresden: Verlag der Kunst.

Stolberg, Marie, and Andrea Lehmann. 2020. 'Best-practice guidelines, research methods and tools'. In *Provenance Research Today: Principles, practice, problems*, edited by Arthur Tompkins, 54–67. London: Lund Humphries.

Stone, Dan. 2023. *The Holocaust: An unfinished history*. London: Pelican.

Strahl, Antje. 2017. 'Geraubte Bücher: Außergewöhnliche Erwerbungen der Universitätsbibliothek Rostock zwischen 1933 und 1945'. *Zeitgeschichte regional* 21 (1): 11–20.

Truman, Charles. 1991. *The Gilbert Collection of Gold Boxes*. Los Angeles: Los Angeles County Museum of Art.

Ulbricht, Josephine. 2022. *Das Vermögen der 'Reichsfeinde': Staatliche Finanzverwaltung und Gegnerverfolgung im nationalsozialistischen Deutschland*. Berlin: De Gruyter.

US Department of State. 1999. *Proceedings of the Washington Conference on Holocaust-Era Assets (November 30–December 3, 1998)*. Washington, DC: Government Printing Office.

Victoria & Albert Museum. 2019. 'Acquisition and disposal policy, approved by Trustees Collections Committee in July'. https://vanda-production-assets.s3.amazonaws.com/2019/08/05/10/09/13/da802e17-9355-4aae-afec-838b361f5a9f/2019%20Acquisition%20and%20disposal%20policy.pdf (accessed 6 December 2023).

Victoria & Albert Museum. 2023. 'Size of the V&A collections on 31 March 2022'. https://vanda-production-assets.s3.amazonaws.com/2022/07/07/13/05/43/bf86e130-ef90-467c-bff8-1f9d0079dd98/V&A%20Size%20of%20Collections%20Statement%20March%202022%20(1).pdf (accessed 6 December 2023).

Voigt, Vanessa-Maria. 2018. 'Silber aus "ehemals jüdischem Besitz": Erwerbungen des Historischen Museums der Stadt München vom Städtischen Leihamt 1939/40'. In *'Ehem. jüdischer Besitz': Erwerbungen des Münchner Stadtmuseums im Nationalsozialismus*, edited by Henning Rader and Vanessa-Maria Voigt, 166–77. Munich: Hirmer.

von Falke, Otto. 1912. *Die Kunstsammlung Eugen Gutmann*. Berlin: Meisenbach Riffarth & Co.

von Leers, Johann. 1933. *Forderung der Stunde: Juden raus!* Berlin: NS Druck und Verlag.

von Leers, Johann. 1934. *Geschichte auf rassischer Grundlage*. Leipzig: Reclam.

von Lüttichau, Mario-Andreas. 2014. '"Crazy at any price": The pathologizing of modernism in the run-up to the "Entartete Kunst" exhibition in Munich in 1937'. In *Degenerate Art: The attack on modern art in Nazi Germany, 1937*, edited by Olaf Peters, 36–51. Munich/London/New York: Prestel Verlag.

von Papen-Bodek, Patricia. 2004. 'Anti-Jewish research of the Institut zur Erforschung der Judenfrage in Frankfurt am Main between 1939 and 1945'. In *Lessons and Legacies VI: New Currents in Holocaust Research*, edited by Jeffry M. Diefendorf, 155–89. Evanston, IL: Northwestern University Press.

Wachsmann, Nikolaus. 2015. *KL: A history of the Nazi concentration camps*. New York: Farrar, Straus and Giroux.

Waite, Robert G. 2002. 'Returning Jewish cultural property: The handling of books looted by the Nazis in the American zone of occupation, 1945 to 1952'. *Libraries & Culture* 37 (3): 213–28.

Walk, Joseph. 1981. *Das Sonderrecht für die Juden im NS-Staat*. Heidelberg: Müller.

Wechsler, Helen. 2005. 'US museums and the Nazi-era assets issue'. In *Vitalizing Memory: International perspectives on provenance research*, edited by American Association of Museums, 12–15. Washington, DC: American Association of Museums.

Wechsler, Helen, and Erik Ledbetter. 2004. 'The Nazi-era provenance internet portal: Collaboration creates a new tool for museums and researchers'. *Museum International* 56 (4): 53–62.

Weiler, Katharina. 2019. 'Die Kunstobjekte Maximilian von Goldschmidt-Rothschilds: Biographie einer Sammlung im Spiegel der Geschichte des Museum Angewandte Kunst, Frankfurt am Main'. In *Gesammelt, gehandelt, geraubt: Kunst in Frankfurt und der Region zwischen 1933 und 1945*, edited by Evelyn Brockhoff and Franziska Kiermeier, 139–53. Frankfurt am Main: Societäts Verlag.

Weiler, Katharina, and Grit Weber. 2019. 'Collected. Stolen. Obscured: The Pinkus/Ehrlich Collection and the Museum Angewandte Kunst'. In *Bought, Collected, Looted? How things came into the museum. Documentation*, edited by Angela Jannelli and Gottfried Kößler, 46–53. Frankfurt am Main: Heinrich Editionen.

Weitz, Ulrich. 2020. 'Recently identified Asian objects from the Eduard & Margarete Fuchs Collection'. *Journal for Art Market Studies* 4 (2): 1–15.

Wessels, Fritz. 1991. 'Die Reichspogromnacht und das Ende der jüdischen Gemeinde in Weener'. In *Frisia Judaica: Beiträge zur Geschichte der Juden in Ostfriesland*, edited by Herbert Reyer and Martin Tielke, 279–306. Aurich: Verlag Ostfriesische Landschaft.

Wetzel, Juliane. 1993. 'Auswanderung aus Deutschland'. In *Die Juden in Deutschland 1933–1945: Leben unter nationalsozialistischer Herrschaft*, edited by Wolfgang Benz, 412–98. München: Beck.

Wiesel, Elie. 1999. 'Opening ceremony remarks at the United States Holocaust Memorial Museum'. In *Proceedings of the Washington Conference on Holocaust-Era Assets (November 30–December 3, 1998)*, edited by US Department of State, 13–17. Washington, DC: Government Printing Office.

Wildt, Michael. 2009. *An Uncompromising Generation: The Nazi leadership of the Reich Security Main Office*. Madison: University of Wisconsin Press.

Wildt, Michael. 2012. *Hitler's Volksgemeinschaft and the Dynamics of Racial Exclusion: Violence against Jews in provincial Germany, 1919–1939*. New York/Oxford: Berghahn.

Winkler, Richard. 2005. '"Händler, die ja nur ihrem Beruf nachgingen": Die Münchner Kunsthandlung Julius Böhler und die Auflösung jüdischer Kunstsammlungen im "Dritten Reich"'. In *Entehrt. Ausgeplündert. Arisiert: Entrechtung und Enteignung der Juden*, edited by Koordinierungsstelle für Kulturgutverluste Magdeburg, 207–45. Magdeburg: Koordinierungsstelle für Kulturgutverluste.

Woodhead, Charlotte. 2021. 'United Kingdom'. In *Museums and the Holocaust*, edited by Ruth Redmond-Cooper, 51–73. 2nd ed. Builth Wells: Institute of Art and Law.

Yeide, Nancy H. 2009. *Beyond the Dreams of Avarice: The Hermann Goering Collection*. Dallas, TX: Laurel.

Yeide, Nancy H., Amy L. Walsh and Konstantin Akinsha. 2001. *The AAM Guide to Provenance Research*. Washington, DC: American Association of Museums.

Zuschlag, Christoph. 1995. *'Entartete Kunst': Ausstellungsstrategien im Nazi-Deutschland*. Worms: Werner.

Index

www.ingramcontent.com/pod-product-compliance
Lightning Source LLC
LaVergne TN
LVHW051013110926
847653LV00008B/38